State and nation in
multi-ethnic societies

State and nation in multi-ethnic societies

The breakup of multinational states

Edited by
Uri Ra'anan, Maria Mesner,
Keith Armes and Kate Martin

Manchester University Press
Manchester and New York
Distributed exclusively in the USA and Canada by St Martin's Press

Copyright © The Institute for the Study of Conflict, Ideology & Policy, Boston University 1991

Published by Manchester University Press
Oxford Road, Manchester M13 9PL, England
and Room 400, 175 Fifth Avenue, New York, NY 10010, USA

Distributed exclusively in the USA and Canada
by St. Martin's Press, Inc., 175 Fifth Avenue, New York, NY 10010, USA

British Library Cataloguing-in-Publication Data
A catalogue record for this book is available from the British Library

Library of Congress Cataloging-in-Publication Data
State and nation in multi-ethnic societies / edited by Uri Ra'anan . . .
(et al.).
    p. cm.
   Revised contributions originally presented at a conference held in
Vienna in Jan. 1991, sponsored by the Institute for the Study of
Economic Culture, Boston University, Institute for the Study of
Conflict, Ideology, and Policy, Boston University, and the Renner
-Institut.
   Includes index.
   ISBN 0–7190–3711–5
   1. Representative government and representation—Congresses.
2. Minorities—Political activity—Congresses. 3. Ethnic groups–
–Political activity—Congresses. 4. Ethnic relations—Political
aspects—Congresses. I. Ra'anan, Uri, 1926– . II. Boston
University, Institute for the Study of Economic Culture.
III. Boston University. Institute for the Study of Conflict,
Ideology & Policy. IV. Doktor-Karl-Renner-Institut.
JF1061.S73   1991
323.1—dc20   91-31631

ISBN 0 7190 3711 5 *hardback*

Photoset in Linotron Sabon by
Northern Phototypesetting Co. Ltd, Bolton

Printed in Great Britain
by Biddles Ltd, Guildford and King's Lynn

Contents

Peter L. Berger

Preface

Most of the chapters in this volume are based on presentations given at the conference on 'State and Nation in Multi-ethnic Societies' held in Vienna in January 1991. Wherever necessary, the contributions were revised to reflect recent developments. The conference was jointly sponsored by two research centers at Boston University – the Institute for the Study of Economic Culture (directed by Peter L. Berger) and the Institute for the Study of Conflict, Ideology and Policy (directed by Uri Ra'anan) – and by the Renner-Institut, a research center of the Social Democratic Party of Austria.

The idea behind the conference and the papers is of pristine simplicity: are there lessons to be drawn for contemporary multi-ethnic societies from the experience of the Austro-Hungarian monarchy in its last decades? More specifically, can some of the thinking about the relation of state and nation that occurred during that period within the ambience of Austrian Social Democracy have possible applicability today?

Karl Kraus, the great Viennese satirist, called Austria-Hungary 'the dress rehearsal for the apocalypse.' He was more right than he could possibly have known at the time. One area in which Austria-Hungary served as a 'dress rehearsal' – or, if one prefers, a prematurely ended laboratory experiment – was that of ethnic turmoil. Indeed, the two parts of the monarchy constituted a sort of controlled experiment for two very different policies regarding what was then called the 'nationalities problem.' The Hungarian elite understood its political entity as a modern nation-state *tout court*, the nation in question was the Magyar nation, and other nationalities (Slavs, Germans, Rumanians) were subjected to powerful pressures (a mix of coercion and cajolery) to magyarize. By contrast, the

Austrian half of the monarchy developed clearly in the direction of a multinational, multicultural political structure. It did so without a coherent theory, without political élan, in a muddle of halfhearted steps. Nevertheless, in retrospect it constituted one of the first cases of a modern state that could or can genuinely be described as a deliberately multinational polity.

Nor should one too readily accept the conventional view that this experiment failed. The Austro-Hungarian state perished as a result of its defeat in a war provoked by its own disastrous foreign policy. Neither the war nor the defeat were the result of domestic ethnic problems (though of course the foreign policy goal of destroying Serbia was related to the monarchy's problems with its domestic Slavs). Historians differ as to the likely further development of this very peculiar political structure if World War I had either been avoided or had been won by the Central Powers (both perfectly 'thinkable' counterfactual scenarios). Be this as it may, the problems of this long-extinct state have a strikingly contemporaneous quality about them, and the idea of taking another look back is not at all outlandish. The ethnic earthquakes currently shaking the Soviet Union and the countries of East-Central Europe (many of them, of course, 'successor states' of the monarchy) give an added timeliness to such an intellectual exercise.

More specifically, Austrian Social Democracy (the party celebrated its one hundredth anniversary in 1990) was very much involved in the debates over the 'nationalities problem' in the monarchy around the turn of the century. Two of its pre-eminent thinkers, Karl Renner and Otto Bauer, wrote highly influential monographs on the subject, and their ideas were embodied for a number of years in the party's program and applied in some practical policies (notably in Moravia).

The recommended solutions of the 'Renner/Bauer model' were cast within the context of the prevailing ideology of that ambience at that particular time – so-called Austro-Marxism. The Marxist elements of this ideology were not exactly helpful in enhancing its Austrian applicability – as, for instance, the mistaken belief that the 'real' issues were those of class and class struggle, and that the 'irrational' and ultimately irrelevant matter of nationalism should be expeditiously taken care of, precisely so that energies could be turned to the 'real' issues. All the same, the 'Renner/Bauer model' had at its core an original and potentially historic idea – the so-called 'personality principle,' according to which national rights should be accorded to individual persons rather than exclusively to territorial groupings. That is, the idea suggested that, under certain circumstances, the concept of nationality might be divorced from the possession of a national territory, or be exercised outside such a territory. Thus Renner and Bauer, at least implicitly, challenged the axiom of modern nationalism that every nation must have sovereignty over a specific piece of real estate – or, as a 19th-century English wit put it, that every language must have an army.

The circumstances in which Renner and Bauer believed their principle to be relevant were those in which national or ethnic groups were so interspersed geographically that any neat division between 'their' territories was impossible. They then proposed quite ingenious constitutional arrangements to take into account the national aspirations of these landless groups. It so happens that the world today has a surfeit of such circumstances, in virtually every part of the world, both less developed and developed. Again, the look back proposed here is intrinsically plausible. As Renner and Bauer themselves believed, and as was reiterated frequently during the Vienna conference, it is unlikely that the goal of territorial sovereignty – a national flag waving over a clearly defined national territory – will be easily given up by any nationally conscious group in the modern world. The nation-state continues to be everybody's 'first prize.' But, as was pointed out by one of the participants, Bobby Godsell from South Africa, the first prize is not always attainable. In such cases it may well be that arrangements along the lines of the 'Renner/Bauer model' may come to be seen as a tolerable *second* prize.

The conference brought together a group of historians and social scientists (not all presented papers). As always on such occasions, there were some difficulties in communication between the two groups. Historians are often irritated by the theorizing proclivities of social scientists, and social scientists do not like their theories to be disturbed by annoying historical details. Still, given these professional handicaps, the discussions during the conference were unusually open, stimulating and productive of new insights. Unusually for conferences of this type, there was an absence of individuals relentlessly pursuing their own monomaniacal agenda regardless of anyone else's. And some participants, historians and social scientists both, discovered a shared ironic sensibility, savoring the notion that ideas thought up a hundred years ago by a couple of

Central European intellectuals could suddenly be relevant and timely today in places like, say, South Africa.

Thanks are due above all to the participants in the conference and the authors of the articles, and to Uri Ra'anan and Maria Mesner as well as to Keith Armes and Kate Martin, for editing the volume. I also want to thank Erich Fröschl, director of the Renner-Institut, and Thomas Nowotny of the Austrian Foreign Ministry, who established contact between the Renner-Institut and Boston University. On this side of the Atlantic, our appreciation is owed to Kate Martin and Cara Shockley for taking care of the rather complicated logistical arrangements. Jeffrey B. Miller and Rhonda K. Brown are thanked for their contributions. Last but by no means least, we are in the debt of the four institutions whose funding made the project possible – the Lynde and Harry Bradley Foundation, the Sarah Scaife Foundation, the United States Institute of Peace and the Arthur Vining Davis Foundations, Inc.

Institute for the Study of Economic Culture
Boston University
March 1991

Part 1
Concepts

Uri Ra'anan

Nation and state: order out of chaos

For some 40 years after World War II, only a handful of skeptics refused to succumb to the fashion of the time, which had accepted as gospel the hypothesis that modernization and democratization somehow would cause ethnic self-assertion and conflict to fade away. It was customary, moreover, to believe that state sovereignty was about to dissolve into regional, transnational, and supranational institutions and associations. (Viewed superficially, of course, the development of such entities as the European Community seemed to bear out this expectation.) Few were the voices protesting that certain significant indicators, if anything, pointed in the opposite direction – i.e., toward the emergence of sub-state actors capable of breaking down existing entities into smaller units.

Misreading the trend

The skeptics suggested that aspirations of a primarily ethnic nature had been submerged, temporarily, by the proliferation of repressive régimes both east of the Elbe and south of the Mediterranean, and by the revulsion in the West from the excesses that chauvinism had wrought in the 1930s and 1940s. They stressed that, in the developed areas, the post-Industrial Revolution, with its attendant social and geographical dislocation and resulting alienation, was likely to impel individuals to ask 'who and what am I?' – now better known as 'searching for [ethnic] roots.' Moreover, the removal of oppressive régimes, imposed from the outside as far as Eastern Europe was concerned, could be expected to release the drive for self-determination with all of its national manifestations.

Today, of course, these views have become axiomatic, in the light of current events behind what used to be the Iron Curtain, in much of the Third World, and, not least, in the West (to mention only Northern Ireland, Québec and the Basque provinces).

Semantic confusion

The reason that realization of the facts came so belatedly has to do with the semantic confusion which has beset much of contemporary political thought, particularly in English-speaking countries. One of the significant expressions of this confusion is the proliferation of the term 'nation-state,' based upon the assumption that the international arena of our time is occupied almost exclusively by 'nation-states' or (at least in developing regions) 'nation-states-to-be.'[1] If the surface of this planet really were dominated by genuine 'nation-states' (as defined below), then aspirations for national autonomy or independence presumably would have been fulfilled well-nigh universally. In that case, there would be little reason to anticipate a resurgence of ethnic self-assertion.

In American English, 'state' and 'nation' are used almost interchangeably – in which case, the term 'nation-state,' of course, is tautological. On the other hand, if this phrase is to be taken literally, in the historical and anthropological sense, then a 'nation-state' would have to refer to a polity whose territorial and juridical frontiers coincide with the ethnic boundaries of the national entity with which that state is identified, frequently by its very name.

If the latter concept applies, as it should, then the simple fact of the matter is that very few genuine 'nation-states' can be found on the contemporary map of the world. Of the approximately 170 more or less sovereign countries existing today, Iceland, metropolitan Portugal, Norway and one or two others constitute exceptions in terms of homogeneity; practically all the rest are ethnically heterogeneous.

'States' larger than 'nations'

In very many cases, the state is larger than the 'nation' – that is the

[1] The concepts employed in this paper were developed by the author in his book *Ethnic Resurgence in Modern Democratic States* (New York: Pergamon, 1980) and in his chapter on 'The Nation-State Fallacy' in *Conflict and Peacemaking in Multiethnic Societies* (Joseph Montville, ed., Boston: Lexington Books, 1990).

juridical limits of the state extend considerably beyond the area settled by its *Staatsvolk*. (Unfortunately, there is no English equivalent for this term, which denotes the ethnic group that created the state, is largely identified with it, constitutes the bulk of its élite, and is the source of the predominant culture.) Thus:

1 Great Russians comprise barely one-half the population of the U.S.S.R. Even if, by a very wide stretch of the political imagination, one were to accept as 'co-*Staatsvölker*' the 14 other national groups for which the various union republics were named, the boundaries of the Soviet Union would still embrace some 28 million additional citizens who belong to 'other' or 'minority' ethnic entities and occupy considerable stretches of the country. (Indeed, if one were to add the individuals who live outside 'their own' union republic, the total would increase to well over 60 million Soviet citizens who cannot be considered part of a *Staatsvolk*.)

2 In the Yugoslav case, the original *Staatsvolk*, the Serbs, amount to little more than 40 percent of the population. Even if Croats, Slovenes, Macedonians, and Montenegrins, whose names the other Yugoslav republics bear, were to achieve genuine self-government within Yugoslavia, this would still leave the country with minorities numbering nearly one-fifth of all citizens and inhabiting considerable stretches of territory.

3 France, *the* classical 'nation-state' of the political textbooks, contains – in contiguous areas adjacent to its outer limits – German-speaking Alsatians, Italian-speaking inhabitants of the Riviera and Corsica, Catalans and Basques at either end of the Pyrenees, Celtic Bretons, and Flemings southwest of the Belgian frontier. Altogether, these ethnic groups amount to nearly one-tenth of metropolitan France's citizens, without counting another eight percent composed of foreign laborers (North Africans and others) residing permanently in the country.

4 In the Canadian case, quite apart from the existence of two *Staatsvölker*, of British and French (Québécois and Acadian) descent, each occupying and dominating a major (more or less contiguous) geographic region, there is still a 'third Canada.' It consists of Indian and Inuit peoples who inhabit considerable stretches of contiguous territory, primarily in the north and northwest. (Others, including Scandinavians, Germans, Dutch, Ukrainians, Italians, Jews, and Poles, are scattered throughout the country, replicating the immigration patterns of the United States

where ethnic pockets are visible primarily at the ward and precinct levels of urban centers.)

5   Even the island state of Japan, despite its long history of relative isolation, is far from homogeneous. It includes a sizeable and unassimilated Korean minority, not to mention the aboriginal Ainus, who cling tenaciously to the country's northernmost regions.

'Nations' larger than 'states'

In these and over 100 other instances, the state is larger in size than the area inhabited by the *Staatsvolk*. Nor can one speak appropriately of a 'nation-state' in any of the many instances in which the boundaries of the nation exceed the territorial limits of any one state:

1   There is a German nation, but until recently there was the German Federal Republic, the German Democratic Republic, and West Berlin (which constituted a separate entity); it is arguable whether Austrians fall within the definition of 'Germans.'

2   A Korean nation exists, but it is divided into two states, not to mention the sizeable Korean minorities in the P.R.C., just north of the Yalu River adjacent to North Korea, in the eastern portions of the U.S.S.R., and, as mentioned above, in Japan.

3   Many observers, within and outside the Middle East, would argue that in spite of some historical, ethnic, linguistic (at least in terms of dialect), and religious differences, the various Arab groups constitute one single nation, whereas currently there are 21 Arab states (many of their constitutions, in fact, refer to 'the Arab nation.')

4   There is a Hungarian state, but the frontiers imposed upon it by the post-World War I and II settlements exclude nearly 3 million Magyars from their motherland (although they live in most cases adjacent to Hungary's frontiers).

5   There are two Chinese states (actually three, if Singapore is viewed ethnically) without including the Chinese inhabitants of Hong Kong or the millions of 'overseas Chinese' in Southeast Asia.

6   Even in relatively homogeneous Scandinavia, Sweden fails to include 500,000 Swedes in neighboring Finland, right across the Gulf of Bothnia.

These examples indicate that in the overwhelming majority of independent countries existing today, the state either is considerably larger or much smaller than the area inhabited by the corresponding nation or *Staatsvolk*. Consequently, genuine 'nation-states,' far from constituting the rule on the contemporary political map, remain an exceptional phenomenon – if a high degree of ethnic homogeneity and congruity between the geographic outlines of the state and nation are regarded as the primary criteria of the 'nation-state.' (If these are not the criteria, then one has to ask what meaning attaches to this term.)

The historical record

If this is true today, it applies even more to earlier decades and centuries. After all, our century, at least since World War I, has become notorious for efforts – usually brutal – to 'clean up' the ethnic map. These have included genocidal measures, forcible expulsion, population exchanges that were rarely voluntary, and attempts to obliterate entire nationalities by means of 'census games.'[2]

Despite such reprehensible measures, genuine nation-states have remained the exception on the political landscape, as has been noted. Prior to 1912, there were even fewer instances of ethnic homogeneity, the map being dominated by three great multinational entities – the Ottoman, Habsburg, and Romanov empires (only the last of which was succeeded by an equally polyglot state). Moreover, in the first half of the 19th century, there were 39 separate German and 9 Italian states. Nation-states, therefore, have been even more exceptional in history than on the contemporary political scene.

The fact of life is that multi-ethnic states, rather than posing an obstacle, constitute a breeding ground for the growth of nationalistic manifestations. Awareness of national differences and a perception of incompatibility of interests are far less likely to develop in ethnically homogeneous societies, where individuals usually do not encounter, in their daily lives, problems caused by the need to function (during study, work, or litigation) in a language other than their mother tongue. Nor do they have to adjust to unaccustomed and incomprehensible cultural traditions, or to compete economically and socially with personalities molded by an entirely

---

[2] Poland between the two world wars invented a new nationality ('natives' or 'people from here') for certain areas in which Belorussians predominated. The result, of course, was to diminish considerably the size of Poland's regions in which Belorussians constituted the majority. Yugoslavia, during the same period, decided that Macedonians did not exist as a nationality and forced them to register as 'Southern Serbs,' with the result that Serbo-Croats (defined as a single nationality) appeared as the overwhelming majority of all Yugoslav citizens.

different background and heritage.

Conversely, the sudden impact of one ethnic group on another – whether because of invasion, annexation, migration, or simple fluctuation in the language or cultural frontiers between two peoples – is likely to give rise to some, most, or all of these problems. That is likely to be aggravated if the nationalities concerned find themselves within the frontiers of a single state, in which case they are likely to seek satisfaction of their aspirations through a struggle for political control of the entire country or, at least, portions of it.

It is not the intention of the author to attach normative attributes to the concept of ethnic heterogeneity; this chapter is concerned with observations rather than prescriptions. In this context, it may be useful to review the origins and antecedents of the fashionable misapprehensions of recent decades:

It was one of the pathetic fallacies of the period which began in the closing stages of World War II and continued after its termination, to assume that the great wave of nationalism, which had swept across Europe between the Napoleonic and Hitlerian eras, had fulfilled its aspirations through the creation of a series of supposed 'nation-states' and would somehow ebb.

It was taken for granted, moreover, that the general direction in which national fervor supposedly had begun to fade away was eastward:

After all – so most economic and political planners of the 1940s and 1950s argued – the concept of the modern 'nation-state' was born during the 16th and 17th centuries, in the bureaucratically centralized, post-medieval societies of Western Europe – Britain, France, the Netherlands. By the 19th century, so they claimed, following the French Revolutionary elaboration of the idea of 'la nation,' and in reaction to the Napoleonic expansionist drive for conquest, nationalism had reached Central Europe, leading eventually to the formation of unitary states in Germany and Italy, and then had moved eastward to the Balkans, East-Central and Eastern Europe, which became known, par excellence, as the hotbeds of national strife. By the 20th century, the wave had moved still farther east, to the so-called Middle East, and, eventually, it had reached the rest of colonial Asia and Africa.

By this time – it was taken for granted – the West (i.e., Western Europe and the Western hemisphere), where, supposedly, 'nation-states' had been achieved centuries ago, had already 'recovered' from, or had even proven 'immune' to, the 'infantile malady' that was now ravaging less fortunate lands. This was believed so firmly that Western states like Switzerland, France, and the United States were held up as the classical examples of societies that had 'solved' the 'national problem.'

Needless to say, events in recent years have demonstrated that these obituary notices even of Western nationalism were, to put it mildly, premature: Belgium has become the arena of revived Flemish and Walloon separatism and the end is not in sight; France has been confronted by national movements of the Bretons and the Basques – and Spain by the Basques and Catalans; the growth of French separatism in Quebec has been meteoric. Then there is, of course, Ulster, not to mention the rise of Welsh and Scottish nationalism in the United Kingdom. Finally, in the classical home of supposed national resolution – Switzerland – a very sharp conflict broke out between the German Protestant majority of the Canton of Berne and the predominantly Catholic and overwhelmingly French population of the Jura, in the north of the canton.

One might ask why the prophets of the 1940s and 1950s have turned out to be so mistaken. All too many of them seem to have been economists or adherents of certain categories of political science, especially those with a functionalist bias. Professionally, they have tended to be enamored of sheer size, 'efficiency,' and 'viability.' To most of them, it has appeared axiomatic that large territorial units, with rich and variegated resources, would prove to be more competent and, thus, more desirable members of the global community, than smaller, poorer and more struggling states. Hence their prejudice in favor of sizeable federations and other large polities, and against national individuality and self-expression. Since, however, most of the academicians and commentators have been products of a democratic environment and, therefore, uncomfortable with open denial of self-determination, they have been compelled to pretend, to themselves and others, that existing states, however arbitrarily their frontiers might mutilate ethnic units, are, in fact, 'nation-states' or 'nation-states-to-be.' Thus, they have hailed large post-colonial states, based upon entirely artificial administrative entities of the colonial period, as laboratories of a supposed process of 'nation-building;' conversely, they have bitterly scorned movements for national autonomy or separation of 'minority' nationalities, such as Ibos or Kurds, as mere retrogressive moves toward 'tribalism' or

'Balkanization.'

Most historians and anthropologists, on the other hand, have been inclined to doubt whether, even under modern (i.e., post-medieval) conditions, artificial 'nation-building' really has been successful to any degree, except perhaps temporarily in a couple of West European instances and in some immigrant societies, in as far as they were based upon the voluntary confluence of separate cultural and ethnic mainstreams and as long as geographic and ethnic lines did not coincide,[3] as they do in Quebec.

Moreover, historians have been well aware that the Sultans in five centuries were unable to 'build' an 'Ottoman nation' out of Turks, Arabs, Armenians, Kurds, Greeks, etc., the Tsars in several centuries could not 'build' a single nation out of Great Russians, Ukrainians, Belorussians, Poles, Finns, Georgians, etc., nor could the Habsburg Emperor-Kings, in a similar time span, 'build' one nation out of Germans, Hungarians, Czechs, Croats, etc.

Toward a new typology

Conceivably, the misconceptions described might have been avoided, but for the well-nigh impenetrable semantic confusion, especially in the West, that has enveloped the entire topic under discussion here – a confusion which, this author believes, is due partly to the fact that there exist in the world at least three quite distinct concepts of nationality and nationalism, and that these terms, therefore, have entirely different connotations in various regions of the world.

---

[3] Because of these very considerations, the United States, like certain other immigration societies (but not Canada), constitutes a special case. With three exceptions (American Indians, most Afro-Americans, and those Chicanos who were incorporated in the U.S.A. as a result of the war with Mexico) the populations consists of individuals who – themselves or by choice of their ancestors – *voluntarily* became Americans, knowing that there was likely to be a trade-off between the assets of a free society and the possible atrophy of the cultural heritage of the 'old country.' The latter was likely to be maintained and to be developed only where immigrants of one ethnic group settled in one major region of the new country (e.g., Quebec), which then became their culturally homogeneous home. In the United States, however, this has happened rarely beyond the ward or precinct level of urban concentrations at least as far as 'voluntary Americans' are concerned. Consequently, while Canada has witnessed a 'nationality conflict' along traditional European lines, this has not been typical of the United States.

The 'Western' approach

In the West (i.e., roughly Europe west of the Rhine and the Western hemisphere), a primarily territorial concept of nationality (having much in common with the legal concept of *jus soli*) has developed during the modern era. Western Europe was the one area where classical feudalism, in the full sense of the word, really flourished. Historical myth notwithstanding, feudalism of this type did not necessarily breed anarchy but rather provided, in several cases, a congenial environment for the growth of centralization and bureaucratic statehood, as evidenced by the history of the early Norman-Angevin Monarchy, from William I to Henry II, and of Norman Sicily.

On the basis of this heritage, the post-medieval, absolutist West European monarchies of the Tudors and the Valois were able to establish modern, bureaucratic and centralized states. In these instances – and, perhaps, in these instances alone – some degree of 'nation building' can be demonstrated really to have occurred. In a sense, it was these new *states* that assisted the process of creating modern French and British *nations*, rather than the other way around (although, as has already been pointed out, even in these cases, this process, extended over many generations, has not been entirely completed to this very day). Consequently, allegiance to the state, residence therein, and submission to its jurisdiction, are the hallmarks of the Western idea of nationality – to the point where, in American English, one speaks of a 'national' of a country when, actually, one means a 'citizen.' The two terms have become synonymous. It is an individual's place of residence and his passport that largely determine his nationality in the West, i.e., primarily territorial and juridical criteria (precisely as in the case of *jus soli*). For the same reasons, 'state' and 'nation' have tended to become almost synonymous in the English language, to a degree that causes many to refer to 'national interests' when, in fact, they mean state interests,' while others speak simplistically of a world of 'nation-states.'

However, since, as has already been demonstrated, there are actually rather few instances in which the limits of the state and its constituent nation (*Staatsvolk*) really coincide, loyalty and commitment to the state and to the nation often not only are not synonymous, but may be directly in conflict with one another. In order to unite a nation split asunder by official boundaries or to win independence for a nationality lacking sovereign territory, men sometimes feel impelled to fight the states in which they dwell and whose formal citizenship they hold. In the pre-1938 Austrian Republic, to be a 'nationalist' meant supporting an *Anschluss* between Austria and the German Reich, i.e., attempting to obliterate the republic and to submerge it in a Greater Germany. Thus, to be a 'nationalist' and an Austrian 'patriot' were antithetical terms. The interests of the 'state' and the 'nation' simply were incompatible. The same, of course, was true of any of the particularist German and Italian states in the first half of the 19th century. Similarly, to be a Jordanian or Lebanese 'patriot' and a pan-Arab 'nationalist' who happens to be a citizen of Jordan or Lebanon are antithetical concepts. The creation of a pan-Arab Empire – whether ruled from Cairo or Baghdad – effectively would mean the end of independent Jordanian and Lebanese states. In multinational states, it may be possible to be a 'patriot' and a 'nationalist' simultaneously – provided one happens to be a member of the *Staatsvolk*; it is, however, hardly feasible for 'minorities:'

In Czechoslovakia, a Czech can, at one and the same time, support his state and his nation. However, an ethnic Magyar from Southern Slovakia cannot simultaneously and without contradiction support the Czechoslovak state, whose passport he holds, and the aspirations of the Magyar nation which, presumably, would desire eventual separation of Magyar-speaking Southern Slovakia from Czechoslovakia and its reunion with the Hungarian motherland.

Because the practical identification of state and nation occasionally has rested upon *some* degree of reality in *Western* history, most Westerners assume that it prevails today throughout most of the world; actually, it has been, and remains currently, a very exceptional phenomenon. The whole Western political glossary suffers considerably from the semantic confusion which derives from this misapprehension.

The fallacious assumption that certain Western concepts which, in fact, have remained rare and unusual products of a particular historical environment and experience, actually have universal application, has led both Westerners and many Western-educated Afro-Asians to think and speak in such terms as 'nation-building.' They have taken it for granted that some exceptional Western historical developments can and should be copied in the Third World and that what, usually, are accidental and artificial Afro-Asian state frontiers (a heritage of arbitrary administrative lines drawn by colonial powers) constitute a suitable framework for the rapid 'creation' of a single 'nation' out of several distinct and antagonistic nationalities, just because something of this sort may have happened two or three times in Western history. (What is forgotten, of course, is that even in the West this process required many centuries and often has remained incomplete.) That does not mean, of course, that a centrifugal process within Afro-Asian (and, for that matter, Western) states should be instigated by outsiders. On the other hand, there is also no justification for outsiders, including Western scholars, to man the barricades against such a process, and to resort to invective against what they see fit to term 'Balkanization' (as if the population of the Balkan peninsula really was better off living under the ramshackle, multinational Ottoman Empire than under somewhat more homogeneous, separate successor states).

In any case, what many Western analysts simply do not seem to grasp is that their essentially territorial concept of nationality, according to which citizenship, loyalty to the nation and to the state are treated as interchangeable terms, may not be the accepted approach elsewhere and that, both historically and at present, it has been and remains very much a minority view.

The 'Eastern' approach

In a majority of ancient communities, as of most contemporary non-Western societies, the criteria determining a person's nationality were derived not from *jus soli* but rather from *jus sanguinis*. According to the latter concept, it is not *where* an individual resides and which state has jurisdiction over him that determines his nationality, but rather *who* he is – his cultural, religious and historic identity, i.e., his ethnicity, a heritage received from his ancestors and carried with him, in mind and body, irrespective of his current place of domicile. Consequently, one is dealing here with *personal* (as opposed to the Western *territorial*) criteria of nationality.

For instance, following the Germanic invasions of many provinces of the Roman Empire, there lived, side by side on the same territory, and under the sway of the same 'Barbarian' ruler, ex-Roman citizens and members of one of the Germanic tribal confederations (such as Goths, Vandals, Burgundians, Franks, Lombards, etc.). Yet, in most cases, and over a considerable period of time, the two groups remained distinct entities and, before the law, it mattered *who* the defendant was and not *where* he was living. Usually, Romans were judged by Roman law and the new Germanic settlers by their own Germanic customary law. Both groups regarded this practice as proper and, indeed, as a precious safeguard of their respective rights and privileges.

It is from this general model that two current, slightly differing but related, non-Western concepts of nationality are descended: the Eastern (covering roughly Europe east of the Rhine) and the Southern (covering the southern and eastern rims of the Mediterranean, i.e., the successor states of the Ottoman Empire). Both are based upon personal rather than territorial criteria, but the Eastern approach tends to focus upon cultural touchstones of ethnicity (including ancestral language and name), whereas, in the Southern view, religion is one of the primary hallmarks of nationality, so that the existence of a separate religious community frequently is a precondition for the successful development of full-blown nationhood.

The Eastern concept, of course, long antedates the rise of communist régimes. In the democratic Czechoslovak Republic, 1919–38, Czechoslovak citizenship was quite distinct and separate from *nationality*. There *was no* 'Czechoslovak nationality;' in the Czechoslovak census, Czechoslovak citizens regarded themselves, and were regarded by others, as belonging to one of seven primary nationalities (Czechs, Slovaks, Sudetengermans, Magyars, Ruthenians, Jews, and Poles) and registered accordingly – e.g., Citizenship: Czechoslovak; Nationality: Magyar; Religion: Catholic; Marital Status: Single; etc. The Czechoslovak state, at least in theory and to some extent in practice, recognized the right of each of the nationalities to its own educational, linguistic and other facilities (in order to preserve its distinct identity), as well as to a reasonably proportionate share of official appointments, particularly in the respective areas in which the population of each of the ethnic groups was concentrated.

Again, in the U.S.S.R. today, while there is Soviet citizenship, there is no 'Soviet nationality;' the Soviet census (and the Soviet internal passport or identity card) requires the registration of each citizen as a member of one of the more than 100 separate nationalities – Great Russian, Ukrainian, Belorussian, Uzbek, Georgian, Armenian, Jewish, etc. Regrettably, in the Soviet case, unlike pre-1938

Czechoslovakia, such identification did not necessarily ensure the grant of corresponding cultural and national privileges (although these are promised in the Soviet Constitution), but, on the contrary, frequently became the basis for discrimination. However, the present analysis is concerned primarily with political concepts rather than the question whether these concepts are abused currently rather than followed. The acknowledgment that there exist various separate nationalities, side by side with a single citizenship, is in line with the historical traditions of the region, dating back many centuries. According to the personal rather than territorial touchstones embodied in these traditions, a Georgian living in Moscow and, perhaps, even born there, who may well speak Russian more fluently than his ancestral Georgian tongue, will still regard and register himself – and be regarded by others – as a Georgian rather than as a Great Russian. What matters is not where he resides, nor even necessarily which language he now speaks best, but what his ancestry and cultural heritage is, i.e., who he is, or rather, whom he perceives himself (and others perceive him[4]) to be. In recognition of this aspect, the Soviet census contains a special category comprising members of ethnic groups who no longer speak the ancestral language of their nationality, presumably because they are dispersed, but have adopted another tongue, usually Russian. They are still registered as Ukrainians, Georgians, etc., but, with a comment to the effect that they now command a language other than the mother tongue of their nationality (the percentage of such persons being particularly high among Poles, Germans, and Jews in the U.S.S.R.).

The 19th-century cultural and political history of many of the 'revived' nationalities of east-central and south-eastern Europe in all probability reinforced the tendency of the Eastern approach to apply personal rather than territorial touchstones. Peoples whose state had disappeared from the map as a sovereign entity centuries earlier and

---

[4] In current Soviet practice, it is, in fact, the bureaucracy implementing the census or issuing internal passports that decides such questions, rather than the individual citizen responding to the questionnaire. There are, for instance, specific official instructions how children of ethnically mixed marriages are to be registered. Moreover, if a citizen with a typically Jewish or Polish family name or patronymic were to declare himself a Great Russian or Ukrainian, the bureaucrat filling in the official form probably would register him as Jewish or Polish anyhow, or would request to see the internal passports of his parents to verify how their nationality had been registered.

whose national tongue had degenerated into a peasant dialect with out a literature, being superseded as written and spoken forms of élite communication by the language of the conquerors, usually initiated their national renaissance by resuscitating their ancient language in modernized and literary form. In many cases, this cultural thrust, as well as the subsequent moves to ignite the spark of national insurrection, emanated not from the segments of the population that had remained settled on the soil of the old homeland, but rather from individual members of the intelligentsia living abroad, in the diaspora.

Modern Greek language and literature owes much to a few Hellenic writers living in Italy, and the Panhellenic movement originated with the sons of Greek merchants in Odessa and of Phanariotes in Bucharest. The modern Serb language and literature was largely the creation of a handful of Serbs in the Habsburg Empire and the Bulgarian Uprising was initiated by members of the Bulgarian Diaspora in Odessa and Bucharest. Similarly, the revival of Hebrew as a modern spoken language with a secular literature and the establishment of a Jewish national movement, Zionism, were the products of the diaspora of eastern and east-central Europe. In all of these instances, individuals permeated with national sentiments helped to resuscitate an ancient language and culture and, then, to organize a national movement, in this way reviving the nation as a whole, which, in turn, proceeded to recreate the old national state. In other words, whereas, in the West, there were some cases in which a state created a nation, in the East individuals sometimes revived nations which, then, recreated states. It is a reasonable assumption that these factors played a role in accentuating the personal criteria of the Eastern – as opposed to the territorial criteria of the Western – concept of nationality.

The 'Southern' approach

In the areas south and east of the Mediterranean, formerly dominated by the Ottoman Empire, a third, Southern view of nationality prevails, bearing close resemblance to the Eastern approach, in so far as it lays stress upon the individual's heritage and personal identity rather than his domicile or passport. However, according to the Southern concept, a more significant role in determining national identification is played by religion than by other cultural factors.[5] A very important cause for this phenomenon may be found in the history of the Ottoman institution known as the *millet*. For centuries after their appearance upon the political scene, the Ottoman Turks regarded themselves essentially as an army engaged in an ongoing Holy War, that had settled down temporarily during one of the truces which interrupted that war, rather than as a normal, permanent state.

Consequently, their ideas of governance were rather rudimentary: they were interested mainly in collecting from the conquered peoples financial contributions for the upkeep of the Ottoman armed forces, as well as an occasional tribute of male children, to be converted to Islam and serve as recruits in the élite corps of those forces; on the other hand, as far as administration was concerned, the Ottoman Sultans were content to set up a skeleton framework in which their authority was exerted by nominated representatives (who, in remote areas, tended to become semiautonomous and even hereditary).

Since these representatives dispensed the Sultan's justice mainly in accordance with Koranic precepts, those of the conquered who were non-Moslem 'infidels' were allowed largely to see to their own internal civil governance, in line with their respective religious canons. Because the aristocracy and warrior caste of the various

[5] There is a considerable area of overlap along the frontiers between the Eastern and Southern views of nationality. It must be recalled that, at one stage, Ottoman rule extended to the Carpathians and to the lower Dnieper and Don, embracing not only the Balkans but even portions of the Ukraine (borderland). Under the influence of Panslavism and other 18th- and 19th-century ideologies, these regions eventually became 'Europeanized' and part of the Eastern zone, as far as the nationality question is concerned. However, there are distinct remnants of the Southern (Ottoman) approach, focusing upon religion as an important criterion of nationality: For instance, Bosnian Moslems, who speak the same language and are of the same ethnic descent as their Orthodox or Catholic Serbo-Croat neighbors, simply having been converted to Islam under Ottoman rule, are now recognized in the Yugoslav census as a separate nationality, 'Yugoslav Moslems:' for that matter, Serbs and Croats are essentially one ethnic group, speaking practically the same language, the main difference being that the Serbs are Orthodox, employing the Cyrillic alphabet (reflecting their Byzantine heritage), while the Croats are Catholic, employing the Latin alphabet (reflecting their Roman heritage) – yet the Yugoslav census and constitution treat them as separate nationalities. Until recent years, the Orthodox Ukrainians and the 'Ruthenes,' the western branch of the Ukrainian people, of the same ethnic stock and speaking the same tongue, were regarded as different nationalities, because the 'Ruthenes' had become Uniates (Greek Catholics) while under Polish rule. For a long period, the Bulgars and their 'Pomak' kinsmen were treated as distinct ethnic groups, merely because the 'Pomaks,' although perfectly good Bulgars, had been converted to Islam during the period of Ottoman domination.

subject peoples often had been decimated during the course of the Ottoman Conquest, the only group left with the necessary literacy and experience to cope with juridical and organizational functions usually was the clergy. Consequently, the limited civil law autonomy of the conquered peoples, de facto became a form of clerical and religious self-government, applying canon law – particularly with respect to matters of 'personal status,' i.e., marriage, divorce, and inheritance. Under this *millet* system (as under the Eastern concept of nationality), what mattered was not where an individual lived, but who he was. Members of the Armenian Orthodox *millet* (i.e., community) paid certain taxes to its clergy, elected its officials, and were judged by it in civil matters, primarily personal status issues, irrespective of whether they lived in the predominantly Armenian-populated provinces of eastern Anatolia or as a scattered minority in the large Turkish cities.

As a result of the *millet* system, national identity in the regions south and east of the Mediterranean eventually became almost synonymous with religious identity – the Armenians being simultaneously a distinct nationality and a distinct religion (disregarding the small minority of Armenian Catholics), the same being true of the Jews, the Druzes, and, to some extent, of the Maronites, the Greeks, the 'Alawites, and others.

It is not widely realized that several Middle Eastern states inherited and incorporated into their system of government various aspects of the *millet* concept – which, for instance, constituted the key to Lebanon's ingenious internal 'compromise,' whereby the President, Premier, and Speaker of the House were chosen from the Maronite, Sunni, and Shiah *millets* respectively and a fixed proportion of Members of Parliament represented each of the various *millets* (30 always being Maronites, 20 being Sunni Moslems, 6 Druzes, etc.). Israel, via the British Palestine Mandate, has inherited another aspect of the Ottoman *millet* system – the exclusive jurisdiction of the various *millet* religious courts over questions of 'personal status' – marriage, divorce and inheritance.

To summarize briefly, it has been suggested here that there are essentially three major approaches to the national question: a Western, territorial, concept, and an Eastern and Southern, personal, concept (with East and South respectively emphasizing different – i.e., cultural or religious – criteria of nationality).

The Renner-Bauer typology: the concept

Having thus attempted to distill some measure of analytical order out of the current confusion in the semantic and conceptual areas alike, a further dimension should be added to the slightly simplified typology proposed in this chapter. Writers from that great experimental laboratory of national conflict resolution – the late Habsburg Empire, and particularly, Karl Renner (*Das Selbstbestimmungsrecht der Nationen*), have proposed a somewhat different analytical schema.

In Renner's typology, there are 'atomistic' views, according to which the only legally and constitutionally recognizable entities (with the possible exception of the economic field – i.e., corporations and trade unions) are the indivisible, centralistic state as a whole and the various individual citizens, who have no collective status, but merely form an unconnected, haphazard, atomized aggregate of persons; there is no intermediate, constitutional entity between these individual parts and the state as a whole.

Renner emphasizes that, opposed to these 'atomistic' concepts, there are 'organic' approaches which do give legal and constitutional recognition to politically intermediate units (frequently of an ethnic nature) between the state and the individual citizen. According to Renner, 'organic' approaches may, in turn, be divided into those that follow the 'territorial principle' and the 'personal principle' respectively.

Under the 'territorial principle,' autonomy may be granted to a specific administrative area (province, canton or, as in the U.S., state), preferably one that has a separate historic identity and tradition of its own or that is populated predominantly by a single ethnic group; these autonomous areas then are constitutionally recognized as legal entities and linked to each other by bonds of federation or confederation.

Under the 'personal principle,' individual members of an ethnic group, irrespective of their domicile, and without regard to whether they constitute a regional majority or are living as a dispersed minority throughout the state as a whole, are joined together in an autonomous organization (not unlike the '*millet*') that is then also constitutionally recognized as a legal entity;[6] the autonomous organizations of the various nationalities coexist with the central government of the state and its local administration, but have the special constitutional prerogative and duty to carry out certain functions (or to act as monitors and 'ombudsmen' over their implementation by the regular central and local government organs). Such functions presumably would include the establishment, maintenance and development of the appropriate educational and cultural institutions and facilities, through which the ethnic group in question, irrespective of size, may preserve and enhance its particular linguistic, historical, cultural and religious heritage. Also included would be the implementation of measures ensuring that, in their contact with judicial, administrative and other facets of regular government, and in their dealings with general public institutions, no individuals of any ethnic group should be disadvantaged (by regulations or practices that take insufficient account of their preferences and abilities, and their cultural and religious customs).

Closer analysis will show that the typology suggested in this chapter and Karl Renner's methodological framework are not, in fact, incompatible, but can be synthesized without too much effort.

The 'atomistic' approach, of course, relates easily to the Western concept of nationality, since the inhabitants of an 'atomistic' state, by virtue of their very domicile and citizenship, are identified nationally with that state, irrespective of their true ethnic affiliations. Thus, all such centralistic polities regard themselves as 'nation-states' whether they are, in fact, ethnically homogeneous or not.

Even Renner's 'organic' approach, so long as it follows the 'territorial principle' and establishes autonomous administrative areas based upon historic factors rather than ethnicity, can be encompassed within the Western view, as defined in this chapter.

On the other hand, that same 'organic' concept, when applying some aspects of the 'territorial principle,' but leading to the creation

---

[6] Much of what follows in this paragraph represents not only Renner's approach, but the refinements conceived by his Socialdemocratic colleague, Otto Bauer (*Die Nationalitätenfrage und die Sozialdemokratie*). Dissatisfied with his party's 1899 nationality program which, in para. 4, called simply for 'national minority rights,' Bauer demanded that it be expanded to read: 'Within each region of self-government, the national minorities shall form corporate entities with public juridical status, enjoying full autonomy in caring for the education of the national minority concerned, as well as in extending legal assistance to their co-nationals *vis-à-vis* the bureaucracy and the courts.'

of autonomous areas based upon ethnic or religious (as opposed to historic, geographic, or economic) criteria, could be compatible with the Eastern or Southern views, respectively. (That compatibility derives from the fact that, in delimiting the autonomous areas-to-be, the touchstone would be the cultural identity and individual nationality options of a majority of their prospective populations, rather than some long-established or arbitrarily drawn administrative line on the map.) Finally, Renner's 'organic' approach, if it follows the 'personal principle,' especially as refined by Bauer, is entirely in line with the Eastern and Southern views of nationality (and is partially reflected by Southern *practice*, i.e., the '*millet*'). Some contemporary illustrations may help to concretize the Renner-Bauer conceptual framework.

'Atomistic' approaches

A typical example of an 'atomistic' state would be France since the Revolution (which abolished the 36 ancient provinces, with their distinctive local institutions, regulations and traditions, and substituted the 90 lifeless *départements*, that correspond to no historic or ethnic units and lack any genuine autonomy, being mere administrative extensions of central state power in Paris). France does not give constitutional status, at least within her metropolitan limits, to any intermediate territorial or ethnic institution between the centralistic state and the individual citizen. The 'regions' in which *départements* have been grouped are administrative rather than organic political entities.

Italy, from her unification in the second half of the 19th century to the post-World War II period, had consciously followed the 'atomistic' model of her Great Latin Sister, with a highly centralistic state subdivided into 92 minute provinces lacking real tradition, autonomy or life of their own. However, in recent years, Italy has moved away from the French example toward a somewhat more 'organic' approach, utilizing the 'territorial principle,' but applying historical rather than ethnic criteria in granting limited autonomy to 20 'regions' (into which the 92 provinces have been grouped). These 'regions' in most instances coincide geographically with Italy's old separate kingdoms, duchies and republics. However, only in a single instance, the (French-speaking) Valle d'Aosta, was a 'region' established with boundaries that follow strictly ethnic lines. In two other cases, considerable trouble was taken to 'gerrymander' the 'regions' in such a way as to outnumber a non-Italian nationality with an artificially created Italian majority. Thus, the historical and geographical artefact 'Friuli-Venezia Giulia' contains the provinces of Trieste and Gorizia with a considerable number of Slovenes, plus the much larger province of Udine with a huge Italian population; similarly, 'Trentino-Alto Adige' has added the overwhelmingly Italian Trentino to the predominantly German (South Tyrolese) province of Bolzano.

'Organic' approaches: along historic-territorial lines
In following primarily historical rather than ethnic lines, Italy's 'regions' are not unlike the Swiss cantons (and, for that matter, the states of the U.S.A.). Of course, Switzerland and the U.S.A. are more genuinely 'organic' states, since they are *federations* of intermediate entities established according to the 'territorial principle,' while Italy still remains essentially a *unitary state* granting limited autonomy to these entities. The similarity between these three countries arises only from their mutual disregard of ethnicity as a criterion for delimiting their territorial subdivisions. Not less than four Swiss cantons contain two or more ethnic groups, and another five contain two religious groups, that live not intermingled but in geographically separate areas, clearly demarcated on the linguistic and religious maps, on the basis of which it would be simple to create relatively homogeneous new cantons (or half-cantons). Indeed, the French-Catholic population of the Jura (in the north of the predominantly German-Protestant canton of Berne) demanded the creation of such a canton and seceded from Berne. However, only in one other case since the establishment of their confederation have the Swiss responded to a request of this kind – when Appenzell was divided into the Catholic half-canton of Inner-Rhoden and the Protestant half-canton of Ausser-Rhoden.

A number of countries, including Belgium, Yugoslavia and India, although starting, like Switzerland, with an 'organic' approach – applying the 'territorial principle' in accordance with primarily *historical* criteria – have felt compelled, in due course, increasingly to resort to *linguistic* and other ethnic criteria, although not consistently or entirely successfully.

The boundaries of Belgium's nine historic provinces have been adjusted recently to follow the Flemish-Walloon language frontier (so that Hainault now has a French-speaking outlier within West

Flanders, and Limburg a Flemish-speaking outlier in Liège). However, the existence of the partially bilingual Brussels area, which constitutes a non-Flemish-speaking enclave in primarily Flemish territory, has rendered a clear-cut linguistic-territorial solution very difficult. (Many of the Flemish-descended inhabitants of Brussels speak French much better than their own ancestral tongue; the city's Flemish-speaking suburbs are afraid of being engulfed in a metropolis that is colored by a predominantly French cultural overlay.) Nevertheless, support for a federal scheme based upon linguistic criteria, with a Walloon and a Flemish territorial unit, has been growing from election to election and each of the three main political parties has divided into Walloon and Flemish wings.

India began with a mosaic of historic provinces and princely states, but, under public pressure, converted to a system of ethnic-linguistic states; however, the Indian government proved curiously reluctant to implement this conversion consistently and wholeheartedly, leaving such anomalies as Bombay and the Punjab, until further crises and conflicts compelled the regime to divide these two provinces also along linguistic-cultural lines.

The provinces of Yugoslavia, immediately after its creation at the end of World War I, replicated almost entirely the historic units out of which the new state was formed. For a brief period, King Alexander attempted to destroy even these historic entities and to turn Yugoslavia from an 'organic' into an 'atomistic' state, following the centralistic French model, by dividing the country into a number of lifeless Governorates, named after geographic features and cutting across historic and ethnic lines alike. However, after his murder, the first steps were taken toward national reconciliation with the 1939 *Sporazum*, which not only recreated the historic Croat state, but modified its frontiers in accordance with ethnic criteria, by adding to it the Croat districts of Bosnia-Hercegovina.

'Organic' approaches: along ethnic-territorial lines
Tito's Yugoslav reorganization, initiated during World War II, was ostensibly not only a move toward a fully 'organic' state, i.e., a federation, but, moreover, one consisting of territorial units based on Yugoslavia's nationalities. However, of the new republics and autonomous regions, only Slovenia, Montenegro, Kossovo, Serbia, and, to some extent, Macedonia, could be considered reasonably homogeneous from the ethnic point of view. Vojvodina was given

frontiers which ensured that the Magyar population would be outnumbered by Serbs and Croats, including immigrants who were
brought in to replace the expelled German population of the region.
Croatia was left with a sizeable Serbian minority, but without the
Croatian districts of Bosnia-Hercegovina, while that republic
became one of Yugoslavia's constituent republics despite the fact
that it had no predominant nationality at all, but contained Serbs,
Bosnian Moslems and Croats alike.

The U.S.S.R., at least in theory, had been established as an
'organic' state, applying the 'territorial principle' in accordance with
ethnic criteria which, supposedly, form the basis of the 15 union
republics, 20 autonomous republics, and 18 autonomous or national
districts, of the which the Soviet Union is composed. In reality, of
course, this federal system until recently was a hollow shell, since the
Soviet communist party and state bureaucracy exercised tight
centralistic control over every facet of life. Even so, in addition to the
substance, the form of ethnic self-determination was not applied
consistently either. The frontiers of the Tatar Autonomous Republic,
for instance, exclude 73 percent of the Soviet Tatars from their 'own'
state on the Upper Volga (in which they constitute only 48 percent of
the population). Their southern kinsmen, the Crimean Tatars,
deported from their homes in Central Asia by Stalin, have not been
permitted officially to return to the Crimea, which has been
colonized in the meantime by Great Russians and Ukrainians. The
boundaries of the Bashkir Autonomous Republic have been drawn
in such a manner as to leave the Bashkirs in a minority of 22 percent
of the state's population, being outnumbered by Russians who constitute 39 percent. A centrally directed stream of colonization, in the
1960s and 1970s, to Kazakhstan's 'virgin lands' by Great Russians,
Ukrainians, and Belorussians ensured that the Kazakhs, in spite of
their high rate of natural increase, constitute only a plurality and not
a majority of the Kazakh Republic's inhabitants. In the so-called
Jewish Autonomous Region of Birobidzhan, Jews are 0.4 percent of
the total population and only about 0.6 percent of all Soviet Jews live
there; moreover, in spite of its name, the region does not contain a
single Jewish school or other Jewish cultural institution.

'Organic' approaches: the 'personal principle'
As for 'organic' states following the 'personal principle,' in accordance with the Renner-Bauer conceptual framework, there has been

reference already in this paper to the practices, past and present, of governments employing the *millet* system (or some aspects thereof). However, it should be emphasized that the Renner-Bauer approach envisaged much loftier status and far broader prerogatives for the (constitutionally recognized and guaranteed) autonomous representative body of each individual nationality, than those enjoyed by the *millet* or outlined in the provisions of the 1919 peace treaties intended to safeguard ethnic minorities. (Not to speak of British colonial practice – which frequently applied the 'personal principle' to the extent of having separate electoral rolls and representation for mutually antagonistic ethnic or religious communities, but confined all representatives to a subordinate role under essentially paternalistic authoritarian colonial government.)

The detailed considerations of a conceptual, methodological and historical nature, to which much of this analysis is devoted – including illustrative references to customary and traditional approaches, as well as contemporary practices – are intended to pave the way for a more systematic treatment of the issue of ethnic conflict resolution, unencumbered by some of the current substantive and semantic confusion and misapprehension. The complexities of the national question are such that one-dimensional approaches, relying exclusively upon a single concept – Western, Eastern, or Southern – are likely to prove counterproductive.

The Renner-Bauer typology: some questions

In this connection, a further examination of the applicability to ethnic conflict situations of the various categories of the Renner-Bauer typology may be helpful.

Problems of 'atomistic' states

'Atomistic' states, however much consideration they might show for the *individual* democratic rights and liberties of the citizen, and however egalitarian their practices might turn out to be, are averse, by definition, to recognizing intermediate, constitutionally enshrined entities between themselves and the individual. Consequently, they cannot deal constructively with the issue that lies at the very core of ethnic conflict, namely *group* rights and autonomies, whether through application of the 'territorial principle' or the 'personal principle.' In the last resort, the 'atomistic' state, if democratic, is likely to produce *majority* rule, and, if authoritarian, rule reflecting the concepts of the élite. In either event, it is the interests of the *Staatsvolk* that most probably will find satisfaction at the expense of other (or 'minority') nationalities, which will remain unprotected by group autonomy, along territorial or personal lines. The principle of (democratic) majority rule is likely to be fully equitable only in culturally homogeneous societies; otherwise, it can lead to the imposition of one (alien) ethos upon another.

As for authoritarian rule in 'atomistic' states, it usually rests upon some degree of identification between the leader and the 'national aspirations,' i.e., the real or presumed interests, of the *Staatsvolk*. This remains true, even when the autocrat himself is an alien, like the Corsican Napoleon, the Austrian Hitler, or the Georgian Stalin (if, in this context, one may treat the U.S.S.R., between the 1930s and 1980s, as an 'atomistic' society, even though theoretically, it remained an 'organic' federal state). Napoleon pursued French ultra-expansionism, as Hitler strove for extreme Pan-German aims, and Stalin during World War II and afterward, identified with Great Russian chauvinism, frequently even at the expense of fellow-Georgians.

Problems of 'organic' states

To a very major extent, the same objections apply to those 'organic' states that apply the 'territorial principle' according to historic, geographic, economic or other *non-ethnic* criteria. The autonomy of such territorial units (cantons, regions, states, provinces, etc., in a federation or other non-centralistic system) underwrites group rights, to be sure, but the groups in question tend to be somewhat haphazard entities thrown together by *residential* factors which, especially in modern, mobile societies, frequently constitute bonds of a very temporary kind at most. The more 'natural' and permanent groups of a cultural, linguistic, or religious type, which are the object of much deeper feelings of solidarity and commitment, are not only ignored in such systems, but as examples cited earlier in this analysis demonstrated, are often deliberately fragmented by arbitrary provincial boundaries or diluted by 'gerrymandering.' Such practices are intended to ensure that the *Staatsvolk* will dominate not only the state as a whole, but also most or all of the autonomous territorial units (e.g., the carefully manufactured Italian majority in 'Trentino-Alto Adige' and in 'Friuli-Venezia Giulia'). In other words, from the aspect of ethnic desiderata, such a system of territorial autonomy has few, if any, advantages over 'atomistic' states, at least so long as it eschews criteria of nationality in delimiting the territorial units. (Of course, occasionally the boundaries of historic provinces happen to coincide with ethnic lines.)

Many of these serious objections disappear in the case of 'organic' states applying the 'territorial principle' according to *ethnic* criteria, and doing so fairly and consistently. Regrettably, however, even this approach is not devoid of major pitfalls and shortcomings. The fact is that, within its own area of jurisdiction, each of the autonomous territorial units to be established will, to some extent, constitute a miniature 'atomistic' state. However carefully and equitably it may have been delimited with regard to ethnic considerations, such a territorial entity is almost bound to contain some linguistic, cultural or religious minorities, and for *them*, the autonomy granted to this region, province or canton provides little solace, since it ensures merely that they will be subjected to the majority rule of the local *Staatsvolk*.

Moreover, it is precisely the drawing of 'ethnically just' demarcation lines between the various autonomous territorial units that constitutes a well-nigh unmanageable task, especially in the absence of some higher authority within the state, magically endowed with superior wisdom, objectivity and power, yet totally disinterested and acceptable to all the parties. As was pointed out earlier, national antagonisms develop and are fought out particularly in linguistic or cultural frontier areas, where two ethnic groups overlap and mingle, and where each feels most exposed and threatened, rather than in the compactly settled, homogeneous and secure heartland of either group. Moreover, these embattled frontier zones are the very areas through which the boundaries between the autonomous regions will have to be drawn – boundaries that will determine under whose local rule future generations will have to live.

It is precisely this prospect, of course, that will exacerbate still further the conflict between the ethnic antagonists. It will spur the efforts of each, in these frontier areas, to achieve numerical superiority linguistically, culturally or religiously, as well as domination over educational and other key institutions, so as to ensure that the contested zones will be included in its own autonomous provinces or regions. It is exactly within this context, that the serious limitations become apparent of proposals to 'solve' conflicts between the *Staatsvölker* of two independent countries by means of a 'federation' between them.[7] Frontier struggles, to be sure, are painful enough when occurring on the international scene – but by internalizing them one does not resolve them. Within a federal entity, boundaries still have to be drawn between the respective autonomous regions and, for the reasons enumerated, this means merely that a previously external conflict becomes an internal one.

Yet it is hardly a lesson of history that civil wars are more pleasant and innocuous than clashes between sovereign countries! Nor is it feasible to evade such frontier struggles by the artificial device of 'neutralizing' a contested key area, i.e., withholding it from the autonomous regions or cantons of either of the antagonists, and declaring it to be a 'federal district,' 'federal capital,' 'binational' or 'international' area. If nature abhors a vacuum, politics certainly does not tolerate a no-man's land (unless, perhaps, it is totally uninhabited). Within such a 'neutralized' district, there is likely to be total ethnic deadlock, rendering representative government non-feasible.

Thus, conflict will descend into the streets and/or an even fiercer linguistic, education, communications media, and demographic struggle will be waged to ensure eventual domination over the district by one or other of the contestants.

(This is painfully evident from the unsuccessful attempt to resolve the Belgian linguistic conflict through the creation for 4½ Flemish provinces – including the Louvain district of Brabant, 4½ Walloon provinces – including the Nivelles district of Brabant, and a 'bilingual' Greater Brussels area, which, as a result, had become merely the focus of even sharper struggles between the two ethnic groups).

It is apparent, therefore, that all efforts to deal with nationality issues on a purely territorial basis (whether 'atomistic' or 'organic,' 'territorial-historic' or 'territorial-ethnic') are subject to grave limitations, since territorial 'solutions' all imply some degree of subjection of minority entities to majority rule by the *Staatsvolk* (whether

---

[7] American advocates of this particular 'solution' are misled frequently by the relative successes of the 18th-century Founding Fathers of this country and are inclined to regard 'federation' as a universal panacea. They tend to forget that the 13 original colonies were largely composed of populations descended from the same, or similar ethnic stocks, with a common cultural endowment and political experience, and a tradition of mutual respect, tolerance and reverence for law, strengthened by interaction with the British mother country during the 18th century.

throughout the country as a whole or within various local autonomous units). The attempt to deal with the problem through the creation of autonomous territorial units, delimited according to ethnic criteria as fairly and consistently as is feasible, should be deemed preferable to the other aforementioned approaches only in as far as it is likely to reduce the proportion of the population having to endure ethnically alien majority rule.[8]

Problems of the 'personal principle'

Finally, the application by 'organic' states of the 'personal principle,' in accordance with the Renner-Bauer definition, contains, at least theoretically, the elements of the most equitable solution, since, in a way, it means that no individual anywhere is relegated to 'minority' status. All, regardless of domicile, would enjoy the protection of their respective country-wide ethnic organizations, and none would be subject, therefore, to territorial majority rule, at least with regard to educational, cultural and religious matters. The Renner-Bauer approach constitutes, in a certain sense, the complete reversal of the *cuius regio eius religio* formula of the 16th-century Treaty of Augsburg – that famous triumph of the 'territorial principle' which 'abolished' (religious) minorities by the simple expedient of confronting all subjects residing in a prince's territories with a stark choice between conversion to the prince's creed, or expulsion. (This formula, or a more brutal version thereof, applied to ideological rather than religious creeds, became the basis for Stalin's division of Europe after Yalta, Teheran and Potsdam).

However, the application of the 'personal principle,' pure and simple, is not devoid of major problems and difficulties of its own. Modern societies cannot dispense entirely with territorial jurisdiction of one kind or another, if only because contemporary life – at least in such fields as criminal or business law – can hardly function without the existence of a single code of behavior and penalties, equally valid for all and implemented uniformly by the duly constituted and recognized authorities within a given state, province, etc. While it is entirely feasible that persons residing in the same area should be members of different country-wide ethnic

---

[8] A territorial approach, based on ethnic criteria, can constitute a very positive contribution to conflict resolution and thus be exempted from the criticism and strictures voiced here, *provided* its implementation is linked integrally to the 'personal principle,' in accordance with the Renner-Bauer concept.

associations (paying dues to them, voting for their representative bodies, benefiting from their assistance, and adhering to their respective educational, cultural, and religious institutions and regulations), it seems inevitable that such a system would have to coexist with some form of territorial government (responsible for those issues which affect each citizen as an individual rather than as a member of an ethnic or religious group). With several forms of jurisdiction, personal and territorial, functioning within each state or province, it is difficult to avoid some measure of constitutional complexity, as well as grey zones in attempting to delimit the areas of competence of the various authorities concerned. In the absence of an ethnically 'neutral,' superior judicial authority, such problems might be difficult to disentangle.

Ethnic conflict resolution: a model

Now, it may be possible to simplify this system to a considerable extent but, paradoxically enough, only in states in which a high degree of ethnic polarization exists. This would apply to countries containing two antagonistic nationalities, with a very limited measure of social, marital and other assimilative processes at work to blur the lines between them (where, consequently, all, or practically all, citizens, without much hesitation, doubt, or equivocation, would feel and declare themselves to be members of one ethnic group or the other and would opt for affiliation with the corresponding ethnic association). In such a case it might be feasible to have one and the same political body serving as a territorial authority in one part of the country and as a personal-ethnic authority in another.

To illustrate this point: The population of country X, composed of two ethnic groups, the A's and the B's (with very few, if any, citizens regarding themselves as A-B's), is allowed to opt for affiliation either with ethnic association A or B. The duly elected representative organ of association A may then exercise personal-ethnic authority to promote and protect the culture and institutions of all its members (in effect, probably all A's), wherever in country X they may reside: At the same time, however, association A also might exercise territorial authority over those of country X's autonomous provinces or regions (delimited, as far as possible, according to ethnic criteria), in which nationality A constitutes a majority of the population. The equivalent prerogative, of course, would be granted to the representative body of ethnic association B.

The objections voiced previously to the 'territorial principle,' even when applied in accordance with ethnic criteria, would be far less valid in this instance, since the jurisdiction of the territorial authorities would be modified and checked by the personal-ethnic authorities, which would be acting as watchdogs and ombudsmen for numerically weak groups. Thus, in the autonomous regions governed by ethnic association A, its counterpart, ethnic association B, would promote the culture and protect the rights of the scattered groups of B's settled in those areas.

In such a case, it might be possible even to constitute the federal government of country X – confined to a relatively small number of central functions – from leading members of the representative bodies of ethnic associations A and B, perhaps chosen in equal numbers, if the numerical ratio between the two nationalities is no greater than 3:2. To prevent deadlock, there might be a functional division of tasks, with the representatives of A and B respectively having the last word in certain fields of central government that are of particular interest to their own ethnic group.

To sum up, there would be essentially a three-tier structure: at the lowest level – municipal and rural councils – the citizenry as a whole, irrespective of ethnic affiliation, would vote and be represented. At the intermediate level, the representative organs of the various ethnic associations, elected by their respective memberships, would act both as the territorial authorities in the autonomous regions or provinces where their own nationality constituted a majority, and as watchdogs and helpers in areas where their ethnic group was scattered in small numbers. Finally, at the highest level – central government – leading members of the various ethnic associations' representative organs would work together, with a functional division of tasks between them, leaving each nationality with the last word on those matters that were of particular concern to it.

The model: shortcomings
The purpose of the model is not to present a detailed blueprint for utilization in any and all cases of ethnic conflict. In the absence of accompanying case studies in depth of specific conflict situations, with consideration of the gamut of appropriate responses in each instance, such abstract draftsmanship would constitute a fairly

useless exercise. Indeed, the author is fully aware that, even as idealized presentations, the model suffers from serious shortcomings. One of two elements would seem to be required to make the scheme fully functional: (1) There has to be a minimal measure of goodwill between the contending groups and a sincere desire to make the structure work, so that elaborate constitutional safeguards may not be nullified in a clash between incompatible authorities (a goodwill and sincerity that may not be consonant with the very word 'conflict' which is the topic of this chapter): or (2) The presence of some absolutist authority is needed, with the power to enforce the provisions of the scheme (a power that is not compatible with the assumptions of representative government, upon which this chapter is based).

As may be gathered from the many instances of ethnically centrifugal tendencies in multi-ethnic states cited earlier on, it is entirely conceivable that the trend toward separatism may become so strong that relatively few multi-ethnic societies may survive the next century at all. All these caveats notwithstanding, the model presented here may be helpful in illustrating how some of the concepts defined in this chapter would work in action, as well as demonstrating that the gamut of imagination and innovation has not necessarily been exhausted in this field.

Above all, it is hoped that some of the extant semantic and conceptual confusion may be dispelled, at least in part, by the attempt to present two mutually compatible typologies, one of the author's own making and the other distilled from the work of Karl Renner and Otto Bauer. Without minimal conceptual clarity and consistency, practical attempts at ethnic conflict resolution would appear to be foredoomed.

Theodor Hanf

Reducing conflict through cultural autonomy: Karl Renner's contribution

The road to World War I ran through Sarajevo, the road to World War II through Danzig. Although not an exclusive cause of either, conflicts between nationalities were an important triggering factor in both wars. There have been numerous attempts to eliminate this factor: although the methods have differed, the result has been the same – failure.

At the end of World War I the multicommunal Hapsburg and Ottoman empires were dismembered and Germany's borders redrawn. The Paris treaties concluding the war were supposed to establish new borders on the principle of giving nations their own states. In reality, they created new multicommunal states: a few vast imperial 'peoples' prisons' were replaced by numerous small 'people's jails.' Separate treaties on the protection of minorities were intended to ameliorate the shortcomings of the new 'national' states. However, they failed to satisfy many old or prevent new separatist or irredentist movements.

During World War II, National-Socialist Germany pursued a policy of homogenization by genocide and enforced germanization. Only the Allies' victory prevented its complete success. The victors in turn pursued a policy of homogenization by mass expulsion, in particular of Germans and other nationalities identified with Nazism in wide areas of central and eastern Europe. Genocide and expulsion did leave some states more homogeneous than before, especially Poland, but most states in eastern and southeastern Europe still included significant minorities within their borders. The Marxist-Leninist form of socialism was able to suppress the 'nationality question,' but, as had become obvious to all by 1990, not to solve it. Today it cannot be excluded that the Soviet Union, the successor to the Romanov empire, the third of the pre-World War I great continental empires, ultimately will share the fate of the other two. The end of the East-West conflict, settled not by a Third World War, but by free competition between economic systems, clears the stage for the same issues that occupied it before Sarajevo and Danzig. However, today these issues are relevant beyond Eastern Europe. They preoccupy large parts of Africa, the Near and Middle East, and Asia. For in these areas other huge multi-ethnic conglomerates have dissolved, i.e., the colonial empires. Just like the successor states of the empires shattered by the First World War, the vast majority of the post-colonial states are in turn multi-ethnic creations. Ninety percent of the global society of ostensible nation-states consists of multi-ethnic states.[9]

The former colonial powers as well as the leaders of most of the new states generally agreed that problems arising from ethnic, linguistic or religious heterogeneity should not be ignored, but overcome quickly and conclusively. They adopted an approach different from that previously practised in Eastern Europe and the Near East. The borders of the colonial territories were accepted as those of the new states. No attempt was made to adapt them to, or to erect new states for, ethnically, linguistically or religiously homogeneous populations. Instead, they concentrated on creating new nations by an act of will, irrespective of differences between the population groups concerned: i.e., 'nation-building.'

In many cases, however, the will required existed only among the political elites of the new states, the politicians, civil servants and army officers, i.e., that stratum that lived off rather than for the state, and hence had a vested interest in its existence. The new order of states in the Near East and Africa resembled in many respects Metternich's, and proved no more durable. Some of the new states fell apart during the process of decolonization: India, Palestine and Cyprus were partitioned after bloody conflicts; colonial federations in West, Central and East Africa collapsed. Many others are racked by permanent conflict. In some instances, nations straddling borders

[9] There are a number of terms in use. 'Multicommunal states,' 'multinational state' and 'multi-ethnic state' are used virtually synonymously. The English literature tends to favor 'multi-ethnic state.' 'Ethnicity' is not used in the original Greek sense, but to indicate identity on the basis of origins, language or religion. In this article, 'ethnic group' or 'community' denotes a group that defines itself in terms of one or more cultural characteristics ('markers'), and 'multi-ethnic state' or 'multicommunal' state a state that embraces more than one such ethnic group or community.

want to break up the states that sunder them: 'The states tear the nations apart; it is not surprising that the nations want to tear the states apart.'[10] What Karl Renner wrote of the Austro-Hungarian Monarchy is equally true of the Arab world today. In other cases, the colonial borders have forced together peoples who were traditionally hostile already in pre-colonial times, as in the Sudan, Chad and the Philippines. If the 'internationalization of nationalism' was the catch phrase of the decolonization phase, today's fashionable internationalisms are concepts of irredentism and separatism. In large swatches of the Third World and Eastern Europe, deterministic nationalism is the order of the day, a nationalism of peoples defining themselves by ethnic, linguistic or religious markers, who are dissatisfied with the existing order of states and want to live in a different state, or in their own state.'[11]

The attempts to homogenize have failed, i.e., both the adaptation of states to existing nations and the creation of nations for existing states. At the end of the 20th century the question facing large parts of the world in which different peoples and nationalities live among one another, as 'hodgepodges' of peoples – mostly areas formerly part of a supranational empire – is much the same as at the start. Can different groups that define themselves as peoples and nations live together within a single state, and how can they organize their coexistence? This question taxed minds and fired debate in the autumn of the Dual Monarchy. One product of that vital discussion is of interest today, a concept that offers an alternative to unsuccessful concepts of homogenization, viz cultural autonomy based on the principle of personality.

The concept was first formulated in 1866 by an Austrian Liberal, Adolph Fischhof.[12] Several decades later in 1902, the socialist thinker and politician Karl Renner developed it further, and in 1918 he refined his ideas.[13] Otto Bauer, another leading Austro-Marxist,

---

[10] Rudolf Springer, *Der Kampf der Österreichischen Nationen um den Staat* (Leipzig and Vienna: Franz Deuticke, 1902), 33. Rudolf Springer is the pseudonym of Karl Renner. Revised edition: Karl Renner, *Das Selbstbestimmungsrecht der Nationen in Besonderer Anwendung auf Österreich* (Leipzig and Vienna: Franz Deuticke, 1918).

[11] Hans Kohn distinguished between 'subjective-political' and 'objective-cultural' nationalism. The former is a voluntaristic concept, the latter deterministic.

[12] Adolph Fischhof, *Österreich und die Burgschaften seines Bestandes* (Vienna: Wallishausser'sche Buchhandlung, 1969).

[13] See Footnote 10.

took it up again in 1923 and 1924.[14] But by then the old Austria no longer existed. Initially, the concept left little trace in the history of ideas.[15] It was discussed by the Russian Jewish *Bund* in Zurich in 1905 and by the Mensheviks under Trotsky's chairmanship in Vienna in 1912. It influenced the Jewish proposals on the redrawing of Eastern European borders presented to the Versailles Conference. It was given legal expression in the short-lived independent Republic of the Ukraine in 1918 and in the law on language rights in interwar Estonia. In the 1930s the concept played a role in the debate on the future of Palestine within the Zionist movement.[16] It then more or less disappeared from political consciousness, partly because Lenin had rejected it,[17] but above all because of the new order of states erected in accordance with the will of the victorious allied powers.

Only in very recent years, as criticism mounted against 'real existing socialism,' did the Western European Left rediscover Austro-Marxism and with it the concept of the personality principle. It there is any logic to history, then it is only right that an old idea should be reconsidered in historical circumstances similar in many ways to those in which it was originally developed.

The potential effects of events that did not occur are by definition not demonstrable. It will never be known whether Renner's concept might have saved the Austro-Hungarian Empire had it been put into practice. However, it is sensible and possible to ask whether cultural autonomy and similar mechanisms have been practised in other multicommunal states, and to assess their success in regulating conflict and in comparison with other mechanisms of conflict reduction.

Karl Renner: personality principle and cultural autonomy

Renner regarded the personality principle as a mechanism that would facilitate coexistence in multicommunal states; it was an

[14] Otto Bauer, *Die Österreichische Revolution* (Vienna: Wiener Volksbuchhandlung, 1923); *Die Nationalitätenfrage und die Sozialdemokratie* (*Marx-Studien* 2) (Vienna: Wiener Volksbuchhandlung, 1924).

[15] On the history of its influence, see Heinz Kloss, *Grundfragen der Ethnopolitik im 20. Jahrhundert. Die Sprachgemeinschaften zwischen Recht und Gewalt* (Vienna and Stuttgart: Wilhelm Braumüller Universitäts-Verlagsbuchhandlung, 1969).

[16] See Frans Ansprenger, *Juden und Araber in einem Land* (Munich and Mainz: Kaiser und Grünewald, 1978), 46, Fn. 22.

[17] Vladimir I. Lenin, *Über die Nationale und die Koloniale Frage* (East Berlin: Dietz, 1960), 118–22.

alternative to the territorial principle. 'The ethnic territorial system has ... a major drawback: It requires partially self-contained, compact linguistic areas that also form a suitable basis for the performance of all the state's other duties.'[18] Where peoples or groups within the state form a hodgepodge this prerequisite is not fulfilled. Under such circumstances, territorial demarcations, whether unitary or federal, create majorities and minorities in a way that excludes any possibility of a change of power. Therefore the only way to act in the interests of all ethnic groups is to constitute *'nations as associations of persons instead of as areas of domination.'*[19] Renner demands that nations constituted on this basis should enjoy complete cultural autonomy and equality with one another in cultural matters, i.e., be safeguarded against domination.

Fischhof had already raised this demand decades before Renner. His goal was a Nationality Law that would 'regulate equality of the languages ... in schools, churches, the civil service, justice and legislation in words so clear and unequivocal that the national minorities would be assured against any encroachment by the majority.'[20] To guarantee this, legislative bodies might 'deliberate together, but should vote separately in national curiae.' Only those draft statutes 'which found a majority in each curia'[21] should be accepted as law.

This proposal is borrowed from the *Itio in Partes*, an article of the Treaty of Westphalia. During the perpetual Imperial Diet that met in Regensburg from 1663 to 1806 it was applied with great success, viz hardly at all – seven times in a century and a half. For as a rule the right of veto alone induced recourse to preventative compromise.[22]

This formula of the Treaty of Westphalia regulated coexistence between the confessions. But its writ ran beyond questions of the *status confessionis* to any question that one of the confessional parties regarded as important. Fischhof's proposal applied this principle to coexistence between linguistically defined nations. However,

---

[18] Rudolf Springer, *op. cit.*, 34.
[19] *Ibid.*, 36.
[20] Adolph Fischhof, *op cit.*, 188.
[21] *Ibid.*, 189.
[22] See Martin Heckel, *Itio in Partes. Zur Religionsverfassung des Heiligen Römischen Reiches Deutscher Nation*, in *Gesammelte Schriften. Staat, Kirche, Recht, Geschichte*, vol. 2, ed. Klaus Schlaich (Tübingen: 1989)', 636–736; *Parität*, in ZRK Kan. (Savigny Foundation), 80 (1963), 261–420.

he reserved the veto system of curial voting to 'questions of national interest.'[23] These included in his view legislation on schooling and language, but also certain matters beyond the cultural field, such as constitutional amendments and changes in the electoral law.

Renner's concept, in turn, goes beyond the power of veto. His concept is *radical cultural autonomy* – almost cultural sovereignty – but at the same time an autonomy restricted solely to the – broadly defined – cultural sphere. He deprives the state of virtually all responsibility in cultural matters.[24] The state would retain only general powers in formal and material matters. 'The separation of the spheres of interest is rooted in the respective natures of the state and the nation: The former provides the material culture and the latter the spiritual. Schooling, art and literature belong to the nations. However, as general education itself is an essential precondition of material culture, the state determines at all levels of schooling the minimum of education that the nations have to guarantee. At the same time, the state guarantees the poorer, undeveloped nations the means to provide this minimum. For the rest, it leaves schooling entirely in the hands of the nations . . . .'[25]

In Renner's view, nations are constituted in the same way as the confessions, that is, as corporations under public law. Just as the principle of *cuius regio, eius religio* in religious affairs had been abrogated, so the principle of *cuius regio, eius lingua* should no longer hold in cultural affairs.'[26] Just as membership of a religious community was a personal decision – 'a moral matter, not a legal one' – so membership of a nation had to be also: 'Membership of a nation is determined solely by an individual's declaration of nationality to the competent authorities. This right of the individual to self-determination is the correlate of every nation's right to self-determination.'[27]

This *principle of free association* is the basis of the cultural and linguistic nations. They should exercise legislative, executive and administrative powers. All nations, including the small minorities, should be adequately involved in governance. To achieve this, pro-

---

[23] Adolph Fischhof, *op. cit.*, 190.
[24] It was this point in particular that aroused Lenin's opposition. See Lenin, *op. cit.*, 118ff. However, Lenin was in favor of the right to mother-tongue instruction.
[25] Rudolf Springer, *op. cit.*, 84.
[26] *Ibid.*, 61.
[27] *Ibid.*, 65.

portional representation should be introduced at all levels, from the municipality through the district to the supreme state. At the level of the supreme state each nation has its own cultural parliament vested with exclusive legislative authority in cultural affairs.[28] Although municipalities and districts with people from different nations should have a single administration, in cultural matters mayors and district presidents must consult the representatives of minorities and 'may only act by mutual consent.'[29] In other words, minorities are granted the power of veto in cultural matters at the lower and middle administrative levels. Finally, each nation has its own national ministry, headed by a national secretary of state, at the level of the supreme state. This ministry is 'an organ of the state in respect of that authority in which the nation itself as a member of the union constitutes an organ of the state.'[30] The ministry appoints all civil servants in its field of responsibility. In administrative areas that do not fall within the responsibility of the nation the ministry has a right of scrutiny and a power of veto.

By the same token, Renner expects that 'functionaries from all nations will be appointed to posts at the middle and top levels on the basis of proportionality.'[31] To reassure the smaller and smallest minorities, there should be reciprocal agreements between the nations. The language of administration at the level of the supreme state should be chosen 'purely on technical and administrative grounds.'[32] This should not give rise to problems because, on the one hand, the nations already have proportional representation in the civil service, and on the other, 'here language is not an object of dispute but a means of communication.'[33] The state should have no official language.

In summary, Renner proposes that the personality principle, as defined by him, constitutes nations on the basis of the free association of individuals regardless of where they live, and provides them with exclusive powers in the sphere of education, upbringing and culture, as well as their own legislative, administrative and executive institutions; i.e., a perfect form of cultural autonomy. Renner's

---

[28] *Ibid.*, 38.
[29] *Ibid.*, 191.
[30] *Ibid.*, 201.
[31] *Ibid.*, 234.
[32] *Ibid.*, 235.
[33] *Loc. cit.*

proposals go beyond the purely cultural sphere by introducing a system of proportional representation through national lists, as well as proportionality in the civil service by giving the national ministries a voice in appointments. Later, Renner demanded that the nations be granted 'proportional codetermination' in the supreme state, a '*condominium pro parte indivisa.*'[34]

These proposals served a specific object. By granting cultural autonomy, Renner wanted to obviate disputes between nations over language, culture and education. The clearest expression of Renner's motivation is found in his comments on elections with national lists: 'The Czechs do not vote against the Germans, the Germans no longer against the Czechs.'[35] Consequently '. . . within a short time similar groups within the two nations will infallibly form alliances. And this puts an end to the struggle between nations.'[36] Elsewhere he explains that proportional representation will 'break down all nations into analogous groups' and the political parties will form themselves 'on the basis of economic programs,' with the result that in all nations 'the same groups will be fighting the same fight' and 'on the same front.'[37] In short: Renner's concern is to *depoliticize national cleavages*, so that these will no longer distract from the truly political confrontation between programs and interests.

Forms of conflict regulation and mechanisms to reduce conflict in multi-ethnic states

Simplifying by establishing ideal types, we can distinguish between five forms of regulation of ethnic conflicts.[38]

Disregarding genocide, since it would be terminological cynicism to treat it as 'regulation,' the most radical form of regulation is *partition* of multi-ethnic states. Peaceful partition by mutual agreement is rare, and has occurred only where the ethnic groups already lived apart in clearly demarcated regions. Examples include

[34] Karl Renner, *op. cit.*, 128.
[35] Rudolf Springer, *op. cit.*, 194.
[36] *Ibid.*, 195.
[37] Karl Renner, *op. cit.*, 278.
[38] On what follows, see Milton J. Esman, 'The Management of Communal Conflict,' *Public Policy* 21 (1973), 49–78; Theodor Hanf, 'The Prospects of Accommodation in Communal Conflicts: A Comparative Study,' in *Bildung in Sozio-Ökonomischer Sicht. Festschrift für Hasso von Recum*, eds. Peter A. Döring et al. (Cologne and Vienna: Böhlau Verlag, 1989), 313–32.

the short-lived Kingdom of the United Netherlands, the Union between Sweden and Norway and the Federation of Malaysia. More frequently, partition occurs after wars or civil wars. In the former instance it is enforced by the victors, in the latter the new borders usually cement the cease-fire line. Partition is often associated with enormous transfers of population and with massacres, as in the cases of the Indian subcontinent, Palestine and Cyprus.

A second form is domination by one ethnic group over others. This form is frequent, and can prove extraordinarily long-lived – witness the Indian caste system, 'apartheid one thousand years on,' according to Pierre van den Berghe. The methods used to maintain ethnic domination vary considerably: democratic control by a majority, as in Israel; the denial by a dominating group of the existence of other ethnic groups, as in Burundi and Syria; strict regimentation within an ethnohierarchy, as until now in South Africa; and physical repression, as in Ethiopia, the Sudan, Iraq, and many other places. However, the numerous cases of repression show that dominated ethnic groups are not prepared as a rule to accept their situation indefinitely, and that they revolt against domination even in the face of apparently hopeless odds. This frequently leads to prolonged violent conflicts.

Assimilation is a third form of conflict regulation. It is a milder variant of domination by one ethnic group. The dominant group accepts members of other groups, provided that they are prepared to abandon their ethnic, linguistic or religious identity and accept that of the dominant group. This condition is most likely to be fulfilled in the classic immigration countries. In non-immigration countries assimilation policies are often associated with enormous socio-economic pressure to adapt. However, the revival of particularist movements among groups previously regarded as models of successful assimilation demonstrates the deep roots of ethnic identities and their ability to flower again as soon as assimilative pressure is reduced.

Another form of conflict regulation seeks neither the eradication of the dominated cultures nor domination by one ethnic group. In Swiss political terminology this form is called *Konkordanz*, termed 'consociation' in political science.[39] Consociational systems recog-

---

[39] See Gerhard Lehmbruch, *Proporzdemokratie: Politisches System und Politische Kultur in der Schweiz und in Österreich* (Tübingen: Mohr, 1967); Arend Lijphart,

nize the existence of different national, linguistic or religious communities and try to organize their coexistence. Differences of opinion are not regulated by majority decisions but by consensus and compromise. The different groups participate in the exercise of power on the basis of proportionality or even parity. As a rule, the different groups in consociational systems enjoy far-reaching cultural autonomy. Consociation may be practised for a transitional period until political integration has been achieved, as in the Second Austrian Republic. But it may also be intended as a permanent way of organizing politics, as in Switzerland, Belgium, the Lebanon and Malaysia.

Consociational systems are often the result of bloody civil wars, and are based on the insight that none of the groups involved is able to establish domination, or only one that is probably not worth the price. One could term consociation a civilized cease-fire; at any rate, it is the product of an equilibrium of power. For this reason, consociational systems are always susceptible to factors that may affect the equilibrium, such as demographic shifts or foreign influence. Consociational systems take account of ethnic groups, organizing and politically institutionalizing their coexistence.

The fifth type of conflict regulation also recognizes ethnicity, but does not organize it politically. It may be termed political *syncretism*.[40] The ethnic, linguistic or religious diversity encompassed by a state is not only accepted, but appreciated and encouraged as part of the society's wealth. Diversity is valued positively as a characteristic of a transcending unity. This can be achieved only by treating all ethnic groups as strictly equal and respecting their cultural peculiarities, while at the same time depoliticizing them. India, Indonesia and Canada are at least partially successful examples of political syncretism.

Both states with authoritarian political systems and states with

---

'Consociational Democracy,' *World Politics* 21:2 (1969), 207–25; *Democracy in Plural Societies: A Comparative Exploration* (New Haven and London: Yale University Press, 1977); *Power Sharing in South Africa* (Berkeley: University of California Press, 1985); Hans Daalder, 'The Consociational Democracy Theme,' *World Politics* 26:4 (1974), 604, 621; *Consociational Democracy. Political Accommodation in Segmented Societies*, ed. Kenneth McRae (Toronto: McClelland and Stewart, 1974); Brian Barry, 'Political Accommodation and Consociational Democracy,' *British Journal of Political Science* 5 (1975), 477–505.

[40] Used in the original sense of the word: 'two parties combining against a third' or 'combined whole.' Consequently, political syncretism is the idea of a state that is composed of several parts, yet constitutes a distinct entity.

liberal, democratic systems provide examples of the five main forms of conflict regulation, though the distribution differs. As mentioned earlier, partition is seldom a result of democratic decision, but there have been such cases. Most frequently, domination is associated with authoritarian rule. But it can be guaranteed by democratic majority rule, as Sammy Smooha's analysis of 'ethnic democracy' in Israel demonstrates.[41] Assimilation policies are practised by both democratic and non-democratic states. Nowadays, most consociational systems are democratic. However, pre-democratic consociation was practised in the Holy Roman Empire, as well as in numerous post-Reformation city states within the empire. Yugoslavia is an example of a non-democratic consociational system that appears to be breaking apart under the strain of its constituents' staggered transition toward democracy. Finally, political syncretism is usually found in democratic systems, though with considerable reservations in the case of Indonesia.

For the purpose of this chapter, we can exclude partition as a form of regulation, at least in those cases in which it has produced homogeneous states. Where this has not been the case, the successor states practise some other form of regulation.

Most political systems that apply one of the other four forms of regulation try to combine it with efforts to *reduce the conflict potential* of ethnic diversity so as to facilitate its implementation. These attempts usually take one of two forms: federalist decentralization of power or cultural autonomy.

Federalism reduces conflict by allowing those political forces excluded from power at the top the opportunity to exercise regional power. By providing a measure of satisfaction it obviates the total opposition born of desperation. This applies to opposition parties in homogeneous states as well as to ethnic and national opposition. As a rule, systems of domination resort to federalism only in two situations: the ruling group is utterly confident of its control over the state, as in the Soviet Union prior to its current crisis; or domination can be maintained only at the price of concessions to ethnic opposition, as in the Sudan in 1972 at the end of the first civil war and again in 1991 in the hope of ending the second civil war.

In the great majority of cases the dominating groups are not

[41] See Sammy Smooha, 'Minority Status in an Ethnic Majority: The Status of the Arab Minority in Israel,' *Ethnic and Racial Studies* (forthcoming).

prepared to relinquish the power inherent in a centralized state. All assimilative systems reject federalism, since it is an obstacle to their prime political goal. This does not of course apply to assimilative immigration countries. For in such cases assimilation is by and large voluntary: emigration implies a readiness to break with previous linguistic and cultural identities and to integrate into the new country. Accordingly, immigration countries have no cause to fear that federal structures might endanger the process of assimilation. Consociational systems are usually simultaneously federal states. As their interest lies in the broadest possible participation of all groups in exercising power, a territorial division of power has its attractions. Systems practising political syncretism also tend to be federal states. In short: the greater the degree of cultural plurality allowed or desired by a form of conflict regulation, the more likely it is to employ federalism as a mechanism to reduce conflict.

Much the same can be said of the mechanism of *cultural autonomy*. Systems of domination permit it only when the political as well as the cultural ascendancy of the ruling group is beyond all doubt. In such cases, cultural autonomy is a two-edged sword. It preserves the identity of the dominated group; yet because this autonomy is inseparably associated with exclusion from the ruling culture, it is intrinsically discriminatory. All assimilative systems exclude cultural autonomy or reduce it to folklore. In contrast, mechanisms to guarantee different languages, cultures and religions are constituent parts of consociational and syncretist systems.

These two mechanisms of conflict reduction are differently suited to different constellations of multi-ethnic problems. At first sight, federalism appears to be better suited to states with territorially demarcated ethnic groups, and cultural autonomy better suited to hodgepodges. India's decision to redraw the borders of its states along linguistic divides and the Lebanon's rejection of any form of 'geographic federalism' for its extreme hodgepodge seem to support this argument. However, other examples advise caution. The cantonal borders in federal Switzerland are by no means identical with linguistic and religious borders. The two mechanisms can be combined or can exist alongside each other. On the other hand, federalism in hodgepodges without non-territorial cultural autonomy can result in just as much discrimination against minorities as a centralized state without any cultural autonomy. These considerations illustrate the importance of a cultural autonomy rooted in the personality principle, both for centralized and for federal states: it alone can effectively guarantee the cultural identity of ethnic, linguistic or religious groups living scattered and mixed among one another. Where there is an ethnic hodgepodge, cultural autonomy is indispensable for those forms of conflict regulation which are based on the preservation of ethnocultural diversity, viz consociation and syncretism. Whereas federalism facilitates both consociation and syncretism, in a hodgepodge situation cultural autonomy seems to be a necessary condition for the success of either form of regulation.

Cultural autonomy based on the personality principle: experience of its application

The conflict-reducing potential of an institutional mechanism can be assessed empirically with historical data. Within the scope of this chapter a few brief examples must suffice.

A classical case of cultural autonomy within a system of domination is the millet system of the Ottoman Empire.[42] Only members of the community of the faithful, i.e., Orthodox Muslims, could be full citizens of the empire. Christians and Jews who accepted the rule of Islam were given the status of protected persons (*dhimmi*). They were tolerated, but had fewer rights. Assimilation into the ruling group was open to them at all times. Those who did not take this step were subjected to restrictions that were applied with varying degrees of rigor, depending on the time and the place: they paid poll tax, were forbidden to carry weapons, and their word carried less weight in courts of law. Tolerance extended to religion, each religion's laws of family and inheritance, and to confessional educational institutions. The institutions of the religious communities were headed by ethnarchs – the Jewish Resh Galutha

---

[42] On what follows see Emile Tyan, *Histoire de l'Organisation Judiciaire en Pays d'Islam* (Paris: Brill, 1938); Antoine Fattal, *Le Statut Légal des Non-Musulmans en Pays d'Islam* (Beirut: Imprimerie Catholique, 1958); S. Benjamin Braude and Bernard Lewis, *Christians and Jews in the Ottoman Empire. The Functioning of a Plural Society*, vols. 1 & 2 (New York and London: Holmes and Meier, 1982); Karl Biunswanger, *Untersuchungen zum Status der Nichtmuslime im Osmanischen Reich des 16. Jahrhunderts. Mit einer Neudefinition des Begriffs 'Dhimma'* (Munich: Trofenik, 1977). For an excellent brief account, see John Bunzl, *Juden im Orient, Jüdische Gemeinschaften in der Islamischen Welt und Orientalische Juden in Israel* (Vienna: Österreiches Institut für Internationale Politik, 1989), 29–36.

and the Christian patriarchs – who needed the sultan's permission before they could exercise their functions. The religious communities were called millets, i.e., literally 'nations:' subjugated and dependent nations, but nations.

Thanks to the millet system, the Jews and Christians were able to expand their educational system considerably in the 18th and 19th centuries, so that in time their communities were better educated and more modern than the Muslims. From the mid-19th century, reforms were introduced that started a process in the direction of civil equality for Jews and Christians in the empire.

This equality was achieved in most of the Arab successor states of the Ottoman Empire. However, they also abolished the millet system. Arab nationalism had little truck with traditional ethno-religious distinctions; minorities were restricted to the practice of religion in the narrow sense. Syria and Iraq went as far as to nationalize the schools of the minorities. Against the gain in legal equality for the individual there was the loss of institutions that preserved the identity of the minorities.[43]

The position of the Arab minorities in present-day Israel is comparable to the millet system after the Ottoman reforms. Apart from certain restrictions related to security matters, above all the exclusion from military training, Muslim and Christian citizens of Israel have the same civil rights as Jewish citizens. In principle, non-Jews have a share in political power; in practice, however, they are effectively excluded by the majority in a system of 'ethnic democracy.' On the other hand, they are under no pressure to assimilate: laws of family and inheritance in accordance with their own religious teachings are recognized, they may conduct private schools, and the Israeli state has introduced school instruction in Arabic.[44]

The Lebanon is an example of a consociational system with cultural autonomy based on the personality principle. In contrast to the other Arab states, the Lebanon did not abolish the millet system, but modernized it and made it more egalitarian. The 17 religious communities do indeed have the same rights. Each community possesses its own jurisdiction in matters of family law, and enjoys the

[43] For a detailed discussion, see Theodor Hanf, 'Die Christlichen Gemeinschaften im Gesellschaftlichen Wandel des Arabischen Vorderen Orients,' *Orient* 22:1 (1981), 29–49.

[44] See Sammy Smooha, *Arabs and Jews in Israel. Conflicting and Shared Attitudes in a Divided Society*, vol. 1 (Boulder, San Francisco and London: 1989).

constitutional right to private educational institutions. Apart from having cultural autonomy, the communities in the Lebanon also participate in the exercise of political power: there is parity between Christians and Muslims in parliament and the government, and the highest offices of state are divided between the largest communities. The government has executive power, and normally takes decisions by consensus; disputes on important issues, including all that affect the autonomy status of the communities, must be settled by a two-thirds majority, giving minorities a power of veto.[45]

In contrast to consociational systems, political syncretistic systems draw a clear distinction between cultural autonomy on the one hand, and a political role for their ethnic or religious communities on the other. They employ cultural autonomy precisely with a view to reducing or preventing a political role for the communities.

Until the mid-1960s the Netherlands was regarded as a consociational democracy in which the religious and ideological 'pillars' – Calvinists, Catholics, Liberals and Socialists – shared power in broad coalitions. Since then the Dutch have moved towards openly competitive democracy. This transition has been considerably eased by the fact that the far-reaching cultural autonomy of the pillars has been left untouched. Each pillar has its own schools, universities, radio and television stations, all subsidized by the state. Those citizens who wish to remain within their traditional pillar have all these institutions at their disposal; those who wish to be free of their influence can join 'neutral' pillars.[46]

Indonesia borrowed many features of its cultural autonomy from the Netherlands as a precaution against the politicization of the religious communities and ethnic groups. Although the great majority of Indonesians are Muslim, five religions – Islam, Protestantism, Catholicism, Hinduism and Buddhism – are recognized as equal. Private, in particular religious, educational institutions are permitted at all levels, and some are subsidized. Religious instruction is being introduced in state schools wherever 10 pupils of the same

[45] See Theodor Hanf, *Koexistenz im Krieg. Staatszerfall and Entstehen einer Nation im Libanon* (Baden-Baden: Nomos Verlag, 1990); 'Le Liban en Perspective Comparée,' *Revue des Deux Mondes* (September 1990), 49–74.
[46] See Arend Lijphart, *The Politics of Accommodation: Pluralism and Democracy in the Netherlands* (Berkeley: University of California Press, 1975); 'From the Politics of Accommodation to Adversarial Politics in the Netherlands: A Reassessment,' in *Politics in the Netherlands. How Much Change?* eds. Hans Daalder and Galen A. Irwin (London: Frank Cass, 1989).

religious community are enrolled. Indonesia also has a policy aimed against ethnolinguistic particularisms. Instead of choosing the most widely used language, Javanese, as the official language, the government adopted a modernized lingua franca, *Bahasa Indonesia*. As it is the mother tongue of a minute minority, it is generally acceptable. Local languages may be used as the medium of instruction during the first three school years. Other non-institutional practices help to prevent the politicization of religious and ethnic particularisms; for example, minorities are overrepresented in the government, and most civil servants at the local and provincial levels are recruited among the local population, which reduces fears of domination by the majority.

Finally, Indonesia has developed an openly syncretistic state ideology, *Pancasila*, which praises the coexistence of religions and ethnic groups as the essence of the Indonesian nation, summarized in the motto 'unity in diversity.' Indonesia's language policy can be regarded as an unqualified success: Indonesian is now understood even in the most remote villages, and no resentment has been aroused, astonishingly not even among the Javanese, who are gradually losing the ability to write their traditional language. However, religious pluralistic equality is endangered by the spread of Islamic fundamentalism, although the government is vigorously trying to contain it. Ethnic separatism is prevalent in provinces that Indonesia acquired against the will of the local population, i.e., Irian Jaya and East Timor, where even years after annexation there is still sporadic armed resistance. Indonesia's political, and in particular military, leaders hesitate to make the move toward a more open form of democracy than that hitherto practiced. A major reason for this is fear of resurgent Islamic fundamentalist and particularist tendencies. Indonesian syncretism has yet to face the test of democracy.[47]

One country currently facing this test is India, the most populous democracy in the world. Since Pakistan's traumatic breakaway, India has been struggling with the problems of 'communalism' and 'lingualism,' i.e., centrifugal religious and linguistic tendencies. The state's answer to the former is to stress its secularist raison d'être and to practise liberality toward the schools of religious communities as a way of satisfying different religious communities and preventing

---

[47] See Theodor Hanf and Josette Marthelot-Tagher, *Education and Development in Indonesia*, research report (Frankfurt: German Institute for International Educational Research, 1987).

their politicization – apart from perpetuating British tradition. The latter was a source of dispute for decades. In the 1920s the Congress Party – ignorant of the facts – regarded the redrawing of borders in the Balkans as a model for India. After the shock of partition, the Congress leadership feared that it would precipitate the balkanization of India. Finally, after numerous and at times violent clashes between language groups, at the end of the 1970s the country was reorganized along language lines. Twenty-one union states were created, in each of which over 80 percent of the population spoke the same language. In these states the predominant regional language became the official language of parliament, the civil service and school instruction.[48]

However, this standardization was watered down by elaborate protection of minority rights.[49] The federal constitution grants each group with its own language, alphabet or culture the right to preserve it as well as to found and maintain educational institutions as the group sees fit. Nor may the state discriminate against these institutions in its subsidy policies. All states of the union and local authorities are bound by law to create adequate opportunities for children from linguistic minorities for primary school instruction in their mother tongue. A special commissioner for linguistic minorities is answerable only to the state president, who has a direct power of veto.

Decisions taken by the conferences of ministers of culture of the union states, as well as administrative agreements, supplement and give concrete expression to these constitutional provisions. For instance, since 1949 a linguistic minority has the right to a separate teacher if there are 40 pupils in a school from this minority or 10 pupils in any one class. Even in secondary schools minorities may be taught in their mother tongue; at the very least, it has to be offered as a subject.

The protection of linguistic minorities does not stop at education, but extends to the civil service. Prospective civil servants have the right to be examined in their mother tongue; their command of the relevant official language is tested only in the course of their probation. By a decision of a 1961 prime ministers' conference, use of the 'official language' applies only to internal communication in the

[48] Jakob Rösel, *Indien – Die Demokratischen Erfahrungen eines Subkontinents*, research report (Freiburg im Breisgau: Arnold Bergstraesser Institute, 1991).
[49] On what follows, see Heinz Kloss, *op. cit.*, 385–420.

civil service. Dealings with the public must be conducted in the common language of each area. Finally, every Indian even has the constitutional right to formulate complaints in a language current in the union or in a particular state.

According to the constitution, the official language of the union is Hindi. Initially, the official use of English was to be circumscribed. However, owing to the opposition of the Dravidian south, the prescribed limit has been regularly extended. In 1961 a 'trilingual policy' was recommended: In school the relevant official language and English should be taught, and in addition Hindi in the non-Hindi-speaking states and another regional language in the Hindi-speaking states. In practice, the recommendation was widely ignored. In the north Hindi became the lingua franca and in the south the relevant regional language, while English continued to be used in the federal civil service and in official dealings between the union states.[50]

The similarity between the linguistic policies adopted in India and Karl Renner's proposals is remarkable. Renner, too, favored a federal state with as many monolingual districts as possible and, concurrently, generous minority rights in mixed-language districts. If, over a five-year period, an average of more than 40 children of the same linguistic minority are attending a school over four kilometers away while living within a radius of an hour's walk of a village, a primary school offering instruction in the minority language would have to be opened in the village. A secondary school would be required if the conditions for a 'general, grammar, scientific or technical school' were fulfilled.[51]

Agreements adopted by conferences of Indian prime ministers and ministers of culture correspond to Renner's concept of 'reciprocal agreements.' His demands that civil servants speak the language of the people, that the relevant national language be used 'as high up' the civil service hierarchy 'as is at all technically possible,'[52] and that top civil servants be at least bilingual, have been realized in India. As one may assume that Indian politicians had not had the opportunity to study Renner's works, the similarity between Renner's concepts

[50] Robert L. Hardgrave, Jr., *India. Government and Politics in a Developing Nation* (New York, Chicago, San Francisco and Atlanta: Harcourt Brace Jovanovich, 1975), 93–6.
[51] Rudolf Springer, *op. cit.*, 185ff.
[52] *Ibid.*, 234.

and the Indian regulations probably reflects the similarity between the political consequences of linguistic problems in India and the Dual Monarchy.[53] Similar problems call for similar approaches. The fact that India largely succeeded in regulating its problems of 'lingualism' by means of the mechanisms described may well be regarded as one of the most impressive testimonies to the suitability of Renner's concepts for such problems. Today, however, India's problems of religious 'communalism' appear to be greater and more intractable. Sikh separatism and the new-found Hindu fundamentalist militancy have created an explosive situation that seems unlikely to be defused by the state doctrine of secularism and the cultural autonomy of the religious communities alone.

Conclusions

These examples allow us to draw some general conclusions. Cultural autonomy based on the personality principle can be applied as different forms of conflict regulation to fulfill different functions. In systems of domination it can serve to preserve the identity of dominated groups. In consociational systems it serves to ensure equilibrium, but can also ease the transition to adversarial democracy. In sycretistic systems it certainly helps to reduce the potential for conflict, although it is not necessarily capable of eliminating it. It appears to be a 'necessary condition lacking,' i.e., if there is only a cookie instead of a cake to reward adaptation, one result of assimilative educational policies will be the limited co-optation of dominated elites prepared to acculturate. In such cases, educational systems tend to practise rigorous internal selection. The losers tend to ascribe their failure not to the system, but to their own lack of ability. The consequence is usually resignation and political apathy. All in all, the result is satisfactory for the dominant group.

Partial co-optation deprives the dominated group of their most able leaders, while at the same time imparting to the rest a sense of inadequacy that they accept and internalize. Hence, under both favorable and less favorable economic circumstances assimilation may prove to be a more successful strategy of preserving privilege than open domination – at least for a certain time. In the long run assimilation systems must obey their own logic and eradicate group

---

[53] Heinz Kloss was the first to draw attention to this similarity (see *op. cit.*, 416ff.)

privileges. If they do not, or lack the necessary economic means, the true nature of assimilation becomes increasingly apparent, i.e., disguised domination – and, as with open domination, the process of ethnic opposition will gradually gather steam. Assimilation is therefore condemned to succeed – which is possible only in a flourishing economy.

There are further conditions attached to success. As a rule, the culture of the dominating group should have a higher standing than that of the dominated groups. Minorities that take a pride in their culture, like the Québécois and Spanish-speaking North Americans, resist assimilation. Attempts by dominating groups to belittle the culture of other groups are not always successful, as Afrikaner resistance to anglicization and Flemish resistance to gallicization demonstrate. Least successful are efforts to assimilate religious minorities, as illustrated by Christians in Islamic countries and Muslims in the Philippines. Attempts to use educational systems in order to coerce religious assimilation sometimes provoke vehement opposition.

Alfred Pfabigan

The political feasibility of Austro-Marxist proposals for the solution of the nationality problem of the Danubian Monarchy

In a discussion of state and nation in multi-ethnic societies it is useful to consider the fate of the Danubian Monarchy. After all, it was ultimately as a result of the unresolved nationality problem that this major factor contributing to order in Central European politics was destroyed. Part of the German-speaking intelligentsia of the Danubian Monarchy evidently saw its threatening downfall as predetermined by fate: in fact, apocalyptic fantasies are still considered to be characteristic of the culture of Vienna at the turn of the century.[54] However, an important counterforce to the passive attitude of such fatalists arose within the intellectual and political school of Austro-Marxism. Moreover, this school developed binding concepts for the reform and preservation of the integrity of the state by transforming it into a democratic federal state inhabited by different nationalities.

History refused success to these proposals, yet some commentators today take the view that if they had been carried out in practice the Danubian Monarchy would have been saved. Thus the study of the concepts of the Austro-Marxist school may provide an example of what can be learned from history.

Inevitably, in making such an attempt one is obliged to limit oneself to discussing a few principal elements and seeking to establish the fundamental core that can be generalized, i.e., the experiences that still possess validity in a changed historical situation. However, not only the generalizable portions of the reform

---

[54] The 1981 exhibition, 'Vienna Around 1900' in the Hamburg Kunsthalle organized by Werner Hofmann was held under the motto 'End of the World Experiment' (*Experiment Weltuntergang*), and the 1986 Paris exhibition organized by Jean Clair had as its motto 'L'Apocalypse Joyeuse.'

concepts of the Austro-Marxists should be investigated, but also the grounds for their failure. The Austro-Marxist concepts were meant to be viewed as an alternative to nationalism – both the 'hegemonic' nationalism of the ruling ethnic groups and the 'oppositional' nationalism of the groups that considered themselves oppressed. All these proposals have in common attempts to reduce the acuteness of nationality conflicts by advancing various kinds of arguments, to 'demystify' them, to reject the promises of nationalism, and to find ways by which antagonistic nations could settle their conflicts through appropriate procedures.

The first significant argument related to the definition of what in principle should be considered to be a nation. George Brock recently wrote, 'A nation is a people united by a common dislike of its neighbors and by a common mistake about its origin.'[55] While this is doubtless a correct observation, it is not one that could be regarded as a 'definition of a nation.' Brock's witty but valid remark has this characteristic in common with numerous earlier remarks about what constitutes a nation. Even when nationalism first flourished, it was not accompanied by any defensible or generally accepted definition of the term 'nation:' everyone talked about it, but meant something entirely different. However, there seems to have been method in this babylonian confusion of concepts – despite the regularly repeated claim to employ scientific concepts, the idea of 'nation' was a cockpit of irrationalism, not merely in its spiritual expression, but also in its biological, materialistic expression.

The individual attempts to conceptualize the phenomenon 'nation' were based on the competing traditions of similarly competing peoples, were visibly linked to the particular interests of their proponents, and employed ideology-related amalgams of various philosophical schools and scientific commonplaces. Here there was truly a 'Gordian knot' that Otto Bauer 'cut.' Bauer's definition of a nation as a 'community of human beings bound together into a community of character through a community of destiny'[56] contains an eminently demystifying, enlightening element, compared with the politically easily instrumentalized 'naturalistic'

---

[55] Cited in Peter Loewenberg, 'The Psychodynamics of Nationalism,' paper presented at the congress 'European Nationalism: Toward 1992,' Catholic University of Liège, Liège, Belgium, 4 September 1990.

[56] Otto Bauer, *Die Nationalitätenfrage und die Sozialdemokratie* (Vienna: 1907), 135.

concepts of 'nation.' 'History,' and collective experiences created by social destiny, 'culture,' and psychology – not 'spirit,' blood,' and 'nature' – constituted the bond that united human beings into a nation.

The inclusion of empirically comprehensible sociological and cultural factors that result from such a definition has a subversive effect with regard to bourgeois – or petty bourgeois – nationalism. The utopia of a 'community' consisting of individuals of the same nationality was linked with vast promises of future bliss. The Austro-Marxist theoreticians were able to delegitimize this utopia by using the Marxist argument of the class character of capitalist society. However, as long as their arguments restricted themselves to the unresolved 'social question,' their opposition to their opponents' promises had only marginal effect.

On the other hand, Bauer and above all Max Adler,[57] whose arguments reflected the influence of Fichte, also addressed a fundamental aspect of national ideology, i.e., cultural community. Adler deduced from Fichte's *Speeches to the German Nation*, a central text of German intellectual nationalism, the need for a unitary national culture as the precondition for the existence of a nation. At the same time, he taught that the reality of a class society prevents the realization of this postulate of nationalism. In a class society such as capitalism the 'community of destiny' is divided into at least two layers – 'top' and 'bottom' layers that inevitably result from the bourgeois system of domination, and create 'graduated levels' of access to culture. As long as the workers are not able to help themselves they are excluded from the blessings of the (supposedly) national culture.

In Adler's view, bourgeois nationalism and petty-bourgeois nationalism suffer from an insoluble contradiction between their claims and social reality. Ultimately they are capable only of excluding 'outsiders,' not of creating a new collective whole. Since it is impossible for a unitary national culture to arise in capitalist class society, in the final analysis under capitalism there can be no nation, only the idea of the nation. The task of creating nations retains its significance, but ultimately it can be accomplished only by the organized workers' movement that is striving to achieve social

---

[57] See his *Der Sozialismus und die Intellektuellen* (Vienna: 1910). Also Otto Bauer, *Deutschtum und Sozialdemokratie* (Vienna: 1907).

equality. Adler held that socialism was only in appearance a political party like the others, in reality it was 'above all . . . a cultural movement . . . similar to what Christianity was . . . a movement that is thus only secondarily political, indeed represents much more than this, indeed a reconstruction of the people . . . .'[58] In a discussion of the nationality problems of the Danubian Monarchy, Adler's concept is an elegant intellectual formulation that has but little to do with Marxism, and instead is to be ascribed specifically to Austro-Marxist revisionism.

The principal Austro-Marxist texts on the question of how the nations of the Dual Monarchy were to organize their life together are represented by Karl Renner's study *State and Nation* (published in 1899 under the pseudonym 'Synopticus') and his work *The Struggle of the Austrian Nations for the State* (published in 1902 under the pseudonym Rudolf Springer). In Renner's treatment of the question of the relation of state, nation, and territory to one another, we again find the author cutting an apparently insoluble Gordian knot. The postulate, 'a nation is a (territorially based) state' results automatically in an enormous number of conflicts arising from the different sizes of national populations and their unequal territorial distribution – conflicts which frequently lead to collective aggression on the part of national minorities and the defining nation of the state (*staatstragende Nation*) that dominates the territory.

On the other hand, Renner polemicizes vehemently against the assumption (which he brands as backward) that every nation should form its own territorially delimited state.[59] Renner saw a parallel between bourgeois ideas of property and the concept of the national state. Historically, he found the origin of this idea in the sovereignty dogma of the French Revolution, which in terms of Austro-Marxist thinking was a backward view compared with proletarian internationalism. Renner was convinced that this view would ultimately lead to anarchy in terms of international law – it is possible here to see an analogy to the anarchy that Marxism claimed characterized capitalist methods of production based on private property.

As opposed to this, Renner attributes a positive role to the Habsburg multinational state – a positive role, however, that it was

[58] Max Adler, *Der Sozialismus und die Intellektuellen*, 36.
[59] See, for example, Rudolf Springer, *Der Kampf der Österreichischen Nationen um den Staat* (Vienna: 1902), 42.

capable of exercising only after fundamental reforms. As an alternative to the 'atomistic-centralistic' view of the nationality question under the Dual Monarchy – according to which the individual remained unprotected *vis-à-vis* the central state power – Renner posits the idea of a democratic federal state of different nationalities composed of supraterritorial nations, each with its own legal personality. Every inhabitant of this state is to choose his 'own' state and to have the right to be registered on the appropriate nationality roll. The protection of the citizen's national rights is incumbent on 'his' nation, and regular legal procedures were provided for this. In accordance with Renner's personality principle, nationality is no longer determined by birth or place of residence, but by the free expression of the will of the individual. The different ethnic groups coexist in a state that is administered by a democratically elected central government. However, they are autonomous in sensitive areas, such as that of 'national culture.'

Renner's concept thus accords a secure place to nations and their interests, yet prevents these particular interests from dominating the state as a whole. Renner treats national conflicts as legitimate, but at the same time their intensity is reduced by their being subjected to regular legal procedures, and the scope that they can assume is limited. Consequently, at least in terms of the intended aims, numerous areas that otherwise would be conflict-intensive are removed from the jurisdiction of the street and 'brought within the law' (*verrechtlicht*) – one is reminded of Renner's historically successful idea of 'bringing the class struggle within the law.'

Without going into the details of the Austro-Marxist proposals – which were frequently products of their time, comprehensible only when one has detailed knowledge of the complex administrative machine of the Danubian Monarchy – it is possible to honor these precise detailed principles, concerned as they are to achieve fairness, as a 'cultural achievement,' to use Freud's term. In place of an unhampered, aggressive national 'drive' aiming at selfish self-assertion, we find supranational 'reason,' which views social development as a whole. Nevertheless, the Austro-Marxist proposals failed, and this failure cannot be explained merely by the overall lack of influence that Social Democracy had on Austrian policies – after all, the concept of a supranational party organization was also doomed to failure.

Marxist ideological criticism disputed the supposed autonomy of 'reason' and raised the question of its specific nature in a concrete historical situation. In this connection, the 'location' from which the Austro-Marxist protagonists made their proposals is of particular interest. In an attempt to establish generalizable conclusions, one might ask – on the basis of the Austro-Marxist example – whether, in a nationality conflict, proposals for its solution advanced by a party involved in the conflict which renounces force can be successful; how far the striving for fairness and reason is feasible (given their involvement in the conflict); and whether it is likely to be perceived as such by potential negotiating partners.

An analysis of the contents of the Austro-Marxist ideas is less important here than the attempt to determine the consequences that flowed from the nature of the political location from which the Austro-Marxist proposals originated. This location was, of course, not voluntarily chosen. However, one may ask whether the Social Democrats considered sufficiently the possible effects such a base would have on the acceptance of their ideas, or whether the 'political viability' of their concepts was impaired by their origin.

In so far as it made the claim to be an international party with an internationalistic ideology, Austrian Social Democracy was not really predestined to provide sophisticated proposals for improving the health of the Danubian Monarchy and solving its nationality problems. However, as Otto Bauer justly noted, 'Nobody is permitted to absent himself from the struggle for the solution of the Austrian nationality question.'[60]

The national question had poisoned the political culture of the Dual Monarchy to such an extent that there was scarcely a single area that was not burdened by it. The effects of national conflicts created severe incalculable problems even in the smallest organizational units of the Social Democratic Party and its trade union organization, just as they did in other aspects of life. Above all, however, the way in which parliamentary activity was crippled by national obstruction spoiled the political strategy conceived by the Social Democratic leaders. Parliamentarism played a central role in the specific revisionism of the Austrian Social Democratic Party referred to earlier. Despite the oft-decreed opposition to 'parliamentary cretinism,' and to the belief that parliamentary majorities were

---

[60] Otto Bauer, *Die Nationalitätenfrage*, 505ff.

the formative element in politics, the assimilative impact of parliamentarism on originally radical movements made itself strongly felt also in Austro-Marxism.

Although the revolutionary orientation of the party was never abandoned, the concept of revolution gradually acquired a new definition which ascribed a central role to parliamentarism. A passage from Friedrich Adler makes clear this ambivalence – an ambivalence associated with feats of interpretative prowess:

> We do not believe that the legislative machinery can achieve anything on its own, but we have no desire to leave it at the disposal of the ruling classes, who know full well what to do with it. We do not overestimate the importance of parliamentarism, but for us the *energy of the proletariat* is primary. It is this that we want to gather in order to apply it wherever the greatest success is to be obtained. However, in the great majority of cases this will be in the legislative machinery.[61]

Yet it was precisely the functioning of the 'legislative machine' that was severely damaged by national conflicts. The party rightly defined itself as one that first had to conquer the 'ground for the class struggle' or for what it eventually came to understand as class struggle in the context of its revisionist approach – i.e., a modern state system. As in so many other areas, Austro-Marxism played the role of belated helper in completing the bourgeois revolution and took over the work – both programmatically and pragmatically – of carrying out what the revolution had failed to accomplish in terms of (then) indispensable elements of the Social Democratic concepts of development.

The orientation in favor of preserving the integrity of the Dual Monarchy, which was an unquestioned *a priori* of the Social Democratic proposals, can be seen in connection with Social Democratic strategies and development concepts. At that period, Marxism proceeded on the assumption that larger economic units would be easier to socialize. However, the leading brains of the Second International did not judge the Austrian problem by this criterion. As early as 1882, Friedrich Engels had spoken with gleeful optimism of the impending disintegration of the Danubian Monarchy.[62] In 1908, Karl Kautsky also objected to Otto Bauer's views, holding that Austria would become superfluous even for those nations that still

---

[61] Friedrich Adler, 'Der Wert des Parlamentarismus,' *Der Kampf* 4 (1911), 415.
[62] *Marx-Engels Werke* (Berlin: MEW, 1971), 88ff.

believed they needed her.[63]

One may recall the passage from the resolution of the 1896 London Congress of the Second International that deals with the national question. It states, 'The Congress declares that it supports the full right of self-determination of all nations and sympathizes with the workers of all countries that suffer at present under the yoke of a military, national, or other despotism . . . .'[64] This declaration – highly prized by the Left[65] – unquestionably calls for interpretation in the context of the history of the Second International, affected as it was by nationality conflicts. It is, however, striking that this death sentence for the Danubian Monarchy, based on Marxist analysis, similarly was ignored by the Austro-Marxists, just as the later resolutions prescribing the conduct of the national parties in the cases of danger of war or outbreak of war were ignored.

The consequences of this political stance should not be underestimated. Given their automatic and scarcely even discussed preference for the continued existence of the Danubian Monarchy, the Austro-Marxists came under a questionable light in the eyes of those population groups whose feeling of living in a 'prison of peoples' steadily became stronger and stronger. Potential allies for the cause of democratization and social reforms were frightened away by this political position. On the other hand, the same political groups that were the strongest supporters of the preservation of the Danubian Monarchy were also the fiercest opponents of social reforms, and in their political agitation they spread the lie of the Social Democrats being traitors to the fatherland. In a way, the party had maneuvered itself and its political concepts into a battlefield where it had no allies, and it was viewed as a potential opponent by both mutually antagonistic groups, i.e., the governmental elite of the Danubian Monarchy as well as the nations which considered themselves oppressed.

Moreover, the isolation of the Austro-Marxists was heightened by the fact that the authors of this particular political concept that was aimed at assuring the continued existence of the Danubian

---

[63] Karl Kautsky, 'Nationalität und Internationalität,' *Neue Zeit*, Ergänzungsheft 1, Berlin (1908), 36.

[64] See *Die Geschichte der Zweiten Internationale* (Moscow: 1983), 462.

[65] See, for example, Lenin, 'Über das Selbstbestimmungsrecht der Nationen (The Right of Nations to Self-Determination),' *Werke in 40 Bänden*, vol. 20 (Berlin: 1972), esp. 437.

Monarchy were Germans – and thus members of the privileged nation. Robert A. Kann has noted that 'The Germans of Austria, as long as the German character of the empire remained uncontested, were not even aware that their much-praised loyalty to the state was largely determined by their undisputed privileged position.'[66] In the case of the Austro-Marxists, a 'failure' of this nature is particularly remarkable, since they were certainly aware of the connection between the national struggle and the social struggle. Nevertheless, in their work we do not find, for example, any reflection of the circumstance that within the monarchy the German working class enjoyed the status of a kind of privileged 'worker aristocracy.'[67]

The Austro-Marxist discussions of the national question focused on areas in which *everyone* was to profit from staying together within the empire: Max Adler declared that it was not in the interest of any of the nations to lose Austria, and that no better future beckoned to any nation if it were to leave the empire, rather than remain in a 'strong Austria.'[68] Finding a solution to the tangible problem of the inequitable distribution of resources, which had an impact on everyday life, was thus postponed. In their work, their perception of the underprivileged status of the non-German national groups is weak in comparison to their concept of a blissful future. Consequently, despite its recognized striving for fairness in future political arrangements, Austro-Marxism displayed a shortfall of empathy as far as the non-German peoples who saw themselves as disadvantaged were concerned.

This should be considered in connection with the fact that the party leaders of the first generation came out of the German nationalist movement, and a certain Zeitgeist-determined German nationalism was a general characteristic of Austro-Marxist thinking. Of course, Social Democratic German nationalism ought not to be compared with its aggressive bourgeois or petty-bourgeois variant. Nonetheless, its principal component was the damaging assumption of the cultural superiority of German-ness (*Deutschtum*), a superiority that unquestionably was decisive in determining

[66] Robert A. Kann, *Das Nationalitätenproblem der Habsburgermonarchie*, vol. 1, *Das Reich und die Völker* (Graz-Köln: 1964), 60.

[67] See Hans Hautmann and Rudolf Kropf, *Die Österreichische Arbeiterbewegung vom Vormärz bis 1945* (Vienna: 1974), 102ff.

[68] Max Adler, 'Das Österreichische Chaos und seine Entwirrung,' *Die Neue Zeit* 20, vol. 2 (1901/2), 643.

attitudes. This assumption frequently resulted in the Austro-Marxists defining something in all innocence as an interest shared by all that was actually an explicit German special interest, so that, as Hans Mommsen put it, 'frequently unilateral national interests' coincided with 'orthodox international principles.'[69]

The examples of such a misunderstanding of reality extend to Victor Adler's downplaying the importance of the ultimatum to Serbia that unleashed the war, and to Karl Renner's assertion that in the East there was merely additional territory for annexation. Beyond doubt, the Austro-Marxists relativized their own *Deutschtum*, but they did not escape its Zeitgeist-determined magic. It was precisely Otto Bauer – whom we held to be a 'demystifier' – who noted that 'The national ideology and national romanticism affect us all: There are few of us who are capable of pronouncing even the word 'German' without a conspicuous and striking emotional tone in the voice.'[70]

In the light of this statement, one should interpret the Austro-Marxist concepts as also providing a contribution to the solution of inner conflicts. The assumption shared by both liberalism and early Marxism that the Germans were to assume the political, cultural, and social leadership of Central Europe[71] also was accepted by the Austro-Marxists. Kann reports[72] that Marx denied the right to an independent national existence to virtually all the Austrian nationalities – with the exception of the Germans – on the grounds of their backwardness and weakness. Engels bequeathed to us not only the dictum about 'history-lacking peoples,' but also the dictum about 'ruins of peoples' and 'refuse of peoples' (*Völkerabfälle*), whose disappearance would represent historical progress. Faced with these Zeitgeist-determined, quasi-automatic positions, one must raise the question whether their mere existence and their unavoidable influence on the climate of communication (within which the necessary dialogue between the national and social opposition groups in the Danubian Monarchy proceeded) did not make 'reasonable' proposals for solutions impossible.

[69] Hans Mommsen, *Die Sozialdemokratie und die Nationalitätenfrage im Habsburgischen Vielvölkerstaat* (Vienna: 1963), 10.

[70] See Alfred Pfabigan, *Max Adler – Eine Politische Biographie* (Frankfurt/Main: 1982), 70.

[71] See Kann, vol. 2, 160.

[72] Kann, vol. 1, 53.

As far as the Austro-Marxists were concerned, they were obviously just as blind to the fact that even a 'well-meaning' German was scarcely listened to within all the national feuding as they were to the undeniable elements of national arrogance in their own basic thinking. Observing the behavior of the Austro-Marxists, one gets the impression that they were so highly impressed by their own proposals that for a long time they failed to realize the full extent of the centrifugal tendencies within the collapsing Danubian Monarchy — anyone who has ever studied the apocalyptic fantasies (*Untergangsphantasien*) in turn-of-the-century Vienna will note with amazement the degree to which the Social Democrats failed to take this mood seriously.

Correspondingly, the calculation of the Austro-Marxists that the integrity of the Danubian Monarchy needed to be preserved stood on feet of clay. That great symbol of unity, the emperor and the ruling house, hardly played any role in this assumption. What remained was the orientation toward a questionable common interest and the pathos of democratization. After the event Otto Bauer realized that this calculation was wrong: '(Victor) Adler led the fight for democracy in the belief that democracy would be able to transform old Austria, but in reality it was to demolish it.'[73] In this there may be an element susceptible to generalization: the dissolution of authoritarian structures cannot possibly save a supranational entity; instead it initially destroys it and helps to create new national entities that then need to be laboriously democratized.

In any case, the concentration of the Austro-Marxists on their own reform proposals blinded the party leadership to the real course of history. For what actually happened, i.e., the disintegration of the Danubian Monarchy and the independent statehood of the Austrian 'remnant,' no concepts had been developed in advance. The question arises whether one should not conclude from this that anyone who makes proposals for the reform of a multi-ethnic state entity ought to produce at the same time an alternative strategy for his own social unit in case the 'greatest possible catastrophe occurs,' i.e., disintegration — or worse.

[73] Cited in Mommsen, 304.

Part 2
History

Gerald Stourzh

Problems of conflict resolution in a multi-ethnic state: lessons from the Austrian historical experience, 1848–1918

The great temptation of a historian is to get lost in the history of terms, such as 'state,' 'nation' and 'people,' or to get lost in historiography on the topic of conflict resolution, commenting on Carlton Hayes, Hans Kohn, or Eric Hobsbawn, or, again, coming closer to the multinational empire of the Habsburg monarchy, on Josef Redlich, Oscar Jaszi, or Seton-Watson, Jr. and Sr., Robert Kann, and many others.[74] Instead this chapter will plunge directly into a specific theme to which a historian may make a contribution: the problems of conflict resolution in the Habsburg monarchy between 1848 and 1918. Ethnic conflicts have their ultimate root in a fundamental fact of history that has been most pungently expressed by a great British historian of Polish-Jewish extraction, Sir Lewis Namier. 'Unless there be a complete return to the conditions of the horde, the basic element of territory cannot be eliminated; there is no escape from the interplay between groups of men and tracts of land, which forms the essence of history.'[75] Indeed, the interplay between groups of men and tracts of land is fundamental. If groups of men

[74] See Carlton J. H. Hayes, *The Historical Evolution of Modern Nationalism*, 3rd ed. (New York, 1963); Hans Kohn, *The Idea of Nationalism* (New York: 1944); Benedict Anderson, *Imagined Communities* (London: 1983); Ernest Gellner, *Nations and Nationalism* (Oxford: 1983); Josef Redlich, *Das Österreichische Staats- und Reichsproblem*, 2 Vols. (Leipzig: 1920–26); Oscar Jászi, *The Dissolution of the Hapsburg Monarchy* (1929). On Robert Seton-Watson, see particularly the volume published by his sons: Hugh and Christopher Seton-Watson, *The Making of a New Europe: R. W. Seton-Watson and the Last Years of Austria-Hungary* (London: 1981), and the most important work by Hugh Seton-Watson: *Nations and States: An Enquiry into the Origins of Nations and the Politics of Nationalism* (London: 1977). The most significant of Robert Kann's writings remains: Robert A. Kann, *The Multinational Empire*, 2 Vols. (New York: 1950).

[75] Lewis B. Namier, '1848: The Revolution of Intellectuals,' in *Proceedings of the British Academy*, Vol. XXX (1944), 182.

who consider themselves different from other groups of men due to many factors – language, religion, 'culture,' idea of 'origins' (frequently merely imagined, but nonetheless important) – settle on a tract of land where another group is settled, the setting for conflict is there.

Karl Renner wrote the following key sentence in this book, *The Self-Determination of Nations*, published in 1918, a reworking of his earlier *Der Kampf der Österreichischen Nationen um den Staat* (1902): 'Nature knows neither an equality of individuals nor an equality of nations; it (equality) is a creation of law and its greatest benefit for those subject to it.' ('*Die Natur kennt weder eine Gleichheit der Individuen noch eine Gleichheit der Nationen, sie ist eine Schöpfung des Rechtes und dessen größte Wohltat für seine Unterworfenen.*')[76] Thus Renner alluded to two points which are of considerable significance for the understanding of multi-ethnic Austria in the last decades of its existence. First, the nationality problem in the Habsburg monarchy from the Revolution of 1848 onwards, particularly in the non-Hungarian lands of the monarchy after 1867, was dominated by the conflict between the postulate of the equality of rights of the nationalities ('*Gleichberechtigung der Volksstämme*,' as the official formula had it) on the one hand, and inequalities of power sharing and the demographic, social, educational and economic status of these nationalities on the other.

Second, Renner made it clear that the task of ensuring an equality of rights was very much a task of devising procedures and institutions, in other words, a task of a legal, constitutional and administrative dimension. Whatever may be said about Karl Renner as a politician, there is no doubt that Renner's greatest claim to creative inventiveness and originality is in the field of law, particularly administrative law and the sociology of law.[77] Renner was a creative genius in the field of the public law of multi-ethnic societies, and when there is discussion of the Renner-Bauer thesis, it needs to be said that its institutional and procedural originality is due to Renner rather than Bauer.

[76] Karl Renner, *Das Selbstbestimungsrecht der Nationen in Besonderer Anwendung auf Österreich*. Erster Teil, *Nation und Staat* (Leipzig and Vienna: 1918), 148.

[77] His work on the institutions of private law and their social function, published in 1904 (an English translation of which was edited by Otto Kahn-Freund in 1949 at the suggestion of Karl Mannheim for the International Library of Sociology and Social Reconstruction), won him international acclaim.

The equality of rights of nationalities

The Revolution of 1848 added a new dimension to the politics of the multinational empire: while grievances about unjust and unequal treatment of various ethnic linguistic groups were not new, the principle of equality or *Gleichberechtigung* opened up a new era of expectations in the multi-ethnic society of the Habsburg empire. There are sources that demonstrate how the principle of equal rights for all nationalities within the empire was seen as an extension, an application to collective groups, as it were, of the equality of individual rights enunciated by the French Revolution.[78] This new principle or postulate was most impressively formulated in April 1848 by Frantisek Palacky, the Czech historian and national leader: 'The equality of rights of all nationalities (and denominations) was the real legal and moral foundation of the Austrian empire.' This principle, he added, was grounded in natural law.[79]

The principle of equal rights for the peoples of the empire became the central postulate of constitutional reform during the first era of Austrian constitution-making in 1848–49; it also became the central article of the constitutional system of the non-Hungarian lands of the dual monarchy, of Cis-Leithania or Austria proper, between 1867 and 1918.

Before reviewing attempts to put this principle into practice, it is useful to discuss briefly ways in which the inequalities that existed among the ethnic groups of the Habsburg empire may be systematized.

The one distinction that ought to be dismissed once and for all, and has of course been subjected to critical comment, is the well-known differentiation drawn between historical nations and nations 'without history' (*geschichtslose Nationen*). It goes back to Friedrich Engels' writing on the Revolution and Counter Revolution in the Habsburg monarchy early in 1849. Engels used this distinction with a very polemical aim. On a deeper level than the polemical one, the distinction, of course, reflects a view of the historical process that

---

[78] Some references are supplied in Gerald Stourzh, *Die Gleichberechtigung der Nationalitäten in der Verfassung und Verwaltung Österreichs* (Vienna: Austrian Academy of Sciences, 1985), 18, 28–9.
[79] 'Das Völkerrecht ist ein wahres Naturrecht ... Die Natur kennt keine herrschenden, so wie keine dienstbaren Völker.' The passage occurs in Palacky's letter declining the invitation to join the preparatory committee for the German National Assembly to be held in Frankfurt am Main in April 1848. Quoted in Stourzh, *op. cit.*, 1.

confers the dignity of an historical people only on those peoples who were fighting in the cause of progress of history; other peoples, who were enlisted in the cause of reaction, were denied that dignity. Naturally, Otto Bauer did not have such a polemical purpose when he revived the distinction in his famous chapter on the 'awakening of the nations without history' (*'das Erwachen der geschichtslosen Nationen'*) in his book *Social Democracy and the Nationalities Question* (1907).[80] For Bauer, 'nations without history' were those nations which were ruled by ruling classes of another nation, at a time when they had no ruling classes of their own and had no culture of their own when culture supposedly was confined to the ruling classes only.

This view seems mistaken for various reasons. First, it ignores the role of substitute ruling elements in peasant populations like the Ruthenes, Romanians, Slovaks, Serbs or Slovenes at a time when these nations did indeed have no aristocracies of their own. 'Substitute ruling elements' can be translated to mean the national clergy, who in all the five ethnic groups mentioned played a considerable role in preserving the national identity of non-dominant ethnic groups. Second, it denies, in true Hegelian tradition, the dignity of 'historical' existence to oppressed ethnic groups with an undeveloped or underdeveloped social structure. But being part of 'history' is the fate – and the dignity as well – of the meanest individual or group as well as the most powerful or developed one.

A well-versed expert on the small peoples of East Central Europe, Professor Miroslav Hroch, has replaced the Bauer terminology (that incidentally has entered a good many important non-Marxian works on Habsburg history) by the terms 'ruling' and 'oppressed' peoples, emphasizing that he uses the term 'oppression' not in the sense of 'persecution,' but in the technical, morally neutral sense of the 'non-equal cultural or political position of the members of an (ethnic) group.'[81] This comes close to the terminology that was

---

[80] Reprinted in Otto Bauer, *Werkausgabe*, vol. 1 (Vienna: 1975), 49–622. For the relevant chapter, see 270 ff.

[81] See particularly Miroslav Hroch, *Die Vorkämpfer der Nationalen Bewegung bei den Kleinen Völkern Europas* (Prague: 1968), 16–17. In a revised English version of this book, Hroch maintains the distinction between oppressed (or 'small') and ruling nations; he does not seem to be able to do without the formula 'so-called 'nations without history,'' when making a further distinction among oppressed nations. See Miroslav Hroch, *Social Preconditions of National Revival in Europe* (Cambridge: 1985), 9.

proposed several years ago,[82] i.e., the distinction between dominant and non-dominant ethnic groups or nations, a differentiation that in the field of social, educational, legal, constitutional and administrative history might be supplemented by a distinction between privileged, underprivileged or non-privileged ethnic groups.[83] The status of different nationalities in accordance with the distinctions proposed could and did change over time; e.g., the Magyars changed from a non-dominant status in the years after 1848 to a dominant status after 1867. The same might be said of the Poles in Galicia.

It might be objected that among those nationalities described as 'dominant' or 'privileged,' such as the Germans, Italians (in the Adriatic parts of the Habsburg Empire *vis-à-vis* the Slav populations), Magyars and Poles, there were of course social classes that were not dominant or privileged at all. However, in a multi-ethnic society that is at the same time a multilingual society, easy (or easier) access to privileged languages is itself a privilege. There is no question that (with variations over time and strong regional differences) German, Italian, Hungarian, and Polish were languages that eased the paths of vertical mobility and facilitated access to social and economical advancement. The expectation of social and economic advancement was the most important motivating and mobilizing force in what in German is suggestively referred to by the term *Assimilationssog*, i.e., the 'assimilating suction' exercised by ethnic and language groups that held forth greater promise of social

---

[82] Gerald Stourzh, *Die Gleichberechtigung der Nationalitäten in der Verfassung und Verwaltung Österreichs 1848–1918* (Vienna: Verlag der Österreichischen Akademie der Wissenschaften, 1985), 4–6. See this study for a more elaborate treatment with references of the topic of this article. In addition, the present article drawns on the following earlier studies by the author: 'Galten die Juden als Nationalität Altösterreichs?' in *Studia Judaica Austriaca* 10 (Eisenstadt: 1984): 73–117; 'Frankfurt – Wien Kremsier 1848–49. Der Schutz der Nationalen und Sprachlichen Minderheit als Grundrecht,' in *Grund- und Freiheitsrechte von der Ständischen zur Spätbürgerlichen Gessellschaft*, ed. G. Birtsch (Göttingen: 1987), 437–56. Both studies were reprinted in the collection G. Stourzh, *Wege zur Grundrechtsdemokratie* (Vienna-Cologne: 1989).

[83] Between 1983 and 1988 a European research project, 'Governments and Non-Dominant Ethnic Groups in Europe 1850 to 1940,' was undertaken under the auspices of the European Science Foundation (Strasbourg), enlisting the cooperation of more than 90 scholars from 18 European states. The studies prepared by eight working groups will be published in a series edited by Michael Thompson (London: chairman), François Bedarida (Paris), Lothar Gall (Frankfurt), Matti Klinge (Helsinki), and Gerald Stourzh (Vienna).

and economic advancement.

Nationality conflicts in the late Habsburg monarchy – on the local level of the fight for the status of individual persons and families – most frequently consisted of a fight between national organizations or institutions wishing to retain individuals and families within the fold of the less privileged group and those wishing to add them to the socially more prestigious or politically more powerful nationality. This kind of nationality conflict was particularly actute in two areas: schooling and the language census. Examples of both fields abound and have been examined in recent scholarship.[84]

The second point that should be made about dominant/non-dominant and privileged/non-privileged distinctions is the following. As distinguished from wholly democratized or republican multi-ethnic states, the Habsburg Empire possessed at its center and as its centre the dynasty, the emperor and king, his government, his bureaucracy, and his army. The dynasty, or the emperor and king, engaged time and again in changing alliances with certain nationalities to the detriment of other nationalities. Those nationalities (or their leading groups and spokesmen) which enjoyed the favor of the crown for whatever motives – the crown's principal motive certainly being the maintenance (or restoration, as in 1848–49) of the power position of the empire as a whole – thus possessed support that enhanced their relative position within the multi-ethnic empire. The way in which the imperial government sought help from the surrounding nationalities, Croats, Serbs, Transylvanian Saxons, etc., against the Magyars during the revolutionary war of 1848–49 is well known. The way in which the compromise of 1867 favored the Magyars on the one hand, and (with permanent results) the Germans on the other hand, is also well

---

[84] The school instruction question was the object of special study with case references to Bohemia, Moravia, Styria and Carinthia in my book, *Die Gleichberechtigung der Nationalitäten in der Verfassung und Verwaltung Österreichs 1848–1918* (See Footnote 18). The problems of the language census (which regularly, i.e., every ten years from 1880 to 1910, and to an increasing extent was accompanied by vast campaigns passionately aged like electoral campaigns, including boycott threats, petty cheating, etc.), were brought to light with a wealth of new source material in the excellent book by Emil Brix, *Die Umgangssprachen in Altösterreich zwischen Agitation und Assimilation* (Vienna-Cologne-Graz: 1982). One was not allowed to indicate two (or more) languages as one's 'language of communication' ('*Umgangssprache*'). The obligation to indicate one and only one language exacerbated ethnic and language conflict, whereas the possibility of indicating two or more languages would have worked to blur ethnic and language differences, thus contributing toward conflict resolution.

known. The speed with which the emperor and his governments dropped nationalities whose support had been enlisted for specific purposes (e.g., the Croats after 1849, or the Romanians and Saxons of Transylvania in 1865, or the Czechs in 1871) surely is a phenomenon that deserves condemnation by anyone holding the view that the postulate of national *Gleichberechtigung* was a postulate for which a nation should strive. Attempts at 'conflict resolution' by way of shifting alliances were partial and unstable at best, and at worst ultimately acerbated relations among the different nationalities.

There is a third kind of distinction useful in analyzing the multi-ethnic Habsburg Empire that may be useful in analyzing other multi-ethnic states as well. This is the distinction between ethnic groups living exclusively *within* the multi-ethnic state (or empire), and ethnic groups having kinsfolk across the state border. Czechs, Slovaks, Magyars, Slovenes, and Croats were groups that lived exclusively within the confines of the empire, whereas Poles, Ruthenes (i.e., Ukrainians, disregarding denominational differences), Romanians, Serbs, Italians, and Germans were not. It is not the purpose of this chapter to give an account of the 'irredentist' pulls and pushes that increasingly were to unsettle the Danubian Empire, yet it seems relevant to draw attention to this kind of distinction. If Karl Renner wrote a book, *The Struggle of the Austrian Nations for Their State* (1902), one should recall the solidarity from across their borders that certain nationalities were able to enlist, while others were not.

A second main point to be discussed is the great project of conflict resolution by devising procedural and institutional ways for effectively creating or ensuring a kind of equality of rights, *Gleichberechtigung*. The Revolution of 1848 produced both the opportunities and the pitfalls that the constitutionalization and the liberalization of politics hold in store for multi-ethnic states. The opportunities were of course those of representation, of power sharing, of the security against arbitrary and discretionary rule offered by foreseeable constitutional procedures (to the extent to which they were not broken or disregarded, which was to happen not infrequently). The pitfalls were revealed in the discovery that the classic liberal (and democratic) criterion of majority rule[85] did not

---

[85] See John Locke, *Second Treatise of Government*, ch. VIII, para. 96: 'For, when any number of men have, by the consent of every individual, made a community, they

work in multi-ethnic states with compact ethnic minorities.[86]

One of the great achievements of political and constitutional liberalism in Austria was the considerable amount of autonomy granted to self-governing municipalities; some authors have spoken of many little republics permeating the empire of Austria.[87] But the historical evidence shows that the record of self-governing bodies in terms of respect for minority rights is very bad indeed. The author has made a study of about 115 complaints concerned with nationality and language conflict heard by the highest constitutional court of Austria (*Reichsgericht*) and of about 200 complaints also concerned with nationality and language conflict addressed to the highest administrative court of Austria (*Verwaltungsgerichtshof*). This research demonstrated rather unexpectedly that by far the greater number of violations of the constitutionally guaranteed equality of rights of nationalities and of the use of languages (according to Article 19 of the Fundamental Law on the general rights of citizens after 1867) was committed by autonomous bodies, whereas a much smaller number was committed by government agencies proper.

The protection of minority rights thus became (and remains) the major constitutional and political challenge of constitutionalism in multi-ethnic states. Here an important point needs to be made. For the last 51 years of its existence – from 1867 to 1918 – the Dual Monarchy consisted of 'two totally different halves,'[88] as an excellent student of national consciousness in general and Habsburg

---

have thereby made that community one body, with a power to act as one body, which is only by the will and determination of the majority.'

[86] This discovery or realization is most forcefully expressed in a short work, *Das Recht der Minoritäen* (Vienna: 1898) by George Jellinek, a celebrated authority on public law. This study was published also as an article in *Zeitschrift für das Privat- und Öffentliche Recht der Gegenwart*, vol. 25 (1898), 429–66. Jellinek argued in favour of constitutional arrangements providing for a veto right by (large) national (ethnic) groups. He referred to earlier constitutional arrangements that had provided a veto right for denominational groups, as in the Holy Roman Empire after the Treaty of Westfalia (the so-called *itio in partes* of the Corpus Evangelicorum and the Corpus Catholicorum), as well as John C. Calhoun's *A Disquisition on Government* and its theory of the 'concurrent majority.'

[87] Friedrich Tezner, *Handbuch des Österreichischen Administrativverfahrens* (Vienna: 1898), 389.

[88] Frederick Hertz, *Nationality in History and Politics* (London: 1944 [third impression 1951]): 199.

affairs in particular put it. Hungary became a national state with national minorities, which originally were protected by generous liberal nationality legislation,[89] but gradually were more and more strongly confronted with openly avowed claims of Magyar hegemony.[90] The non-Hungarian part of the Dual Monarchy, Cis-Leithanian Austria, made some valiant, though in the end insufficient, attempts to put into effect the postulate of national equality.[91]

Some of the most ingenious procedural and institutional attempts to ensure minority protection remained only on paper as draft constitutions or draft laws that were never put into practice, such as the 'Kremsier' (Kromeriz) Constitution of 1848–49, or the draft nationality legislation of 1871 for Bohemia. Other attempts, like the judicial redress for administrative infringements of nationality rights provided by the *Reichsgericht* and the *Verwaltungsgerichtshof*, were rather successful in safeguarding minority rights. The introduction of nationally separate institutions for the supervision of education, first introduced in Bohemia in 1873 and carried to great perfection in Moravia in 1905, should also be mentioned, as should also the major national 'compromises' in Moravia (1905) and the Bukovina (1909–10). These compromises, particularly the one in Moravia, were, however, measures of pacification by separation, pacification by isolation; they did not lead to a new consciousness of integration, of 'togetherness,' if the expression be permitted.

One feature of 'pacification by separation,' as demonstrated by the new institutional device of nationally separate school boards introduced first in Bohemia and then in Moravia, has received too little attention. This was the introduction of the obligatory option for membership in a particular ethnic group that was taken to considerable length in the Moravian settlement of 1905.

Ethnic membership (the official term being '*Volkszugehörigkeit*') became an inescapable decision. At first, in doubtful cases, it was

[89] The legislation of 1868 largely reflected the idea of Joseph Baron Eötvös, who was perhaps the Habsburg monarchy's most interesting political thinker of the 19th century.

[90] For sources, see Oscar Jászi, *The Dissolution of the Habsburg Monarchy* (Chicago: 1961; originally published in 1929), ch. 3, 'The Chief Tendency of the Hungarian National Struggles: The Move Toward a Unified National State,' 298ff., especially 321.

[91] Oscar Jászi has characterized the 'Chief Tendency of the Austrian National Struggles' as 'The Move Toward National Equality;' see ch. 2 of *The Dissolution of the Habsburg Monarchy*, 283–96.

permitted that ethnic membership be determined by personal choice. In a beautifully worded judgment in 1881, the Austrian Administrative Court held as follows:

> Sowie nun zum Wesen einer Nation, einer Nationalität gehört, daß sie andern gegenüber sich als Einheit und als abgeschlossenes Ganzes erkennt und bethätigt, so wird auch für den Einzelnen die Zugehörigkeit zu einer bestimmten Nationalität wesentlich Sache des Bewußtseins und des Gefühls sein.
>
> Sicherlich wird der einzelne Angehörige einer Nationalität die Sprache der Nation sprechen, wohl auch ihre Sitten theilen, allein auch ebenso gewiß ist, daß die Kenntnis der Sprache, die Bethätigung der Sitten einer Nation auch bei Dritten, Fremden zutreffen kann, weshalb diese Merkmale für sich allein zur Bestimmung der Nationalität nicht ausreichen.
>
> Eben darum wird, wenn im concreten Falle die Nationalität eines Einzelnen in Frage steht und es an äußeren Bethätigungen nationaler Gesinnung mangelt, sicherlich nichts anderes erübrigen, als ihn um seine Nationalität zu befragen und als Angehörigen jener Nationalität zu behandeln, zu welcher er selbst sich bekennt.[92]

Around 1910, this priority of subjective choice gave way to new interpretations – both in the Imperial Court and in the Administrative Court – which stressed the 'objective' principle of determining ethnic attribution – in doubtful cases – even by means of administrative investigation. In the province of Moravia, by 1911, elaborate questionnaires were drawn up by the imperial authorities designed to gather points of information for a final official attribution of ethnic membership. Thus one of the last and most thoroughgoing procedural and institutional innovations aimed at conflict resolution in late imperial Austria – the Moravian 'national compromise' – included the foreshadowing of bad things to come: i.e., *the mandatory attribution of ethnicity.*

Such a mandatory attribution of ethnic membership was

[92] Quoted in Stourzh, *op. cit.*, 205. See the English translation cited in Robert A. Kann, *op. cit.*, 311: 'It is in the nature of a national group to act toward outsiders as a unit and a well-rounded whole. To the single individual adherence to a definite national group means essentially a matter of consciousness and feeling. To be sure, the member of a national group will speak its language; he probably will obey its customs, yet it is equally certain that command of the language and practice of the customs of the national group may apply to strangers as well. Thus these features are insufficient in themselves to determine national status.

Therefore, if in a concrete case the national status of an individual is contested and external manifestations of [his] national consciousness are lacking, it will be necessary to question him about his national status. He will have to be considered a member of that national group to which he belongs according to his own declaration.'

dangerous even when equal citizen rights were guaranteed and maintained, as was the case in late imperial Austria. It was to become terrible in later years, when this was turned against the Jews.

While there is no need to analyze here the unholy alliance between anti-Semitism 'old' and 'new' and various brands of social Darwinism (out of which was to grow national socialist racism), one little known and unsuspected factor ought to be mentioned. In the English language of the late 19th and 20th centuries, the words 'ethnicity' and 'ethnic' were not in use; 'nationality' and 'national' related to political organization; instead, 'race' and 'racial' were the terms used as 'nationality' and 'national' are used now. 'Nationality,' Woodrow Wilson observed in 1900, 'did not mean to Germans what it meant to Englishmen or Americans. The Germans regarded it as meaning race.'[93] The result of Anglo-American usage was that the minority treaties and minority articles in the peace treaties of 1919–20 spoke of 'racial, religious or linguistic minorities,' not of 'ethnic, religious or linguistic' minorities.[94]

The concept of 'racial' or 'race' as embodied in the peace treaties, when combined with the 'objective' attribution of ethnic membership, led as early as 1921 to a most unfortunate decision by the Austrian Administrative Court, turning down the request of a national of Jewish extraction from Galicia in imperial Austria to opt for the Republic of Austria on the basis of his 'German' ethnic membership. A majority of the tribunal held that a person belonging to the Jewish 'race' could not change his ethnic membership to German (decision of June 9, 1921). Subsequent decisions by the Austrian Administrative Court returned to a 'subjective,' more flexible interpretation of ethnic membership along the lines of the 1881 definition quoted earlier.[95] The mandatory attribution of ethnic membership (in cases of doubt) re-emerged in 1930–31 at the University of Vienna in the attempt (short-lived due to a ruling of the Austrian Constitutional Court) to organize the student body along

[93] Quoted in Erwin Viefhaus, *Die Minderheitenfrage und die Entstehung der Minderheitenschutzverträge auf der Pariser Friedenskonferenz 1919* (Würzburg: 1960), 110, from Harley Notter, *The Origins of the Foreign Policy of Woodrow Wilson* (Baltimore: 1937), 104.

[94] See, for example, Articles 8 and 12 of the minority treaty with Poland of June 28, 1919; a similar terminology, referring to persons different from (or similar to) majority populations according to 'race and language' appears in Article 80 of the peace treaty of Saint Germain with Austria.

[95] See Jonny Moser, 'Die Katastrophe der Juden in Österreich,' *Studia Judaica Austriaca*, vol. 6 (Eisenstadt: 1977), 91–2.

'national' – i.e., racial – lines.[96] These were little known preludes to infinitely worse to come – the mandatory attribution of ethnic membership under Nazi rule, accompanied by discrimination, persecution and finally destruction.

In his final paragraph, the historian may be permitted to make a general observation about contemporary phenomena of ethnic autonomy. The recent 'explosion of ethnicity' in parts of Central and Eastern Europe – though part and parcel of a liberating process from totalitarian domination – awakens ominous memories of the past, 'the demons of the day before yesterday,' as an eminent Austrian journalist of Hungarian extraction recently observed. 'Ethnos' and 'demos' are two different sources of two different meanings of 'people' and 'nation.'[97] The German scholar Rainer Lepsius has commented critically on the possible implications of a notion of 'nation' that is one-sidedly ethnically and 'culturally' oriented:

Concepts of a nation that primarily relate to ethnic and cultural characteristics of a collective constitute as a subject of national unity and self-determination ethnic and cultural essences (*Wesenheiten*) whose interests can no longer be determined by means of established procedures. The interests of the 'German People' and 'German Culture,' interpreted in terms of the philosophy of history, cannot be subjected to the principles of majority decision, the institutionalization of conflicts, or pragmatic com-

---

[96] See Brigitte Fenz, 'Zur Ideologie der 'Volksbürgerschaft.' Die Studentenordnung der Universität Wien vom 8. April 1930,' *Zeitgeschichte 5* (1977–78): 125–45; see also her chapter 'Deutscher Abstammung und Muttersprache,' in Brigitte Fenz, *Österreichische Hochschulpolitik in der Ersten Republik* (Vienna-Salzburg: 1990). A moving account of the dilemmas posed by the obligatory attribution of ethnic membership ('*Volkszugehörigkeit*') required of students at the University of Vienna in 1931 is given in Richard Thieberger, 'Assimilated Jewish Youth and Viennese Cultural Life around 1930,' in Ivar Oxaal, Michael Pollak and Gerhard Botz eds., *Jewish, Antisemitism and Culture in Vienna* (London and New York: 1987), 174–84. Thieberger tells how he answered the questionnaire about '*Volkszugehörigkeit*' with 'Österreichischer Jude,' whereupon the anti-Semitic and germanically inclined student official supervising the completion of the questionnaires struck out the word 'Austrian.'

[97] See the most interesting book by Emerich Francis, *Ethnos und Demos. Soziologische Beiträge zur Volkstheorie* (Berlin: 1965). A meaning of 'nation' derived from the 'demos'-source is of course to be found in Ernest Renan's well-known Sorbonne lecture 'What is a Nation?' (1882). This idea of a political nation is by no means obsolete, as not only the United States and Canada, but Switzerland as well as the Republic of Austria have shown in recent decades. See, for example, William T. Bluhm, *Building an Austrian Nation – the Political Integration of a Western State* (New Haven, Conn.: 1973). For a very recent discussion, see Gerald Stourzh, *Vom Reich zur Republik. Studien zum Österreichbewußtsein im 20. Jahrhundert* (Vienna: 1990).

promise, and consequently are unresponsive to constitutional arrangements.[98]

Lest the dangers pointed out by Lepsius prevail, two conditions seem essential. First, ethnic groups that conceive themselves as nations must not conceive themselves as closed entities: consciousness, not origins (*Bewußtsein*, not *Abstammung* with its terrible abusive implications) is important. It is noteworthy that post-World War II definitions regarding ethnic groups: (a) avoid the term 'race' that appeared in the post-World War I treaty provisions; and (b) stress 'subjective' rather than 'objective' factors of ethnic membership. A report of the United Nations Subcommission on Prevention of Discrimination and Protection of Minorities in 1972 defined ethnic groups as 'peoples who *conceive of themselves as one* by virtue of their common ancestry (*real or imagined*), who are united by emotional bonds, a common culture, and by concern with the preservation of their group.[99]

Secondly, there must be no mandatory attribution of or exclusion from ethnic membership.[100] Ethnic attributions in official documents appear to be fraught with the dangers of discrimination.

Thirdly, there must be procedural guarantees for the institutionalization of conflict articulation and conflict resolution. In the case of both individuals and groups, such procedural guarantees need to respect equality of rights, without attempts at conflict resolu-

---

[98] M. Rainer Lepsius, 'Die Teilung Deutschlands und die deutsche Nation,' in *Politische Parteien auf dem Weg zur Parlamentarischen Demokratie*, eds. L. Albertin and W. Link (Düsseldorf: 1981), 443. 'Nationsvorstellungen, die sich primär auf ethnische und kulturelle Eigenschaften einer Kollektivität beziehen, konstituieren als Subjekt der nationalen Einheit und Selbstbestimmung ethnische und kulturelle Wesenheiten, deren Interessen nicht mehr verfahrensmäßig festgestellt werden können. Die geschichtsphilosophisch interpretierten Interessen des 'Deutschen Volkes' und der 'Deutschen Kultur' entziehen sich dem Prinzip der Mehrheitsentscheidung, der Institutionalisierung von Konflikten, der pragmatischen Kompromißfindung, sie sind insofern politischen Verfassungsformen gegenüber indifferent.'

[99] See the 'Capotorti Report,' U.N. Document E/CN 4 (Sub. 2/L. 564, June 19, 1972). Italics supplied.

[100] Valuable information on the question of the mandatory attribution of ethnic membership and the question of objective and subjective criteria is to be found in the history of the German-Polish nationality conflict in Upper Silesia during the interwar period under the provisions of the Upper Silesia Convention of 1922. Article 74 of this convention stated that the question whether a person did or did not belong to a racial, linguistic or religious minority may not be verified or disputed by the authorities. See George Kaeckenbeeck, *The International Experiment of Upper Silesia* (London: 1942), 23–4, 299–300, 319–30, 610.

tion in a multi-ethnic society are bound to fail. It is in this domain that the experiments attempted and the theories developed in Austria during the period between 1848 and 1918 may again be of interest to the contemporary world.

Zdenek Kárník

Attempts to achieve a German-Czech *Ausgleich* in Habsburg Austria and the consequences of its failure

In September 1990, preparing a paper concerning textbooks on German history for a German-Czech symposium, I was impressed by a book that dealt especially accurately with developments in Habsburg Austria. This work was one of the few to appraise positively the German-Czech *'Ausgleich'* (compromise) in Moravia (the *'Mährenpakt'*); however, it merely listed other attempts at *Ausgleich*, naming only the most important. The book even went so far as to state that the language regulations and all the other preparatory activities (in 1880, 1882 and 1897) were 'causes' of the outbreak and spread of the national skirmishes and struggles which ultimately proved so disastrous to the Danubian Monarchy. This was not surprising, in view of the great popularity among historians of the general thesis that, west of the Rhine, 'nation states' would help to solve the problem of managing society without major conflicts. Polities in countries east of the Rhine had, however, been unfortunate in that new nations – i.e., 'linguistic' or 'cultural' nations – had developed whose boundaries did not coincide with the state frontiers that had been established for various historical reasons at other times and under different conditions. This chapter is designed to correct unjustified assertions concerning Central Europe since space does not allow for a discussion of other weak points in that work's thesis.

This is not the place to delve into extensive theoretical concepts of the birth and development of modern states in Central Europe. However, the principal facts need to be established. As early as the middle of the last century national movements existed, especially among the Germans, the Poles, the Hungarians and the Czechs. These ethnically based movements were so autonomous and so well developed that they became a traumatic problem for the Danubian Monarchy, as well as for the States of the German Federation (although in a very different way). In none of them could the center in Vienna find an integrating force strong enough to counterbalance the others automatically. Instead, the more patent the problem became, the more Vienna sought refuge in 'suprapatriotism.' Simplifying somewhat, one could call these efforts a more or less conscious attempt to create a 'Greater Austrian Nation' or an 'Austrian Supranation.' All aspects of national independence were to be integrated into this 'nation,' and with them a particularly significant characteristic of burgeoning or reborn nations – i.e., language and culture. This integration was to have been established essentially without compulsion, as a result of the 'natural' assimilative power of the mainly German-Austrian core of the empire. However, the widespread cultural feature of bilingualism (e.g., German-Czech, German-Polish, German-Hungarian, and German-Italian bilingualism) was granted permanent status, not just the right to existence 'in principle.' One needs only to study the writings of Count Leo Thun, a typical representative of German-Czech patriotism, in order to convince oneself of this.

'Supranationalism' sought to find its sociopolitical basis in the most important pillars of the monarchy:

1   The emperor, the Habsburg dynasty and the policies of the court – indeed reverence, friendship, even love for the imperial house

2   The aristocracy, which was systematically promoted and supported as the élite of the country that penetrated all parts of the state organism. As a result of its national hetereogeneity or changing national identification, the aristocracy remained loyal to old Austrian patriotism, as well as retaining its particular narrow 'national' or 'provincial' loyalty to its own nation or province, although there were a few not unimportant exceptions (e.g., Hungary)

3   The church, particularly the Catholic Church, which constituted a natural spiritual basis for the Habsburg Monarchy. (Indeed, the church reciprocated the trust placed in it by the throne, of which it was its most devoted pillar.)

4   The civil service, constituting the backbone and nervous system of the empire (which, as the result of its secure status in society and its prestige and power, enjoyed an importance comparable to that of the army in neighboring Germany)

5 The repressive elements that existed primarily in the army, but also in the local and state police, as well as the gendarmerie.

The Austrian (later Austro-Hungarian) state lost its case in the court of the 20th century, with the result that many debts and unsettled IOUs were billed to it. However, it is easy to underestimate the extent of worship and trust the emperor inspired if one judges 19th-century Austria from the viewpoint of a republican society. Similarly, the aristocracy was not just a survivor from medieval times. It included an intellectual élite, professional statesmen and politicians, as well as entrepreneurs. Indeed, it controlled entire agro-industrial complexes. Even the church awoke from its rigor mortis – at least by the end of the century – and began to devote attention to social problems. Even if belatedly, the church was at the origin of a modern political movement. (Of course, next to the ruling dynasty, the church was the greatest landowner in the monarchy). In terms of officialdom and the army, what is significant is not the real physical power they possessed, but their social prestige and the aura of supranational authority that they projected.

It is well known that all these forces sought to find their legitimation in the past and in tradition, and that they were not flexible enough – particularly in Austria – for the age of technological 'revolutions,' wars conducted by machines, and global imperialism. As a result, their ability to preserve 'Austrianness' as the fundamental concept and spiritual basis of the empire constantly diminished. Nevertheless, in their attempts to adapt and to preserve the principle of Austrian identity, these forces demonstrated a remarkable fortitude and persistence, even if in so doing they rather resembled soldiers on the retreat. In this way, the Austrians became a famous nation of 'Privy Councillors' (*Hofräte*), as Löwenstein recently noted in a stimulating study of civil movements and national orientations in the mid-19th century.[101]

Did any additional integrating element exist in the Danubian Monarchy capable of helping to secure the future of the state? In brief, there was indeed such an element – the process of industrialization of the country – and concretely those who were responsible for it (i.e., industrialists, bankers, workers and others). Politically, they were represented by the Liberals, the Progressives

---

[101] Bedrich Löwenstein, 'Hnut: Mestanstva a Národní Orientace v Polovine 19. Století. Nekolik Úvah,' *Cesky Casopis Historicky* 4 (1990), 499-513.

and the 'Socials,' while the highest level of the Austrian bourgeoisie became increasingly integrated into aristocratic court circles. These groups constituted the basic opposition to the conservative forces and fought against them for supremacy in the country, promoting their own interests with a firm hand.

Within Austria (in the double sense of all Austria prior to 1867 and Cis-Leithania after 1867), the 'modern' element was distinguished from the conservative forces in another respect. Capital and industry were dominated by German-speaking Austrians, including Jews, the majority of whom opted for 'German-ness' (*Deutschtum*) during the period of economic expansion in the industrial regions of the monarchy. Initially linked with elements of Bonapartism, industrialization in the course of its further development was supposed to bring about a melting pot, in which national differences were gradually reduced until they finally disappeared, at least as far as the middle classes and officialdom (aptly termed 'white collar workers') were concerned. In the areas where industrialization occurred, a special system of factory organizations promoted linguistic unification among the workers as well as other groups involved in industrial development. The development of a 'cultural (ethnic or linguistic) nation' into a state nation (*Staatsnation*) thus led in the direction of 'Austrianness' – defined, however, exclusively in German terms.

The automaticity of this process was strikingly powerful. Suffice it to cite the area around Ostrau: in the last quarter of the 19th century and in the years preceding World War I it developed into an industrial region in which half the production capacity of the leading industries in Cis-Leithania (i.e., coal, iron, steel) was concentrated. For the topic of this chapter, this area is of particular importance. After Vienna, it attracted the most immigrants of any region of the monarchy. Moreover, it bordered on the areas of settlement of three different ethnic groups (i.e., Germans, Czechs, and Poles), while the principal area of settlement of a fourth ethnic group (i.e., Slovaks) was only a short distance away. Not fortuitously, under the influence of the processes of civilization and industrialization quite new 'inter-ethnic' groups with multiple language variants developed, such as the 'Water Poles' (*Wasserpolen*), i.e., persons who originally had been Poles and had spoken Polish, but had lost their Polish identity in the course of time, or the 'Schlonzaken,' who originally had been

Silesians, although essentially indifferent about their nationality.[102] In the Ostrau (Vítkovice) iron foundries, the largest and most modern industrial plant in the region, 'automatic Germanization' occurred not only during the era of the monarchy, but even after the creation of Czechoslovakia. It was only here in the Bohemian provinces that the Czech workers (as well as others) were organized almost entirely into nominally international, but in fact non-national, trade unions directed centrally from Vienna. 'In theory, industrialization should have been able to create an all-Austrian melting pot by removing local barriers and creating a large market, strengthening economic links and increasing mobility, freeing up land, unifying laws, reforming trade and handicraft legislation, etc., ' and consequently to 'isolate the majority of the population that sought prosperity from the bearers of the ideas of political freedom and of nationalism.'[103] This comment is valid for the entire process of industrialization. Regrettably, however, the hope that such isolation could be achieved represented only a pious wish inherited from the age of absolutism.

By the final half of the 19th century, people had good reason to believe no longer in such automatism. Thus German Liberalism, which was *obliged* to put its trust in German nationalism, became the political expression of the 'melting pot' of industrialization. Moreover, historical events occurring over a compressed period gave an even faster spin to the fateful wheels of nationalism. The Austro-Prussian War of 1866 made Austrian Germans second-class Germans – i.e., German Austrians. The Habsburgs responded to the crisis of Austrian German-ness (*Deutschtum*) by introducing political dualism, which brought these Germans Cis-Leithania as a fiefdom – in return for the abandonment of the Hungarian Germans.

The German Empire established in 1870 became the supreme goal of all Germans. This empire successfully demonstrated its hegemony over the European continent by its victory over the French arch-enemy. The 'all-Austrian' melting pot was now destined to become a 'German-Austrian' one, following the pattern of Imperial German industrialism – which had been far more rapacious and successful.

---

[102] See, in particular, the chapters on industrial development and demographics in the Ostrau industrial region in the collection published by the Schlesisches Institut der Akademie der Wissenschaften: *Ostravská Prumyslová Oblast v 1. Polovine 20. Století* (Ostrava: 1973), 205ff.

[103] Löwenstein, *Hnutí Mestanstva*, 505.

Thus Austria could only make sense as an Austria 'with a German backbone,' i.e., an extension of German-ness, bringing the light of industrial civilization to the less developed (or even backward) nations – above all the Slav nations of Central and Eastern Europe. Many historical studies have convincingly shown how German Liberalism disintegrated into a number of different political movements and parties, the 'Austrian' wings of which were recruited from 'still-Austrian Germans' who remained loyal to the 'extended' Austrian homeland mainly for pragmatic reasons.[104] Against these were ranged those who already quite openly (and strictly speaking, treasonably) acted in the interests of a Greater Germany, seeing as their future homeland a great Germany comprising the German Empire and Austria with its Slav 'border-nations' (not accidentally the latter were referred to by the technical term 'adjoining lands' [Nebenländer]).

The laws of industrialization never were and never will be narrowly nationalistic. It is impossible to direct industrialization on a nationalistic basis. Thus in the last quarter of the 19th century, the Czech national movement had begun the process of economic emancipation, as had other such movements. By the end of the century the Czechs possessed not only a certain industrial potential, but also their own banking system. During the first decade of the 20th century the Zivnobanka not only had penetrated into the Austrian provinces, but had extended its activities to Hungary, Galicia, the Balkans and Russia as well. It co-operated successfully with the German Empire's Deutsche Bank, and there was no choice but to include it in the group of major Viennese banks. In this way it became internationalized, while remaining national. Even before World War I, the capacity of the Czech economy became the second largest in Cis-Leithania, thus competing with the German-Austrian economy.

As far as the decidedly German-oriented German-Austrian industrialization program is concerned, the fact that it enjoyed a 'popular base' had much more catastrophic consequences. In many towns in

---

[104] Apart from a few essays and monographs in German, see in particular the following Czech studies: Jan Kren, *Konfliktní Spolecenství – Cesi a Nemci 1780–1918* (Prague: 1986); '*Die Böhmischen Länder in der Krise 1870–1871*,' *Bohemia* (1987), 312–30; Otto Urban, *Ceská Spolecnost 1848–1918* (Prague: 1982); also the earlier work by Zdenek V. Tobolka, *Politicke Dejiny Ceskoslovenského Národa od r. 1848 az do Dnesní Doby, vol. 3*.

Bohemia and Moravia which until that time had preserved their (sometimes artificially created) German majority, one German town hall fell after another. The lignite area of northeast Bohemia, which had originally been German, changed to a mixed national area with several definitely Czech islands. In addition to the German-Austrian directed industrialization, a Czech industrialization took place that was initially weaker but grew steadily. However, its importance should not be exaggerated. The actual situation is indicated by estimates made at the time of the collapse of the monarchy and the birth of Czechoslovakia. These figures are not precise, and are constantly being revised. It suffices to note that in the Bohemian provinces, where about three-quarters of Cis-Leithanian industry was concentrated (with a population that was 66 percent Czech and 32 percent German), 20-30 percent of industry was dominated by Czech capital and Czech entrepreneurs.[105] The principal characteristic of this development was the tendency for Czech industrialization to proceed faster than German industrialization.

With regard to demographic developments, it was not so much the absolute rates of growth that mattered as the fact that the Czech rural population moved from the interior into the industrial areas, which were mainly located in the border regions, thus changing 'closed' German areas into mixed national ones. During this period, Vienna, where it is estimated that 250,000–500,000 Czechs lived, became the greatest Czech metropolis.[106] Dismayed by this development, German nationalists warned of the end ('*Untergang*') of 'German-ness' in Bohemia, and sought refuge in Pan-Germanism. Not accidentally, in 1897 one of its founders and best known representatives, Georg Ritter von Schönerer, won four out of his party's total of five seats for deputies from the Bohemian provinces, and it was here that in 1904 the German Workers' Party was founded, later

[105] See *Otázky Vyvoje Kapitalismu v Ceskych Zemích a v Rakousku-Uhersku* (Prague: 1957), particularly 203–10. According to more recent estimates, the proportion was approximately 20 percent. See, for instance, Vlastislav Lacina, '*Zivnostenská Banka behem a pred Svetovou Válkou (1907–1918),*' *Cesky Casopis Historicky*, 3 (1990), 276–303.

[106] These figures are taken from various Czech sources regarding national minorities. On the other hand, Michael John, Albert Lichtbau, Ceská Víden (see '*Von der tschechischen Großstadt zum Tschechischen Dorf,*' *Archiv 1987e*, Jahrgang 3 (Vienna: 1987), 36–55), use figures that refer to the language used on an everyday basis (*Umgangssprache*), and consequently count the Viennese Czechs (who were assimilated in varying degrees) as German-speaking. According to these figures, Czech Prague was bigger than Czech Vienna.

to become one of the precursor organizations for the Nazi movement (although no direct connection can be established).

There is no doubt that the Czech entrepreneurs did not want to isolate themselves, but instead wanted to be integrated into the all-Austrian framework as equal partners. The conditions that prevailed in Austria were important in determining the future of the relationship between industrialization and a multinational society held together by a state apparatus. All hopes that this framework would help the process of industrialization to overcome national frontiers were doomed to failure.

In a certain sense the fears of the German nationalists are comprehensible. The Czech policy, as pursued by the majority, concentrated on systematically taking over positions in the social life of Austria, particularly in the state apparatus, cultural life, the school system, the civil service, the army administration, and the police administration. On the other hand, against a background of growing national consciousness and the intensification of national conflicts a strongly nationalistic trend arose, resulting sometimes in a refusal even to negotiate with the German side (e.g., the policies of the Czech National-Socials and Constitutional Radicals). The nature of the demands made on the basis of Czech constitutional law (i.e., recognition of the historical rights of the provinces of the Crown of St. Wenceslas – Bohemia, Moravia, and Silesia), the proponents of which formerly had been the political representatives of the Czech bourgeoisie and a nationally divided 'patriotic' Bohemian aristocracy, underwent an essential change: they began now to be advanced in order to legitimize the supremacy of the Czechs, who represented the majority in the Bohemian provinces, over the Sudeten Germans, who were in the minority. In Moravia, for instance, in 1910 only 27.6 percent of the population was German – thus approaching the magic minimum of 20 percent, at which a minority was recognized. It appeared unimportant that over a period of 30 years the percentage of Germans in Moravia had declined by only 1.7 percent, that before World War I Czech capital investment in the Bohemian provinces was only one-fifth of the German level, or that the majority of the population in the Northern Bohemian lignite regions was still German.

The trend of events was totally unacceptable to the Germans in the Bohemian provinces, since they felt part of the ruling nation in the country, indeed a component part of the totality of Central

European German-ness, which was moving toward leadership of the continent. In the course of three or four hundred years they had never met with such a reversal as occurred in Bohemia. The German Liberal camp thus considered itself indubitably in the right with regard to the 'nationalization' process, and was proud to stand on the side of progress as opposed to obsolete constitutional laws and a conservative aristocracy – as well as the backward Slav nations.

The drama of successive successes and defeats of the German-Czech and Czech-German *Ausgleich* in Austria was played out against the background briefly outlined above. All in all, the Czech politicians reacted to the catastrophe of the Austro-Hungarian *Ausgleich* in a striking fashion, notably with gestures such as the pilgrimage to St. Petersburg, including an audience with the czar, and a series of assemblies inspired by the Hussite 'Mountain Pilgrimages,' each of which was attended by crowds hitherto unseen in Czech history. As early as August 22, 1868, the Czech representatives presented a resolution that demanded nothing less than 'trialism' instead of 'dualism.' The failure of these activities led to negotiations that eventually resulted in the Imperial Rescript of September 12, 1871 and the so-called 'Fundamental Articles' (the main author of which was Count Heinrich Clam-Martinic, representative of the Czech constitutional aristocracy).

Despite certain compromises, the Czech question was to be solved on the basis of the constitutional law of the Bohemian kingdom. The nationalities law constituted only a portion of this solution. Nevertheless, it did represent the first fully formulated law of the kind. Moreover, unlike, for example, the Austro-Hungarian *Ausgleich*, it did not aim to 'sacrifice' the Germans. On the one hand it called for German and Czech administrative units (*Bezirke*), but at the same time it also provided for the creation of nationally mixed boroughs, with the criterion for recognition of a minority being a minimum population of 20 percent. But the plan failed because it encountered intense opposition from the Austrian – especially the Bohemian – Germans. This was not due to any real menace to their national existence, but because of the threat to their traditional privileges. For understandable reasons, the Hungarians did not agree either: they wanted a duopoly. The newly created Germany of Bismarck also chose camps and came out against the proposed legislation. The government, and finally the emperor, gave in, and thus nothing came of the 'Fundamental Articles.' The Bohemian parliamentary deputies consequently adopted a policy of passive opposition – i.e., they refused to exercise their functions – maintaining this attitude until 1878.

In this way, the path to a constitutional settlement proved impracticable for the Czechs, and all that remained to them was a cultural-linguistic solution within the existing constitutional framework. What had been noticeable as early as 1867-1871 now became increasingly evident. The greatest enemies of a Czech *Ausgleich* were the German Liberals and the Progressives, whereas its principal supporters were the imperial court and the aristocracy.

At this point it would be appropriate to include a description of the most important stages in the efforts to achieve a German-Czech *Ausgleich* in Austria. However, for reasons of space it must suffice to note that these attempts were characterized increasingly by the disapproval of the liberals and nationalists on the one side and the relative concurrence of the imperial court and the conservative aristocracy on the other. This unfavorable constellation was made even worse by the growing nationalism of the German camp and heightened Czech national consciousness, as well as by the fact that the government had recourse to increasingly absolutist attempts at solutions in the search for an escape from a situation that was becoming more and more hopeless. The situation remained unchanged despite the success of the Moravian Pact of 1905, which was due to special factors. The final defeat of the Bohemian Diet, paralyzed by German obstruction, was confirmed by rapid action on the part of Stürgkh – the so-called Anna Patents of July 26, 1913. Its abrogation by the German side in February 1914 represented merely a formal confirmation of an already existing situation. The aristocracy – represented this time by its ultraconservative wing, i.e., Count Erwin Nostitz-Rhieneck in accord with the Heir to the Throne, Franz Ferdinand, and the Prime Minister, Count Karl von Stürgkh – made a final hopeless attempt at reconciliation. Then war broke out.

In theory the German-Czech *Ausgleich* would have had some prospect of succeeding, but only if the trends of development had reversed themselves: if Austria-Hungary had not acted more and more aggressively in the Balkans, if it had reduced its dependence on the German Empire, if the Austrian Germans as the decisive national force in Cis-Leithania had slackened their striving for hegemony and the establishment of Austria as a German national state with Slavic minorities, and finally if, in addition to all this, the chauvinistic elements which were becoming more powerful in Czech politics had been suppressed.

All this might have been possible if Austria had had not just months and years, but decades to achieve peaceful development. However, not only Austria and the entire Habsburg monarchy, but the whole of Europe, was heading toward conflict and war. Its outbreak might have been prevented, but such an outcome became ever more improbable. At the same time, a positive German-Czech solution likewise became increasingly improbable, as was demonstrated during the first few days and months of the war with terrifying clarity.

On the domestic front, the Austrian militarists and the German nationalists, who had put all their hopes in the victory of German arms, wanted to exploit a German victory in order to fulfill their chauvinistic dreams. With the drastic methods of oppression that they employed they in fact impelled the Czech politicians to join the anti-Austrian camp, and drove the most loyal Czech Austrians into despair and isolation. Undoubtedly, blame attaches to both sides. But above all it was German chauvinism which would not permit a German-Czech *Ausgleich* and ultimately destroyed Austria, since it had no alternative basis on which it could exist. The Austrian Germans acted in this way, not because they were Germans, but because they were members of a ruling nationality – who were neither willing to admit this to themselves, nor able to draw the necessary conclusions from it. As for the Czechs, at a later date when they had their own state they were to behave more democratically and in line with a higher standard, but they also failed to cope successfully with a comparable situation. The fault was not that of any individuals who can be singled out for blame, but that of nationalism as a phenomenon, which proved unwilling to grant freedom to other nations.

At this point it is worthwhile to focus on the possible application of the nationality programs of Renner and Bauer. In historical terms, the importance of a program can be assessed only after it has been implemented and become political reality since historical reality changes all theories fundamentally and permanently. Before World War I, the nationality programs of Renner and Bauer remained only theories, or more precisely, topics of political discussion. The parties that advocated these concepts played no part at all in government or the active formulation of policies.

This does not mean that the two Social Democratic Parties – the Czechoslovak Party and the German-Austrian Party – did not participate in the relevant debates in the *Reichsrat*. Two major events demonstrated that neither party was invited to form part of the bodies that prepared the vital draft legislation, and thus could neither contribute to nor reject the legislation. During the discussions of one of the greatest successes of the German-Bohemian *Ausgleich*, the so-called 'Moravian *Ausgleich*,' the two parties and their worker adherents mostly fought shoulder to shoulder – but in opposition to the legislation, organizing protest meetings and demonstrations. In fact, the Moravian *Ausgleich* was above all a compromise between the politically conservative wings of the German and Czech populations of Moravia. Although undemocratic, it proved acceptable above all to the Czech liberals, as well as to the Germans, only because at that point in time it seemed hopeless to attempt to obtain satisfaction of more extensive demands.[107]

In Bohemia also, the Czechoslovak Social Democrats took a very lively part in the parliamentary deliberations (indeed, they had campaigned for the introduction of universal suffrage in *Landtag* [provincial assembly] elections). In the elections for the *Reichsrat*, 36 percent of the Bohemian voters supported them, with the result that they became the strongest party in the province. However, they were not represented in the Bohemian *Landtag* or in the commissions that debated the *Ausgleich*, since no one had invited them. Thus if the party wanted to influence the course of the debates, it could do so only by means of demonstrations and protest meetings. The situation was particularly paradoxical, since at the time the party under the leadership of Dr. Bohumír Šmeral had produced a relatively sophisticated nationality program reflecting the outcome of the 1899 Social Democratic Party Congress in Brünn.

On the opposite side stood the conservative forces from the nobility, who were also represented in the government (such as the Statthalter Fürst Franz Thun-Hohenstein).[108] The only opportunity that the Austrian Social Democrats – this applies to the Czech, Polish, Italian, etc. parties almost as much to the German Party

---

[107] See Josef Kolejka, ' "*Moravský Pakt*" z Roku 1905,' *Ceskoslovensky Casopis Historicky*, 4 (1956), 590–615.
[108] On this, see the major unpublished study by Karel Kazbundas of the so-called Anna Patents (July 1913) in the archives of the Prague National Museum (Karel Kazbundas Bequest).

under the monarchy – had for practical political activity was during the sessions of the *Reichsrat*. But even in the legislature, they followed a policy of opposition on principle. They took the view that individual questions could be seen only as portions of a complex solution – however, the time was not yet ripe for any such solutions. Indeed, their experience in connection with some partial questions (as for example the minority school question in 1909–10) was such as to constitute initial grave disappointments for these parties as far as the possibilities of *Realpolitik* were concerned.[109]

It was not until 1917 – but above all in the spring of 1918 – when the Habsburg Monarchy found itself at an historic crossroads, that a real possibility arose of converting both Renner's and Bauer's (as well as Smeral's) nationality programs into authentic political structures. Of course, reality took a very different course, and the possibility of a so-called 'Third Way' – i.e., the implementation of the Austro-Marxist nationality program – was not exploited. At this time of historical upheaval Austro-Marxism disappointed its proponents – as did other political tendencies[110] – and historical development, following its own inner logic, led successively from the political disintegration of the Danube basin to the Hitlerite (and not socialist, Bauerite) *Anschluss*, to the occupation of the whole of Central Europe by the Nazis, as well as to (among other things) the 'expulsion' of the German population from Czechoslovakia and Poland.

A 'sacred cow' of our historical writing – i.e., the concept of 'progress,' and, closely connected with it, the concept of the 'mission of modern nationalism' (both of which originated in the 19th century) – needs to be examined critically. Every historian is influenced in his work not only by the past but also by present-day

[109] This can be seen clearly from the debates at the 1911 Innsbruck Social Democratic Party Congress (see the transcript of the Congress, especially pp. 92–100, 185–97).

[110] Zdenek Kárník, *Socialisté na Rozcestí. Habsburg, Masaryk ci Smeral* (Prague: 1968). This book remained for twenty years on the index of forbidden books. A German translation is in preparation. In this connection, I would like to point out above all the failure of Bauer's endeavors to bring about an 'Austrian Zimmerwald,' endeavors that reflected merely socialist Anschluss policies, rather than any real hope for the creation of a multinational federation of states of the Danube Basin. Previously unknown material was used by Berthold Unfried in his ' *"Ein Österreichisches Zimmerwald." Versuche zur Wiederherstellung der Österreichischen Gesamtpartei 1917–18: Zur Entstehungs- und Wirkungsgeschichte des "Nationalitätenprogramms der Linken"* 1918,' *Archiv* 1 (987), 194–224.

themes and events. Most of Europe is seeing and experiencing national feelings, their political interpretation, and the political activity that results. This is evident both in what many are wont to describe as progress, as well as in what is obviously to be considered a step backward – sometimes indeed in the direction of almost unbelievably inhumane acts.

In this context, how would the attempts at a German-Czech understanding and a national *Ausgleich* in Austria be rated? According to the theories – including Marxism – that construct history on a socioeconomic basis, the situation appears to be relatively unambiguous: the failure of efforts to achieve a German-Czech *Ausgleich* was accompanied by the failure of the attempts of the Czech people to assure for themselves equal rights of existence within the Danubian Monarchy. From the viewpoint of the history of European progress, however, this was a failure of merely local significance. If one considers the separate stages of the German-Czech negotiations, it was the primarily Austria-oriented Czech national movement that failed, just as did Catholic conservatism, but above all the 'Bohemian' aristocracy, the big landowners, and the Imperial Court. The ultimate victor was Greater German nationalism and chauvinism that was constantly expanding, borne by the rapid social and economic growth of Germany. These were factors that undoubtedly represent social progress – even though one's attitude toward them may be ambivalent.

In light of the further development of Greater German chauvinism, no complex analysis is required for one to entertain the deepest reservations regarding a concept of progress derived on such a basis. Even the initial moves made by Czech Marxists like Smeral to establish links with Austrian Conservatives – initiatives that were doomed not to be further pursued – would lead one to relativize the dogma of considering history in terms of criteria of 'progress.' Can it really be true that 'progress' – i.e., that spiral represented by the development of humankind, which, despite various detours, always strives to advance 'further and higher' – was represented by the forces of technological, social and economic expansion controlled by the German bourgeoisie and upper bourgeoisie in Central Europe, as well as the German nationalist politicians associated with them, if the same elements also led the world, or at least Europe, into the inferno of Nazi horrors? These questions are confronted not only when the problem of nationalism in the 19th century is considered, but also in view of present-day nationalism, which is becoming a nightmare in a Europe that is striving to achieve integration. Europeans today also face the problem of the growth of a technological civilization that contains vast forces of self-destruction. How is it possible that hitherto reliable instruments of knowledge are now falling apart?

Jan Patocka, probably the most important Czech philosopher of the second half of the 20th century and a co-founder of Charta 77, has presented an heretical view of this question in his *Heretical Essays on the Philosophy of History* (see the essay *The Wars of the Twentieth Century and the Twentieth Century as War*). He throws doubt on the central concept of progress, i.e., the concept of revolution:

the party which is leading the struggle against the status quo, and which therefore despite all appearances to the contrary must be characterized a revolutionary party, is Bismarckian Germany. How can such an entity be a revolutionary element, the bearer and agent of world revolution, despite being led by conservative Prussia with its army caste, its ossified bureaucracy and incredibly limited Lutheran orthodoxy? . . . If we accept the current view of revolution, which is typified above all by socioeconomic doctrines . . . then this thesis can be nothing other than a mighty paradox. However, of all the countries of the world (apart from the United States) it is Germany that, despite its traditional structures, most closely approaches the reality of the new scientific-technological age. Even its conservatism ultimately serves a discipline that is pursuing the formative accumulation of energy, vehemently and ruthlessly, with contempt for equality and democratization. It is precisely the scientific-technological trait of its [Bismarckian Germany's] existence that is becoming stronger and stronger. It is also the organizing will of its economic leaders and its technological representatives, who inexorably forge their plans in conflict with the hitherto existing organization of life . . . . Its [Bismarckian Germany's] internal adversaries, the socialists, could not fail to see in it a pit of rapacious capitalist magnates . . . . However, in reality they themselves are co-operating in the organization of this new society of work, discipline, production and planned construction . . . . Long before the war [i.e., World War I], Germany transformed Europe into an energy-producing complex. Despite all the intelligence with which other European countries, and particularly France, progressed in the same direction, their transformation was somewhat slower.[111]

Patocka's words are in conflict with the theses of Marxist historiography regarding Greater German imperialism. However, do his

[111] Jan Patocka, *Kacírské Eseje* (Prague: 1990), 129–31. The essays were originally published in Samizdat in 1975, two years before the author's death.

basic statements on the philosophical interpretation of history really express anything of new and revolutionary significance? No. They are merely 'heretical' in the original sense of the word (the heretic is only a *katharos* within his own religious community). Patocka's opinions demonstrate what, for example, 'industrialization' or 'modern progress' essentially mean or can mean in relation to European history if we remain faithful to the 'current view, typified above all by socioeconomic doctrines,[112] as well as how we are to view our instruments of cognition.

Patocka's skepticism about theories of history, and especially materialist theories, is also evident in his *Vlastní Glosy ke Kacírskym Esejum*, where he in essence makes the following assertion: 'It is precisely history, that domain of the mobile societal being of humankind and the ground of traditions, to which human achievements attach themselves both positively and negatively . . . that is capable of showing that the societal being of humankind is fundamentally free.[113] One may add, free also in the interpretation of historical facts.

Europeans no longer possess an integrated universal philosophical/historical framework. All the schools of thought fail when confronted with the problem of nations and the complexity of modern civilization. Given this mix of opinions, one can only select or reject, according to the need of the moment. Or, as the fashion is at the moment, speak or write of the end of history.

All this is certainly not surprising. The global societal upheavals of the last two centuries have resulted not only in a technological revolution, but also in a crisis of society that threatens the very existence of humanity. In such a phase of history, why should men's views of their past (or for that matter their views of their present and future), be invested with new brilliance? To assume this would be to succumb to the illusion that arose earlier as a consequence of the upsurge of the natural sciences (how such arrogance ends is shown by the downfall of orthodox Marxism). In brief: the crisis of society must also result in a crisis of historiography. It is time to realize this. Renner's and Bauer's nationality program was unquestionably a serious attempt to seek new way of escaping from the confusion that existed at the beginning of this century. The reason that the program

---

[112] *Ibid.*
[113] *Ibid.*, Additional Writings, 158.

was not successful is ultimately not just one of the most important questions for historiography, but also for contemporary Europe – and not for Europe alone.

Peter Sipos

National conflicts and the democratic alternative in the Austro-Hungarian Monarchy and its successors

Since during the first 50 years of its modern history Hungary formed part of the Austro-Hungarian Monarchy, there are few problems related to this period that can be discussed without bearing in mind the consequences of coexistence within the empire. This relates in particular to some highly important issues concerning the nation, minorities and ethnic groups.

In 1867 the Habsburg Empire became a dual state. The two constituent parts, i.e., Austria – or more precisely the territories represented in the Imperial Council ('*Reichsrat*') – and Hungary – comprising the Hungarian Kingdom, Croatia, Slovenia and Fiume (the 'lands of the sacred crown') – had in common only the person of the sovereign, foreign and military affairs, and jointly assumed financial expenditures.

The so-called 'economic compromise,' which was renewed every 10 years, brought about common arrangements for customs, foreign trade, the monetary system, transport and communications. Furthermore, it entitled all the subjects of the empire to engage in trade and commerce.

The provisions of the 1867 Compromise ensured the political hegemony of the Austro-Germans in Austria and the Hungarians in Hungary. However, this division of power did not correspond to the actual national composition of the monarchy, and particularly of Hungary.

A total of 11 nations lived within the borders of the empire. These included 'historical nations' (Austro-Germans, Hungarians, Czechs, Poles, and Croats), which had constituted independent autonomous political entities in the Middle Ages and consequently claimed their share in the governing of the empire on the grounds of their historical rights. The social composition of the so-called 'peoples without history' included no class of landowners, i.e., the class that would naturally assume historically based constitutional endeavors. The bourgeois-intellectual leading strata of these nations took shape during the period of capitalist development following the 1867 Compromise.

One of the peculiarities of the monarchy was that the ruling nations constituted only a relative majority. In this respect Austria-Hungary differed from both the Western national states and from Russia. The existence of Western states was based on the territorial unity of their economies and the ethnic homogeneity of their populations. As for Russia, Russian nationals formed the overwhelming majority of the population. On the other hand, in Austria-Hungary by the turn of the century the Austro-Germans and Hungarians amounted respectively to 24 percent and 20 percent, i.e., only 44 percent combined, of the total population.

Another peculiar feature of the national composition of Austria-Hungary was that it was only the Czechs, Slovaks, Hungarians, Croats, and Slovenes who lived entirely inside the monarchy. The other six nations belonged to ethnic communities of national states that lay outside the borders of the monarchy. The issue of the unity of Romanians, Serbians, etc., who were separated by frontiers, was not on the agenda for many years after 1867 mainly owing to international circumstances; however, this factor was felt more and more strongly during the period of modern capitalist development, coming into its own after the eclipse of the monarchy.

In 1900 Hungary's population of 16.8 million (omitting Croatia) included only 8.6 million ethnic Hungarians (51.4 percent), who thus barely constituted an absolute majority. The composition of the population comprised the following nationalities besides Hungarians: 2.7 million Romanians (16.6 percent); 1.9 million Slovaks and 2 million Germans (each about 11.9 percent); 520,000 Serbs (3.1 percent); 420,000 Ruthenians (2.5 percent); and 190,000 Croats (1.2 percent). The remaining 240,000 (i.e., 1.4 percent of the population) represented a number of other nationalities (e.g., Gypsies).

Between 1850 and 1910 there was a considerable increase in the size and growth rate of the Hungarian ethnic group. Within 60 years its number rose from 4.9 million to 10.1 million (i.e., by 107 percent), while its percentage of the total population grew from 48 percent to 55 percent (including an increase from 28 percent to 34 percent in Transylvania). The main causes of this change in national composition were the facts that, beginning in the 1860s, the Hungarian population surpassed the other nationalities in natural growth owing to changed demographic factors; far fewer Hungarians emigrated than other nationalities; and part of the non-Hungarian population, as well as a majority of immigrants, assimilated with the Hungarians, resulting in a gain through assimilation of 2 million, i.e., the difference between the gross increase of 5 million and the natural growth of 3 million. The composition of this group was as follows: 700,000 Jews, 500,000 Germans, 400,000 Slovaks, 150,000 Romanians, 150,000 Southern Slavs, and 100,000 members of other ethnic groups.

Assimilation came about as a natural and spontaneous process during the second half of the 19th and the beginning of the 20th century. The development of the capitalist economy, bourgeois restratification of society, accelerated residential and social mobility, urbanization, and changes in traditional conditions brought about above all the assimilation of small communities of non-Hungarian nationals living in the central Hungarian language area. Towns played an important role in the process of assimilation as the percentage of Hungarians living in towns jumped from 63 percent in 1880 to 77 percent in 1910. Thus Hungarianization occurred primarily in the Hungarian language area and in towns.

Language frontiers did not undergo any essential changes during this period. Assimilation could hardly 'attack' contiguous territories inhabited by non-Hungarian nationals. In diversely populated zones on the border of two language areas the percentage change varied from village to village, increasing in some and decreasing in others. Hence it was obvious that assimilation was subject to limits, and that consequently it was impossible for multinational historical Hungary to become a purely Hungarian national state.

The process of assimilation, especially in the towns, reinforced a characteristic feature of nationality conditions in Hungary, i.e., an intensive blending together of different peoples, which later rendered the drawing of ethnic boundaries more difficult – indeed in certain areas absolutely impossible. Out of the 423 districts of which Hungary consisted before 1918, there were only 215 (52 percent) in which a single nationality constituted a majority of over 80 percent, while 198 districts had minority populations of over 20 percent. In

41 districts the ethnic blending was so extensive that no single nationality constituted 50 percent of the population.

The Hungarians lived in two large territorial blocs: the central Hungarian language area occupying the most fertile central territories of the country, and the southeastern corner of Transylvania inhabited by Székelys. Eighty-eight percent of Hungarians lived in these two areas, separated by a zone inhabited by other nationals with a total population of nearly one million. In the mountainous border areas that represented one-third of the country's total territory there existed only a thinly scattered Hungarian population, mainly near the language frontiers and in bigger towns. The number of Hungarians grew more rapidly than that of non-Hungarians, especially in the administrative, industrial and trade centers with a greater population of 'national minorities.' In this way Hungarian 'urban islands' evolved in an ocean of villages populated by other nationalities.

Unlike Austria, whose provinces did have a certain minimal autonomy, Hungary possessed a homogeneous sovereign territory and did not contain any autonomous territorial entities with historical traditions. Consequently, the oppression of nationalities prevailed to a more pronounced degree than in Austria, hindering national development to a greater extent than in Cis-Leithania.

During the 1860s the nationalities living in Hungary wanted to transform the country into a federation of autonomous national territories, limiting the jurisdiction of the central legislative and executive organs to the highest and necessarily common levels of state government. Their politicians recognized the unity and integrity of the country, but nevertheless stressed that Hungary could not be consolidated on the Western pattern. They opposed a federative concept based on autonomy, decentralization and democracy, advocating instead a dualistic solution. If their concept had been carried out in practice, Croatia as well as Transylvania would have been granted political and territorial autonomy, while with respect to the national minorities of Hungary *strictu sensu* counties with administrative and ethnic communes would have been established, taking into account the actual 'language frontiers.' In addition, proportional representation in central institutions would have been introduced.

However, in the view of leading politicians, state sovereignty meant exclusive Hungarian hegemony. This precluded the very possibility of a federation; even more significantly, the restricted municipal variant of territorial-ethnic communes was rejected and thus the collective rights of national minorities were not recognized. These politicians deemed it possible to settle the nationalities problem by guaranteeing individual rights and freedom of language use. This attitude was reflected in the 1868 nationality law, which in the spirit of liberalism granted non-Hungarian ethnic citizens the right to schooling and further education in their mother tongue, and the use of their language in lower-level public administration, in the courts, and in church affairs. According to the law a person's nationality 'should not prevent anyone being promoted to any position of dignity.' There is no doubt that such a broad range of possibilities provided under law for language use was unique in Central and Eastern Europe and could hardly be found even in Western Europe. In fact, the law was definitely the most comprehensive of any that had ever been enacted in Europe. This legislation represented the summit attained by Hungarian liberalism.

Yet the law was only partially applied in practice. Hungarian nationalism had a greater impact on local administration and the municipal authorities that were responsible for carrying out the law than it did on governmental circles. During the entire period under discussion the principal demand that the progressive parties and politicians made with regard to nationality policy was that the 1868 law be implemented in its entirety.

In accordance with the programs of the First and Second Internationals, Hungarian Social Democracy espoused the principle of the right to self-determination of peoples as early as 1870–90 – i.e., the first years of the movement's development. The Social Democratic Party of Hungary (S.D.P.H.) valued the compromise and indeed the existence of the Austro-Hungarian Monarchy since it judged that the constitutional dualistic state would ward off both German and Russian imperialism. The party condemned the oppression of nationalities and supported the 1868 nationality law. The 1903 party platform declared the 'total equality of rights for every nation in the country.'

Despite this, on the grounds of the preservation of the country's integrity, Hungarian Social Democrats did not recognize claims of either territorial or cultural autonomy until the autumn of 1918. Naturally, they were aware of the huge potential for tension inherent in the question, and before the outbreak of World War I were haunted by a terrible vision of the impending catastrophe. At the 1913 Party Congress Zsigmond Kunfi, one of the party's leaders, said: 'The Balkan War launched the greatest showdown in the history of the world,' and stated that a general international conflagration was likely to come before long, overthrowing the monarchy, which was 'overloaded with the problems of unreconciled nationalities and oppressed social classes.'

Kunfi went on to say that the only condition for peace and the survival of the monarchy was a 'democratic policy of granting all the nations of the monarchy the means of national, political and social success, and a policy of self-government throughout the empire from the smallest village communes to every organ of the parliamentary and political structure of the country.'

In principle, Social Democrats, who admitted the right of peoples to self-determination, did not object to the possibility of Romanians and Serbs being united with their independent national states. On the other hand, they reasoned that annexation was undesirable since neither of these countries was democratic and living standards and cultural levels were lower than in Hungary. They regarded Slovakia as an independent nation, rejecting the idea of 'Czechoslovakianism.' They also believed that in a future democratic Hungary the peaceful coexistence of Slovaks and Hungarians would be possible. Hungarian Social Democrats opposed Bohemian separatism, labelling it a 'division of power,' since it had resulted in the ethnic splitting of Bohemian Social Democracy. Until World War I the idea of Bohemia's secession from the monarchy did not even occur to them.

During the War, and especially from 1917 on, the party pleaded for restoration of the *status quo* and a peace without annexations or divisions. At the May 1917 Conference in Stockholm the S.D.P.H. delegation expressed its desire that 'The nationality problems of Austria-Hungary should not be solved by partitioning the country but by extending democratic reforms, allowing the setting up of national communes and making free cultural and economic development possible.'

The view of the Social Democrats did not change until the utter defeat of the Central Powers. At its October 1918 Congress the party took a stand in favor of an 'independent and sovereign Hungary' and explicitly recognized the right of every nation to self-determination, while they considered every likely consequence of its exercise. Social

Democrats trusted that 'major economic interests related to the survival of the country in its present form' as well as 'cultural ties linking the masses of laboring people' would provide the cohesive force that would keep Romanians, Serbs, and Slovaks together within the framework of a single state. They hoped that there was a chance the nationalities would not leave Hungary, which was supposed to be turned into a federal state like an Eastern Switzerland. Naturally, it immediately became clear that they were too late, since the nationalities, including their fellow Social Democrats, had already been gravitating away and had begun to cooperate with their 'own' bourgeois parties.

The concept of an 'Eastern Switzerland' was elaborated in detail by Oszkár Jászi, the most important theoretician among the Hungarian radical intellectuals. The core of his conception of nationality policy was advocacy of general democratism over and above constitutional rights and reforms regarding public education in the native languages of ethnic groups. His formulation is still relevant today: 'Peace between nationalities can be achieved provided that two *sine qua non* conditions are fulfilled: first, appropriate education and good public administration in the language of the people; second, acknowledgement of the right of every nation to pursue their culture and to use their language freely. This is what I consider a minimal nationality program and in my view it coincides with the minimal social program.' Above all, he attached chief importance to implementation of classic parliamentary principles as the guarantee of cooperation and mutual confidence between the Hungarians and other nations. He also was of the opinion that the democratic alternative might preserve the monarchy.

In 1918 Jászi realized that the main aim of the nationalities was to create their own national states. He had good reason to fear the dangers of the 'nationalist atomizing concept of the nationality principle.' In order to forestall these dangers he elaborated the concept of the 'United Danubian States.' The members of the federation would have been Austria, Hungary, Poland, Bohemia and Illyria (the Southern Slavic State). According to the ideas that he advanced in November 1918, Hungary would have been divided into self-governing territories inhabited by different nationalities (i.e., cantons, following the Swiss pattern) possessing cultural and administrative autonomy, while the traditional system of counties would be abolished. These territories would all have been represented in the central government.

Postwar power relations made it impossible to put these federative concepts into practice, since there were no political and military forces that supported them, while the neighboring states, together with nationality movements allied to the victorious Entente, carried out a policy of secession. The newly created states regarded themselves as 'nation-states,' in which the ruling nation laid claim to privileges and exclusivity.

'The spectacle is the same in every place I have been,' wrote Jászi in 1926,

the political morals of an oppressed nation undergo a radical change as soon as it comes into power. The former claim of national equality can easily turn into a claim of national supremacy .... At this point only the final step remains, i.e., imperialism, under the aegis of which the occupation of the territories of weaker nations is given the appearance of being the cultural and historical mission of the victorious nations.

The consequences of the 1919 peace treaties which were concluded with the Central Powers and their allies proved the correctness of Jászi's analysis. Instead of the settlement of nationality problems, there were new tensions in the area which made the situation even more complicated than it had been before the War.

The peace treaties abolished historical Hungary. Sixty-seven percent of its pre-1918 territory (190,000 square kilometers) was transferred to neighboring countries, so that only about 90,000 square kilometers remained. Its population was reduced by 56 percent (about 10 million), so that about 8.5 million remained within the new borders of Hungary. According to censuses taken in 1930–31, 2.5 million Hungarians lived in Czechoslovakia, Romania and Yugoslavia. (The corresponding figure from the 1910 Hungarian census was 3.2 million.) The proportion of Hungarians in the total population was 3.3 percent in Yugoslavia, 4.9 percent in Czechoslovakia, and 8.6 percent in Romania. Moreover, there were considerable numbers of Germans in the new states, and the German populations showed a rapid rate of increase.

Apart from the presence of large numbers of 'alien' nationals, there were serious disputes within the new majority-population nations.

The Slovaks did not accept the fiction of a 'united Czechoslovakian nation' and were discontented over their subordination to Czech interests. In Yugoslavia neither the Croats nor the Slovenes accepted Serbian rule. The nationalistic policies of the new countries denied the independence of kindred nations and promoted the hegemonic endeavors of majority nationalities.

The protection of minorities that was to be guaranteed by international supervision by the League of Nations proved to be a fiasco. In practice it provided no protection whatever for the nationalities. The states in question, however, objected to this system since it provided the minorities' mother nations with legal grounds for protests that were invariably deemed 'interference in internal affairs.'

According to the 1930 census, 92 percent of the population in post-Trianon Hungary was of Hungarian nationality, while there were 470,000 Germans (5.5 percent of the population), almost 100,000 Slovaks (1.2 percent) and 3,000–30,000 belonging to other nationalities.

Trianon was experienced as a national trauma by Hungarian society, as it had to accept the fact that about 30 percent of the Hungarian ethnic group had fallen under foreign domination. The shock was made even worse by the one-half million people who fled from the disannexed territories and sought refuge in Hungary. The majority lived in extremely poor conditions for many years and their situation made it more and more difficult for the nation to accept what had happened.

Recovery of the disannexed territories as the main goal of Hungarian foreign policy was supported by the whole of society. For any political group, rejection of the Trianon agreements constituted a precondition for its participation in public life.

The Social Democratic Party was the only movement to give preference to democratization over territorial revision. Social Democrats also regarded the peace treaty as an unjust, imperialistic *diktat*, but they rejected the foreign policy of the leading circles, who endeavored to conclude an alliance with the Great Powers. These circles were upset by the division of Europe into spheres of influence and were ready to bring about the restoration of historical Hungary, even by taking up arms if necessary. According to the Social Democrats, on the other hand, the only possible way of revising the Trianon Treaty was by peaceful negotiation and mutual agreement with the neighboring states. As early as 1928 they sounded a note of warning, cautioning that 'any other measure taken [than negotiation] would lead to armed conflicts that would plunge the country once more into catastrophe.'

In response to the official Hungarian demand, 'Give back everything,' the neighboring states answered, 'We will give back nothing.' The unsolved nationality problems strengthened dictatorial tendencies, and the policy of threatening the use of force promoted the development of fascist movements. Apart from social tensions, the success of the Romanian, Croatian, Slovakian and Hungarian fascist parties owed much to this. At the same time it enabled Hitlerite Germany to exploit nationalist aspirations, ambitions and movements, playing them against one another, and at the same time building up its own empire in the '*Südostraum*.' This process began with the *Anschluss*, followed by the dismemberment of Czechoslovakia and Yugoslavia.

After Munich, Slovak separatism was used by Hitler as a pretext to 'dispose of' Czechoslovakia. While bringing into existence the Croatian puppet state, he declared the formal abolition of Yugoslavia as a state. Hungary and Romania were kept at loggerheads over the problem of Transylvania. Hitler baited Romania with the prospect of gaining back Northern Transylvania, lost as a result of the so-called second Vienna Award. Hungary was duped by Romania's annexation of Southern Transylvania. The Hitlerite policy, which directly or indirectly integrated the successor states of the monarchy into a vast German area, ultimately collapsed in 1944–45.

The states which regained their independence learned a completely distorted lesson from the national catastrophe that they had suffered, beginning the new stage of their existence with the persecution of nationalities. In all of these countries (including Hungary), the principle of 'German collective responsibility' prevailed. The same principle was applied to Hungarian nationals in Czechoslovakia, Yugoslavia, and Romania. Following this 'principle,' hundreds of thousands of Germans and Hungarians were deported from Czechoslovakia, and most of the Germans were expelled from Hungary. With the consent of the political parties, persecutions and bloody atrocities were widespread in almost all of the countries. The sole exception was the Social Democratic Party of Hungary, which protested against the application of the principle of collective responsibility to the German population – although these protests had no effect.

The practice of deportations and persecutions was the common sin of the new 'democratic' states and damaged the strength and validity of their democracies. Democracy is indivisible and if a state discriminates against its citizens by reason of any criterion – whether political conviction, religion, ethnic or linguistic affiliation – the genuineness of its democracy is automatically called into question.

The monolithic and autocratic Stalinist system, which was consolidated in the area beginning in 1947–48, reintegrated all the countries except Yugoslavia into a zone ruled by naked power. Since the democratic social institutions had been liquidated, the nationalities' chances of protecting their common rights disappeared also. According to the dogma in force, once socialism had been established and proletarian internationalism asserted, the nationality problem would automatically be solved.

In fact, during the entire period of their existence the Stalinist and post-Stalinist regimes systematically strove to eliminate ethnic diversity by means of forced assimilation. The following methods were employed: reorganization of territories inhabited by nationalities in order to liquidate ethnic centers; abolishment in practice of officially declared nationality rights, especially the right to secondary and higher education; linguistic and cultural assimilation, using public administration, military service and the mass media; deliberately disadvantageous economic policies in the territories inhabited by nationalities; and acts of violence and coercive measures against population groups.

The 1947 Paris Peace Treaty restored Hungary's old Trianon borders, which resulted in about 2.5 million Hungarians again falling into minority status.

The repressive methods mentioned earlier jeopardized the existence of Hungarians living in neighboring states. During both the Rákosi and Kádár eras the ruling communist party avoided taking a stand in support of Hungarians outside the country's borders. Janos Kádár regarded the unity of the socialist camp as the principal value of international politics. In his view internationalism should not permit any measures in foreign affairs that might offend the declared interests of the countries belonging to the Soviet sphere of interest. He regarded relations between the countries of the socialist bloc as relations between the various communist parties, and believed that they could be defined only on the basis of the canonized principles of Marxism-Leninism. Thus a policy of complete conformity was followed, which in turn made it impossible to raise any question that might be taken as criticism or interference in internal affairs. This attitude made an essential contribution to the Kádár system's gradually losing its 'capital of confidence' among the people.

Following the collapse of the Soviet bloc the area has experienced a growth in the nationalism of small ethnic groups, and messianism has become current policy. This has had two main consequences. On the one hand, disputes between different nations and nationalities have intensified, and the changes in regimes have not altered the subordinate position of minorities. On the other hand, the former coerced relations between countries (i.e., Warsaw Pact, Comecon) have not been replaced by calls for free cooperation, but instead, as Emil Niederhauser, a Hungarian expert on Eastern Europe, has said, 'Everybody is gazing at the West, often forgetting his neighbors . . . . It is to be feared that looking steadily at the West and scrambling for Western aid will result once more in national divisions . . . . The syndrome, 'We are the only ones who belong to Europe,' is spreading alarmingly.'

In one of his last works Otto Bauer maintained that democracy is the primary precondition for national self-determination. Hungary still has a long way to go to achieve this. At the same time, establishing a federation cannot be considered a real alternative. The politician István Bibó was right in saying that 'A federation is like a marriage: One must not undertake it with unsolved problems up one's sleeve, as the whole point of it lies in creating a new perspective and new problems, rather than saving the effort of having to answer previously unclear questions.'

During the course of the 20th century the area has seen three times how integration by force has proved to be a failure, while on two occasions nation-states also turned out to be fiascoes, thus helping the great powers to establish their hegemony. Now it is again the turn of the nation-states. If they fail to cooperate, it will be inevitable that the strongest European power – today Germany – once more will take charge of their destinies, using the means and methods proper to our own age.

Part 3

Contemporary applications

Uri Ra'anan

The end of the multinational Soviet Empire?

Western analysts and commentators have experienced considerable difficulty in attempting to grapple with the nature of the nationalities problem in the U.S.S.R. To start, the term and concept of the 'nation-state' have monopolized the jargon and, to some extent, the views of political scientists, particularly of the 'functionalist' persuasion.

Thus, there are frequent references to a non-existent entity, to wit 'the Soviet nation.' Until recently, the peculiar nature and problems of a multinational state seemed to present serious obstacles to persons trained in disciplines that owe their vocabulary to experiences particular to the West.

To the extent that Western scholars and decision makers came to grips with the phenomenon of ethnic conflict in the U.S.S.R. during the 1980s, they tended to view it in terms of human rights. This would have been a major step forward, but for the fact that an unspoken assumption prevailed, to the effect that the attainment of individual human rights necessarily would safeguard group rights as well.

Consequently, there was an understandable fixation on the Helsinki Final Act of 1975 as the instrument that would resolve the unenviable lot of the nationalities within the U.S.S.R. What strengthened this tendency was the fact that the most courageous and best-known dissidents within the U.S.S.R. made use of Helsinki – not because they shared the Western misapprehension that individual and group rights were necessarily intertwined, but for the very sound tactical reason that, by acceding to the Final Act, the Soviet rulers had left themselves open to charges that they were violating an *international* accord.

The next step forward in Western comprehension occurred in the second half of the 1980s, when it was realized that even the attainment of human rights for individuals would not resolve a wider issue, namely that the major ethnic entities in the U.S.S.R. harbored *political* aspirations. However, this realization was marred by the view that the various Soviet nationalities were simply 'minorities' within a predominantly Great Russian state, and that 'minority guarantees' would suffice (along the lines that were envisaged in the 1919 peace treaties, but never implemented).

Eventually, Western analysts acknowledged that fully one-half of the Soviet population was composed of non-Russians who could no longer be viewed merely as 'minorities.' However, this realization itself was skewed because of a Western penchant for viewing the nationalities within the U.S.S.R. in essentially *territorial* terms: thus, the aspirations of the major non-Russian peoples were equated with the enhancement of the status and powers of the 14 non-Russian union republics.

In other words, it was believed that the desires of the Baltic peoples, the Georgians, the Armenians, or the Ukrainians could be met by mere decentralization – primarily as far as the economic sector was concerned, although more enlightened minds understood that such decentralization would have to affect the cultural, linguistic and educational arenas as well. This concept might have been appropriate if the frontiers of the union republics (and, for that matter, the 'autonomous' republics, regions, and districts) had been drawn to coincide as far as possible with the ethnic boundaries of the nationalities concerned. (However, even in that case, decentralization or other measures short of independence which might have been acceptable during the initial stage of Gorbachev's ascent to power, became offers regarded as 'too little, too late' when years passed before it began to dawn on the Soviet leadership that some such steps were required.)

The case of the Tatar Autonomous Republic (A.S.S.R.) – which is located within the Russian Republic (R.S.F.S.R.) – indicates legitimate grounds for suspecting that frontiers between ethnic 'homelands' within the U.S.S.R. may have been 'gerrymandered.' The Tatar A.S.S.R. has a population of 3,641,000, of whom only 1,765,000 are ethnic Tatars, while 1,876,000 belong to other nationalities. Yet, an additional 3,754,000 Tatars live in the R.S.F.S.R. outside 'their own' republic, and another 1,126,000 are to be found in the rest of the Soviet Union.

Lest it be assumed that the failure of the Tatar A.S.S.R. to contain
more than a fraction of all Soviet Tatars is due simply to the geographic dispersal of the Tatar people, an investigation of the demographic structure of the eight administrative areas (four A.S.S.R.s
and four *oblasti* of the R.S.F.S.R.) bordering the Tatar A.S.S.R.
proves otherwise. These contain 1,790,000 Tatars, i.e., more than
the Tatar A.S.S.R. itself. It seems very unlikely, therefore, that the
frontiers of the latter could not have been drawn so as to include a
considerably larger Tatar population and fewer Russians and others.

As a result of arbitrary frontiers, preferential treatment of some
nationalities at the expense of others, and demographic movement
(mostly directed by the center, in part to promote Russian
'colonization' of other Soviet republics), almost one-quarter of the
U.S.S.R.'s population, 23.6 percent (67,300,000 citizens) is composed of nationalities that either do not have an ethnic territory 'of
their own' or live outside that territory.

The criteria employed here define a nationality's 'own' territory as
one of the 15 union republics, 20 autonomous republics, 7
autonomous regions (*oblasti*) and 10 autonomous districts (*okruga*)
in which that nationality constitutes at least a plurality, if not an
absolute majority, of the population. Only 5 of the union republics –
the R.S.F.S.R., Uzbekistan, Georgia, Azerbaijan, and Tadjikistan –
contain autonomous republics, regions, and/or districts. In these five
cases, the union republic *excluding* the autonomous entities within
its borders is counted as the territorial home of a nationality.[114]

There are two reasons for this approach: (1) The autonomous
republics, regions, and districts themselves are supposed to constitute the homes of ethnic groups other than the titular nationality
of the union republic in which they are located: (2) Gorbachev, in an
effort to undermine union republics that aspire to independence, has
demanded that the autonomous republics be treated like union
republics, as far as their constitutional status is concerned. This
change is aimed, presumably, at disrupting the territorial cohesion of
several union republics. Indeed, Gorbachev has attempted to
diminish union republic status still further by permitting even

[114] This approach coincides with current Soviet practice. Since the fall of 1990, the
distinction between union and autonomous republics has been abolished, de facto,
and the various drafts of Gorbachev's 'Union Treaty' now speak simply of 'republics,'
encompassing both categories. However, most of this chapter, which covers the
period before and after the change was promulgated, has retained the previous
appellations, especially when citing demographic data.

autonomous regions and districts to participate in sessions of his recently upgraded Council of the Federation, which was intended originally to represent the union republics only.

Of the 16 A.S.S.R.s (autonomous republics) on the soil of the R.S.F.S.R., only 8 constitute the national home of the nationality whose name each bears: in the other 8, the indigenous population is actually outnumbered by Russians. (Thus, in the Buryat ASSR, Russians constitute just under 70 percent of the population, while Buryats amount only to 24 percent.) As defined here, therefore, the latter 8 autonomous republics in reality constitute Russian national territories rather than 'belonging' to the titular nationalities.

In all of the 5 autonomous regions within the R.S.F.S.R., Russians constitute a plurality or absolute majority of the population and this holds true also for 8 out of the 10 autonomous districts. Thus, the titular nationality can be viewed as possessing 'its own territory' only in 10 of the 31 autonomous republics, regions, and districts in the R.S.F.S.R., while Russians could legitimately view the remaining 21, in addition to the R.S.F.S.R. itself, as constituting their national home.

Similarly, of the two autonomous republics within Georgia, one – the Adzhar A.S.S.R. – contains no titular nationality but is inhabited by the Georgians themselves, while in the other – the Abkhaz A.S.S.R. – Georgians (46.2 percent) outnumber the indigenous Abkhaz (17.3 percent). Only in Georgia's South Ossetian Autonomous Region does the titular nationality constitute a majority of the population.

In at least 1 of the 15 union republics – Kazakhstan – Russians held a plurality over the indigenous population until recently, and even now the Kazakhs constitute a mere 39.7 percent of the inhabitants, only a fraction ahead of Russians who amount to 37.8 percent. Thus, Kazakhstan is only marginally the national home of the Kazakh people, of whom, moreover, almost one-fifth lives outside the Kazakh Republic.

Altogether, of the 52 union republics, autonomous republics, regions, and districts, only 27 can be considered to be the national homes of their titular nationalities in terms of the demographic criteria set out in this chapter. This fact alone should explain why (even if genuine) mere decentralization and extended self-government of the U.S.S.R.'s extant administrative subdivisions cannot solve the Soviet nationalities problem. It accounts also for the huge number of Soviet citizens – 53,677,000, or 18.8 percent of the population – who can be defined as 'living outside their national territory,' not to mention the additional 13,624,000, or 4.8 percent, who 'have no national territory.' (The latter category would include such anomalous cases as the Jewish Autonomous Region within the R.S.F.S.R., in which Jews are 4.15 percent of the population while Russians constitute 83.13 percent: moreover, only 0.65 percent of all Soviet Jews live in that region. In that sense, Jews can be numbered among those who 'have no national territory.')

It is an entirely different question whether the 27,669,000 Russians who belong nominally to the category of those 'living outside their national territory' really can be defined in this way. To give just two examples:

In the Soviet Ukraine's Donetsk *oblasi* Ukrainians constitute 51.1 percent of the population, while Russians are only 43.0 percent. Does this mean that those Ukrainians are living 'in their national territory' and the Russians are not? If so, why do 1,217 schools in that region have Russian as their primary language of instruction and a mere 63 use Ukrainian?

In the Poltava District, Ukrainians outnumber Russians approximately 10 to 1 (89.2 percent and 9.0 percent, respectively). In Poltava City, which reflects this demographic composition, 26,000 students attend schools in which Russian is the language of instruction, while only 14,000 are able to attend Ukrainian-language schools.[115]

If, as these statistics indicate, 25,265,000 Russians living outside the R.S.F.S.R. thus enjoy a privileged position, that applies even more to the 2,404,000 who dwell in the eight A.S.S.R.s and two Autonomous Districts in which the titular nationality outnumbers Russians, but which (at least until recently) were subordinate to the R.S.F.S.R.

With regard to Russians living outside the R.S.F.S.R., however, an interesting trend may be noted: whereas, since 1970, the percentage of all Russians residing in the European union republics other than the Russian Republic has increased from 10.25 percent to 10.59 percent, in the case of Russians living in the Asian/Moslem republics, a decline from 7.12 percent to 6.83 percent was registered in the

---

[115] The author wishes to express appreciation to Mr Eugene M. Fishel, Graduate Research Fellow at the Institute for the Study of Conflict, Ideology & Policy, from whose work these data on the Ukraine are taken.

1989 census. Moreover, in the last two years, there has been actual flight of Russians from the latter areas to the larger Russian cities where a 'refugee problem' has developed.

This phenomenon has to be viewed within the wider context of the startling growth in the absolute and relative size of the Turkic/Moslem/Asian population of the U.S.S.R., from 38,046,000 in 1970 to 58,927,000 in 1989, constituting an increase from 15.7 to 20.6 percent of the population. During this period, the east Slav and Baltic peoples experienced a natural increase of a mere 10.5 percent, as compared to the 54.9 percent natural increase of the non-European nationalities. As a result, approximately one-half of the population under the age of 19 is composed of non-Europeans, a factor which explains the current estimate that a full 37 percent of draft-age persons this year will be members of the Turkic/Moslem/Asian group.

The east Slav population has decreased from 74.0 percent to 69.7 percent during the same period, a phenomenon which contrasts sharply with statement by Colonel General A. Kleymenov, deputy chief of staff, quoted in *Krasnaya Zvezda* on October 29, 1989, that the general staff consisted of 'Russians 85 percent, Ukrainians 10 percent, Belorussians 3 percent . . . ,' i.e., that 98 percent were east Slavs, and that this reflected the composition of the senior officer corps as a whole. One can imagine what possibilities this leaves for the upward mobility of (the Asian) 37 percent of recruits, who can hope at most for a sliver of the 2 percent of the senior officer slots left for non-Slavs (at least some of which are likely to be filled by other European nationalities).

While much of Western attention has focused on the east Slav/Moslem confrontation, that particular conflict, in fact, is not high up as yet on the agenda of the Soviet nationalities problem. The reason has to do with the nature of governance in Central Asia, where the union republics became and have remained feudal baronies of individual communist party leaders, notorious for corruption. In the Soviet Congress of Peoples Deputies and in the Supreme Soviet, the Central Asian representatives have provided the 'tame' battalions that can be relied upon to produce the necessary votes to carry almost any motion initiated by the party and state leadership. In the March 1991 referendum on Gorbachev's new Union Treaty, the 'Moslem' republics provided the highest percentage of supporters.

The real problem concerns those nationalities which, unlike the

Central Asians, represent *more* developed societies than Russia itself. This applies particularly to the Baltic peoples, the Georgians, and the Armenians (the latter two having rejected paganism in favor of Christianity, for instance, many centuries earlier than the Russians). The Ukraine constitutes a borderline case. In all of these instances, the Soviet leadership has done its best, with varying degrees of success, to play off the sizeable ethnic minorities within those republics against the aspirations for independence of the titular nationalities.

This is the case in Latvia, where Russian colonization is threatening to overwhelm the indigenous Latvian population, which is down to a slim majority: in the capital city of Riga, Latvians now constitute a minority. It applies, in a somewhat different manner, to Georgia, where the Abkhaz and South Ossetian minorities have been encouraged by Moscow center to assert their autonomy – and possibly even their independence – from the Georgian Republic. This approach led to results: while Georgia as such boycotted the referendum on Gorbachev's new 'Union Treaty,' the Abkhaz A.S.S.R. and the South Ossetian Autonomous Region voted to approve the document. Since the Abkhaz are outnumbered within their own republic by ethnic Georgians, this outcome was possible only because of the Georgian boycott. Inter-ethnic relationships in Georgia have deteriorated to the point of bloodshed.

In the Moldavian case, Moscow center went much further: while Moldavia boycotted the referendum, the Soviet authorities invented two new ethnic entities on its territory – the 'Gagauz' and 'Transdniestrian' republics. *Pravda* reported the (favorable) response to the referendum of these fictitious administrative units under the same rubric as the results from the existing union and autonomous republics.

As the developments cited here indicate, the nationalities problem in the U.S.S.R. cannot be tackled successfully just by enhancing individual human rights, or even by extending minority safeguards: nor will simple decentralization suffice – whether it involves greater powers for the republics or is applied down to the level of autonomous regions and districts.

For the initial five years of the Gorbachev period, the population of the U.S.S.R. waited with bated breath, first for a communist party conference that was supposed to tackle the entire nationalities question, and then for a new 'Union Treaty' which was to restructure the

Soviet state in a manner that would resolve the issue. It took several years and repeated postponements before the conference was held finally in the fall of 1988 and it produced clichés, devoid of any innovative approach. In 1989, a C.P.S.U. Central Committee Plenum was convoked to create a commission on ethnic problems, the work of which remained unpublished. Its only contribution was made, indirectly, via two of its members – G. I. Usmanov and A. N. Girenko, both of them new party secretaries at the time – who spoke subsequently at the 28th C.P.S.U. Congress.

On July 5, 1990, Usmanov, addressing himself to the future of the 2,036,000 Germans in the Soviet Union, revealed that several hundred thousand, deported by Stalin from their former Volga A.S.S.R., would be permitted to return, despite the fact that Russians had settled this area in the meantime. He suggested that a country-wide German association be set up, responsible for the remaining 1,750,000 Germans, wherever they might be residing, which would enjoy the same authority as an autonomous republic – although such powers had been reserved previously for territorial entities. The non-territorial German association would provide special cultural, linguistic, and educational facilities for Germans dispersed throughout Central Asia and other parts of the U.S.S.R. In fact, Usmanov appears to have rediscovered the Renner-Bauer approach to the nationalities problem, although one may assume that he knew of their work only indirectly, if at all. (Stalin's booklet on *Marxism and the National Question* had been intended, of course, at least in part as a polemic against the Austrian Social Democrats.)

Sadly, there was no follow-up to Usmanov's suggestion and the draft Union Treaty published on November 24, 1990 (and in supposedly final form on March 9, 1991) contained no reference to these ideas. Gorbachev had held out the concept of such a new Union Treaty as a panacea for the solution of the nationalities problem and had tried to fob off the independence movements in the Baltic and Transcaucasian republics by asserting that the new document would provide ways of responding to their aspirations.

In fact, when the first draft appeared it contained fewer concessions to the restive republics on the Soviet geographic periphery than had the 1977 ('Brezhnev') constitution, at least on paper. Article 72 of the latter document, for instance, had stated that 'Each Union Republic shall retain the right freely to secede from the U.S.S.R.' The new draft initially contained no reference whatever to this right. The 1977 constitution, in Article 70, claimed that the U.S.S.R. was the result 'of the free self-determination of nations' and that it drew together 'all its nations and nationalities.' The 1990 draft, in Section I, Article 1, stated that the U.S.S.R. was the result of 'a voluntary association of republics' but carefully avoided the claim that it had emerged as a result of 'self-determination.' Nor did it contain any reference to 'nations and nationalities:' Section III, Article 11, dealing with the U.S.S.R. Supreme Soviet, used less specific terminology: 'The representation on the Soviet of Nationalities of all peoples living in the U.S.S.R. is guaranteed.'

The revised version of the Union Treaty in March of 1991 weakened this reference still further, changing 'all peoples living in the U.S.S.R.' to 'all national-territorial formations in the U.S.S.R.,' i.e., precluding implicitly self-determination by nationalities that do not already possess a territory 'of their own' (Section III, Article 12).

That the Brezhnev constitution did not affect Soviet reality and was intended for purely cosmetic effect is beside the point. The fact that Gorbachev's initial draft did not offer an improvement upon the Brezhnev document is more relevant.

However, where possible boundary changes within the U.S.S.R. were concerned, Article 78 of the Brezhnev constitution had stated that 'The territory of a Union Republic may not be altered without its consent. The boundaries between Union Republics may be altered by mutual agreement of the Republics concerned, subject to ratification by the U.S.S.R.' Section II, Article 3 of Gorbachev's first draft relaxed this provision by declaring that 'borders between republics may only be changed by agreement between them.' This would seem to allow for such changes without ratification by the U.S.S.R.

(As mentioned earlier, it was this initial draft of the Union Treaty which eliminated, by implication, the difference between union and autonomous republics, referring to them simply as 'sovereign republics.')

The reference to border changes implies at least theoretical recognition of the fact that the existing boundaries bear little resemblance to the ethnic map of the U.S.S.R. and that, without some territorial changes, no meaningful approach to the nationalities question is realistic. Yet, in practice, Gorbachev has shown vehement opposition to the *implementation* of the principle of redrawing frontiers, as demonstrated by the case of the Nagorno-Karabakh Autonomous Region, which is subordinate to Azerbaijan although its population is almost 77 percent Armenian. Despite the ardent Armenian desire for union between their republic and Nagorno-Karabakh, Gorbachev has supported obstinately Azerbaijan's veto over such a move.

On the other hand, where a putative territorial change could be used as a threat against would-be secessionists, Gorbachev has not hesitated to make sinister references to such a possibility. For instance, in the case of Lithuania, he has pointed out that it: (a) received its capital, Vilnius, as a result of Stalin's partition of Poland in 1939; (b) was enlarged to include several small Belorussian districts in 1940 when Lithuania was annexed to the U.S.S.R.; and (c) regained its port and region of Klaipeda (Memel) as a result of the Red Army's defeat of Germany in 1945 (having lost the area in 1939, following an ultimatum by Hitler). All of these areas, Gorbachev threatened, might be lost if Lithuania departed from the U.S.S.R. Moreover, he ensured that Belorussian nationalist demands against Lithuania would back up his warnings.

The revisions introduced in the draft Union Treaty between November 24, 1990, and March 9, 1991, are of interest, but by no means constitute unqualified improvements. Thus, Section II, Article 1, restores the right of secession, although it seems to limit that privilege to the republics least likely to take advantage of that article, namely, the nine that actually adhered to the revised Union Treaty: 'The republics, parties to the treaty, have the right of free secession from the union in the manner prescribed by the parties to the treaty.'

This seems to exclude the six republics that refused to sign: they are precisely the areas that have declared their independence. Section IV, Article 23, appears to underscore this interpretation: 'Relations between the Union and the republics which have not signed the Union Treaty shall be regulated on the basis of the existing U.S.S.R. legislation and mutual commitments and agreements.' The reference, presumably, is to the constitutional provisions passed in March of 1990 which placed elaborate restrictions on the secession process, requiring no less than two plebiscites and the ultimate consent of the Soviet central legislature. An unkind commentator might say that those who do not wish to secede may do so freely, while those who desire independence will have no practical way of achieving their aspirations.

Of course, neither version of the Union Treaty may turn out to have statutory force since, on April 23, 1991, President Gorbachev met with the leaders of nine of the republics (excluding the Baltic states, Georgia, Armenia, and Moldavia) and produced a joint statement which, in effect, superseded both drafts. It called on the participants 'to finalize work on a draft new union treaty . . . . Not later than six months after the treaty is signed, a new constitution of the U.S.S.R., based on the provisions of the treaty on the union of sovereign states, should be prepared and brought up for adoption at a congress of the U.S.S.R. people's deputies.'

In at least one crucial aspect, the joint statement differed from the previous drafts: 'The top leaders of the union republics taking part in the meeting, while recognizing the right of Latvia, Lithuania, Estonia, Moldavia, Georgia and Armenia to decide independently on the question of accession to the [U]nion [T]reaty, at the same time consider it necessary to establish the most-favored-nation treatment for republics signing the union treaty . . . .' Not only did the meeting seem to relegate the former autonomous republics to subordinate status once again, but it appeared to open the way to secession by union republics, through the device of non-adherence to a new Union Treaty (with economic penalties, to be sure).

Whatever the next Gorbachev gyration might entail, in the light of the developments examined a three-part approach to resolution of the Soviet Union's nationalities problem is indicated:

1   The recognition of the right of secession, and its realization if demanded by the democratically elected assemblies of the six republics that absented themselves from the April 23, 1991 gathering. With some relatively minor exceptions, Lithuania, Georgia and Armenia are ethnically homogeneous, while Latvia and Estonia, although subjected to Russian colonization, are widely recognized (as is Lithuania) as independent sovereign entities that were unlawfully seized by the Soviet Union. All of these republics are situated on the periphery of the U.S.S.R., and their subtraction from a new union would not interfere seriously with the economic or security needs of the Soviet state.

2   In the remaining portions of the U.S.S.R., there would have to be far-reaching devolution of authority not only in the economic sector, but with regard to residential qualification, education, cultural institutions, and language of instruction and of official usage. Ideally, borders of union republics, autonomous republics, regions, and districts would be redrawn to adhere more closely to ethno-linguistic criteria. Unfortunately, *Moscow News* (No. 11,

March 1991) has identified no less than 76 territorial claims – most of them mutually incompatible – that are currently advanced by nationalities on the western periphery, in the Caucasus, in the Upper Volga-Urals region, and in eastern Siberia.

3   Usmanov's (actually Renner-Bauer's) concept of country-wide associations of peoples without a territorial base (or who are living outside their territorial base) would have to be applied, giving these non-territorial associations constitutional status equivalent to the expanded authority that would be devolved on union and autonomous republics, at least as far as education, culture, and linguistic facilities are concerned.

Most current discussions on the Soviet nationalities problem are devoted primarily to questions of secession and of decentralization. Hardly any reference can be found to the discrepancies that need to be rectified between administrative and ethnic boundaries and to the large number of citizens whose cultural and linguistic rights cannot be addressed on a territorial basis, even after such adjustments are made. Of course, the fundamental question remains whether anyone in authority at the Soviet center is willing to draw the necessary conclusions.

Dusan Necak

The 'Yugoslav question': past and future

The unresolved national question lies at the root of all the political changes in Eastern and Southeast Europe. At least to the same degree as the totalitarianism of 'real socialism' and the monopolization of power, self-deception over nationality problems contributed to the collapse of the rigid communist systems. This self-deception was attributable to the ideological premise that national questions were the exclusive property of the bourgeois social order and had been eliminated with the establishment of socialism.

Thus, as far as the East European socialist states as well as Yugoslavia were concerned, the nationality question was considered to be solved. With the exception of a short period after the war, however, a difference existed between Yugoslavia and the East European socialist states. After the break with Stalin in 1948, Yugoslav communism as molded by Tito became more adaptable and more open than late Stalinist 'real socialism,' but even so, at the end of the 1950s, the national question raised its head, despite its official demise.

Consequently, although the wave of political changes did not pass by Yugoslavia, it manifested itself in less dramatic form. Nevertheless, it is self-evident that the continued existence of Yugoslavia depends on a solution being found to the national question, not only in the sense of equal rights of co-decision over the fate of the country, but above all in the sense of complete national sovereignty and statehood (*Staatlichkeit*). Several times in the past, the Yugoslav peoples were obliged to make major decisions regarding their destiny, but on earlier occasions the centripetal forces always won over the centrifugal forces.

This situation leads one to ask whether the theoretical legacy of

Austrian Marxism may be able to make a contribution to the solution of national problems in modern society. This legacy consists
principally of the work of Karl Renner and Otto Bauer.

The initial theoretical position of the Austro-Marxist solution to
the national question was stated in the first issue of the Social
Democratic publication *Der Kampf*, which came out in 1907. The
following working thesis was formulated: 'How can one embrace
large cultural differences within the proletariat and keep them all
within the framework of a single party, a single program, and a single
policy?'[116] In contrast to other left-wing theoreticians (e.g.,
Kautsky), the Austro-Marxists – headed by Renner and Bauer –
advocated the preservation of the Austro-Hungarian Empire, since
they believed in its survival. In particular, Renner was aware of the
destructive potential of the unresolved national question and
attempted to depoliticize the question and reduce it to a legal problem.[117]

In fact, the principal characteristic of Renner's views on the
nationality question is his awareness of its destructive political
power. He saw the key to the solution of the problem in the 'personal
principle' and a 'national register,' in which the declared national
affiliation of each citizen would be recorded, as well as in separate
electoral registers for each nationality in territorial or national
bodies with rights limited to administrative autonomy, etc.[118]

Renner advocated a constitutional reform that would confine the
striving for power of the different peoples to its cultural core.
National rights could be asserted only by members of a people, i.e.,
on an individual basis.[119] Hence Renner's theory is termed a 'personal' theory. This characteristic feature is the second relevant factor
when it comes to attempting to apply his theory today. It also is the
basis for Renner's definition of the nation, according to which a
nation is seen as a 'spiritual, cultural, not a material or economic,
community.'[120] This definition of a nation without an economic

[116] See Rudi Rizman, *Marksizem in Nacionalno Vprasanje (Marxism and the
National Question)*, (Ljubljana: 1980), 168.

[117] *Ibid.*; see detailed discussion especially in Karl Renner, *Staat und Nation – zur
Österreichischen Nationalitätenfrage (State and Nation – on the Austrian Nationality
Question)*, (Vienna: 1899).

[118] Rizman, *op. cit.*, 169.

[119] See Helmut Konrad, 'Delavsko Gibanje in Narodnost (The Workers'
Movement and Nationality),' *Nasi Razgledi* [Ljubljana], October 8, 1976, 519–20.

[120] Rudolf Springer (Renner), *Der Kampf der Österreichischen Nationen um den
Staat* (Vienna: 1902), 26.

component is the third and perhaps most significant characteristic of Renner's views on the solution of the nationality question that needs to be considered in the context of the comparison with current efforts being made here. A similar standpoint is found in the so-called Brünn National Social Democratic Program of 1899, which supported national territorial autonomy in all affairs that concern the nationality directly. At the same time, the nationality would not have the right to conduct a unitary economic or foreign policy. However, in contrast to Renner and Bauer, the Brünn Program advocated the idea of a multinational federal state.

Renner's ideas were partially put into practice in Moravia and in the Ukraine, as well as in regard to the granting of cultural autonomy in Estonia. His principal aim was to replace the official protection of minorities by a constitutional recognition of the status of the nationalities (nations) as associated bodies with limited sovereignty.

In brief, Renner advocated a decentralized unitary state with a federal administrative nationality system strictly distinguishing between political interests on the one hand and purely nationality interests on the other. The central government would be responsible for social and political problems, while the problems that affected a nation or a nationality would be dealt with under regular procedures by the decentralized administrative organs.[121] The separation of political and nationality interests as well as a kind of partial statism represent a fourth characteristic that enables one to make a comparison with current attempts to resolve nationality issues.

Otto Bauer took a different view of the national question, defining the nation as a 'community of destiny (*Schicksalsgemeinschaft*) from which a community of character emerges.'[122] Bauer's opinions lead, however, to the same political conclusions. Some commentators are of the opinion that Bauer's nationality theory is superior to Renner's and represents an advance on it.[123] However, Bauer's analysis of the nation, which is oriented toward the psychocultural theory of the nation, pursues the same aim: 'His reduction of the nation to a cultural and psychic question fulfilled the same function as Renner's reduction of the nation to a legal problem, i.e., the function of

---

[121] Rizman, *op. cit.*, 170; Hans Mommsen and Albrecht Martiny, 'Nationalism, Nationalities Question,' in *Marxism, Communism and Western Society – A Comparative Encyclopedia*, ed. C.D. Kernig (Herder and Herder: 1973), vol. 6, 42.

[122] Otto Bauer, *Die Nationalitätenfrage und die Sozialdemokratie* (Vienna: 1907); Rizman, *op. cit.*, 173.

[123] See, for example, Rizman footnote, 173.

depolitization of the nationality question.'[124] For Bauer, national culture and national sovereignty meant everything: in his view, an ideal state is a multinational state with broadly assured cultural autonomy for its ethnic segments.

Renner and Bauer were the first to carry out systematic scientific research on the concept of the nation. They pointed out that, apart from its other interests, the proletariat also had national interests. It was precisely their emphasis on the national as opposed to the international that aroused fierce criticism of Austro-Marxism above all from communist theoreticians, e.g., Lenin and Stalin, as well as Kautsky, on the grounds of nationalist deviation. On the other hand, Kautsky also expressed a positive judgment, stating that after the victory of the proletariat the ideas of Renner and Bauer might become a model for the construction of the future United States of Europe.

For the sake of historical accuracy, it should be noted here that two Slovenes were among the precursors of the national cultural idea. As early as 1865, Matija Majar wrote in an article entitled 'Thoughts on the Austrian Provinces (*Länder*) and Nations'[125] that he saw the solution of the Austrian national question in the consistent separation of 'purely political affairs from national political affairs, and in the introduction of a "nationalities administration".' In 1898 (shortly before the publication of Renner's work *State and Nation – On the Austrian Nationalities Question*), Etbin Kristan arrived at similar proposals for the solution of the Austrian national question on the basis of cultural autonomy and the personal principle. In his article 'Nationalism and Socialism in Austria,'[126] he came out in support of unrestricted autonomy, using the well-known phrase, 'A nation cannot be measured geometrically, only arithmetically.' In his view, a nation is composed not of a community of individuals living on a certain territory, but of a totality of individuals who speak a certain native language and willingly consider themselves to be a nationality. Each individual should carry his nationality and national rights everywhere with him, since in his conception the granting of equal rights, e.g., for the Czechs, would be very problematic, if it were to be recognized only in Prague and

---

[124] Rizman, *op. cit.*, 174.
[125] *Slawisches Zentralblatt* (December 1865, Nos. 10, 11, 12).
[126] *Zeitschrift Akademie* (Prague: 1898).

Pilsen, but not in Vienna as well.[127]

Although chronologically these two Slovene authors published their views before Renner and Bauer, the sociopolitical influence of their ideas cannot be compared with that of the two German-speaking Austrians. However, one can justly claim that the content of Kristan's ideas is still alive to this day in proposals for the resolution of the Serbian national question outside the present borders of the Serbian Republic. This is demonstrated by the way in which the Croatian Serbs are endeavoring to obtain personal autonomy (outside the Serb-populated areas) for individual Serbs who have settled in the major Croatian cities.

The Austro-Marxist vision of a possible resolution of the national question in the Habsburg Monarchy was not adopted by the South Slavic national movements. Moreover, as far as the present situation is concerned, it cannot be said that it would be possible to make use of the legacy of these theoreticians in attempts to solve current Yugoslav national-political problems. This is not only because the theories were developed nearly a century ago in a different historical era. Both then and today, their theories were and still are unacceptable for the Slovenes, the Croats, and the Serbs because of their limited view of the nation, emphasis solely on the cultural component, and de facto denial of complete sovereignty and the right of a people to its own state (*Eigenstaatlichkeit*).

Indeed, all the national programs of the South Slavic peoples – whether under the monarchy or within Yugoslavia – were based on a demand for complete national sovereignty and possession of their own state, whether within or outside a multinational state community. No solution of the national question could be crowned with success if it separated sociopolitical interests from so-called national interests and handed over the economic fate of the nation to another entity that advocated unitarism and statism, reduced the nation to its 'cultural core,' and failed to defend the nation's territory – i.e., the territory on which all national rights, ranging from political and cultural to linguistic rights, belonged to the indigenous population.

Today's Yugoslavia – although now it can scarcely be said to exist any more as a country – arose during World War II as a federative

[127] For details, see France Klopcic, 'Prvi Nastop Etbina Kristana za Kulturnonarodnostno Avtonomijo Leta 1895,' *Sodobnost* (Ljubljana) 1–3 (1965), 201–4. On 204–9 Kristan's article is quoted in Slovene (the original article appeared in German).

community of the Yugoslav peoples and national minorities. The 'Yugoslav idea' is naturally much older, and its realization could not be accomplished without major problems. It presupposed the solution of many questions, above all the question whether the South Slavic peoples were nations in the sociological and political sense or only immature constituent parts of a future unitary Yugoslav nation, as well as the question of the very nature of the Yugoslav idea and the Yugoslav movement, indeed even how to define all these peoples.[128] Until the first Yugoslav state was created, the Yugoslav national programs were distinguished primarily by national unitarism, while the federalistic concept remained essentially the privilege of a few lucid democratic spirits. Nevertheless, despite the polycentric character of the Yugoslav movement, the tendency toward federalism has always been present and active. Indeed, it has frequently made a formal appearance when political decisions that came close to national self-determination were under discussion (e.g., in 1848, as well as around 1870).[129]

The Yugoslav peoples banded together in a common state on the basis of their relationship and in order to unite all the portions of their different peoples within a single state – but above all out of the conviction that if they formed a common state they would be able to protect themselves more easily against the danger represented by the larger neighboring peoples, i.e., the Germans, Italians, and Hungarians, in whose states they had lived until the beginning of this century.

Whereas the Serbian and Montenegrin nations joined the new state on December 1, 1918, as nations who already had their own states, the Slovene and Croatian nations did not possess fully constituted states (*Eigenstaatlichkeit*), since the latter two peoples had lived until the end of World War I within the Austro-Hungarian Monarchy. The most prominent Slovene and Croatian politicians were very conscious of the fact that they would have to build their future on the basis of national sovereignty and possession of their own states. Thus it is not surprising that on the occasion of the founding of the National Council for Slovenia and Istria on August 16–17, 1918, the chairman of the council and head of the Slovenian clericals, Dr Anton Korosec, emphasized in a special communiqué that 'The state rights (*Staatsrecht*) that the Slovene people had exercised and fulfilled in its own state [i.e., the state of Carantania that had existed in the early medieval period] passed into foreign hands for over a thousand years, (but) the self-determination of the peoples will restore them (i.e., state rights) to it and unite all the Slovenes, Croats, and Serbs in an independent Yugoslav state.'

According to Korosec, the Slovene people had elected the National Council precisely in order to be 'prepared for the historic moment when it would assume all the rights and obligations of its own state (*Eigenstaatlichkeit*), together with the Croats and the Serbs.[130] When on October 29, 1918, within the frontiers of the Habsburg Monarchy the so-called 'State of the Serbs, Croatians and Slovenes' was created (within which the Serbs represented a decided minority limited to the Voevodina and the Serb diaspora in Croatia), for the Slovene people as well as for the Croat people this meant the realization of national self-determination and the achievement of an historic situation in which they were able to make independent and sovereign decisions for themselves and determine their entire national development. Consequently, this constituted the national aim of the Slovene and Croatian peoples when the Kingdom of Yugoslavia was founded on December 1, 1918.

On the other hand, the creation of the Yugoslav state represented a success for the Serbian people, since in conjunction with several other political factors – e.g., victory in the war, well-established independence, a ruling dynasty – it created the preconditions required for it to assume the leading role in the state and to 'replace' the Germans or the Hungarians as far as the Slovenes and the Croats were concerned. Above all, the Slovenes found themselves once more in a situation in which they had to fight to maintain their national independence and preserve their equality and national sovereignty. The Kingdom of the Serbs, Croatians, and Slovenes was founded solely to assure the national interests of its peoples. Since it did not fulfill this expectation, it did not justify the grounds for its creation. Social injustices only intensified national contradictions and became an 'explosive constituent part' of the 'national class contradictions' that destroyed the first Yugoslav state.

As in the Habsburg Monarchy, the reasons for this lay in the

[130] Jurij Perovsek, 'Sedemdesetletnica Slovenske Narodne Osvoboditve,' *Komunist*, November 4, 1988, 19.

national – i.e., state – question with which Yugoslavia was beset. This question arose because of limited national sovereignty: while the cultural independence of each people was emphasized and maintained, at the same time the Slovenes' and Croats' economic as well as their broader political interests were handed over to the 'supranational' Serbian state. This approach to solving the national question can be compared in some respects with the Austro-Marxist vision of a depolitization of the national question by means of granting limited statism (*Etatismus*). Instead of relations between sovereign peoples and their state, there was talk of a triple nation – especially during the first years of the existence of the Kingdom of Yugoslavia – a nation consisting of three ethnic groups (*Stämme*) and of a unitary Yugoslav nation. The Macedonians were not recognized at all as a nation.

During the entire interwar period, the idea of a kind of dissolution of Slovenes, Croats, and Serbs in a Yugoslav nation lived on among intellectuals in the liberal political camp (cf. much material in the periodical *Nova Evropa*, Zagreb, 1920–41). After the dictatorship of the king was established in 1929, however, the idea of a unitary 'Yugoslavness' dominated the political scene. The Yugoslav theory and practice of reducing the national question to a cultural question and the attempt to depoliticize the national question by replacing the recognition of complete national sovereignty by a unitary 'Yugoslavness' constituted the principal cause of the collapse of the first Yugoslav state. Yugoslav bourgeois politics became conscious of the destructive forces inherent in the unresolved national question only too belatedly.

The Yugoslav communists who founded the second Yugoslavia that arose in the middle of World War II, during the period of the anti-fascist struggle and the revolution, paid attention to the national question from the very beginning. The principles proclaimed at the session of the Yugoslav anti-fascist war parliament in Jajce in 1943 gave rise to hope that the Yugoslav national question would be resolved in corresponding fashion. The future state was to be a federal state of nations and national minorities with equal rights. The Macedonian nation was recognized. The principles included support for the national integrity of each nation which was to achieve its own statehood (*Eigenstaatlichkeit*) within the framework of the new state. On the formal plane, this situation undoubtedly represented a certain measure of progress compared with the position in the first Yugoslav state, and indeed this resolution of the national question was given corresponding legal embodiment in the first Yugoslav constitution adopted in 1946. However, in many respects this constitution was a mere copy of the 1936 Stalin Constitution, which provided for a highly centralized state. Moreover, as far as the solution of the national question was concerned, the constitution proceeded from the incorrect assumption (discussed earlier) that the national question would resolve itself as a result of the creation under socialism of a just social order. Thus the class principle was given precedence over the national principle.

It was not until 1959, when the Albanian issue again appeared on the agenda, that the Yugoslav state and party apparatus realized that the national question had not been resolved once and for all. Up until 1968 a process of democratization and decentralization went forward, manifesting itself not only in the opening of Yugoslavia to the outside world, but also in the restructuring of the Yugoslav federal state order. In that year the constitutional amendments were adopted that resulted in the strengthening of the 'autonomous provinces' and the role of the Peoples' Council, the parliamentary chamber in which all the Yugoslav peoples possessed equal representation.

The change becomes even clearer when one also takes into consideration the decentralization of the party apparatus thanks to the promotion of the creative role of the national parties *vis-à-vis* the Yugoslav Party. In this way the basis was created for the most recent Yugoslav constitution, that of 1974. This constitution already contains elements of a confederative state order, since it requires a consensus with regard to decisions of importance to the individual republics or nations. However, as a result of the country's constantly deteriorating economic situation — owing to the lack (characteristic of communism) of a successful economic doctrine — the tensions between the different nations increased, and the economic, linguistic, and cultural differences between the various Yugoslav peoples became more pronounced. This applied even to the interpretation of the constitution, which for the economically less-developed southeastern portion of Yugoslavia was too confederative, whereas for the northwestern portion it was too centralized.

The peoples of both parts of Yugoslavia felt economically threatened, which in turn intensified their feelings of national jeopardy. Their political elites began to take measures related to individual state rights that ignored the interests of the state as a whole. The principle of limited sovereignty – i.e., the transfer of part of the sovereign rights of a people to the federal state, so that federal laws take precedence over republican laws, and strategic economic, financial, foreign and defense policy issues fall under the exclusive jurisdiction of the federation – was replaced by the principle of complete sovereignty, i.e., the full responsibility of each people for its own destiny. This was effected by Serbia, Slovenia, and Croatia through their adoption of new constitutions or constitutional amendments that represented state constitutions of the classic type. In addition, in Slovenia a referendum for an independent and sovereign Slovene state was conducted. Slovenia and other republics have adopted a number of laws in the economic, financial and defense areas, which have had the effect of loosening their links with the federal state. These developments have also strengthened the self-awareness of the Macedonians and the peoples living in Bosnia and Herzegovina.

The theoretical legacy of Karl Renner and Otto Bauer was and still is inapplicable to the solution of the national question in Yugoslavia. The times call for different solutions. The country's history has demonstrated that 'cultural autonomy' on the model of Austro-Marxist or analogous thinking cannot be applied to Yugoslavia. The complete sovereignty of all the peoples living in Yugoslavia is a *conditio sine qua non* for the future existence of Yugoslavia as a modern multinational state. Only the legitimate representatives of a people can decide whether any portion of its national sovereignty can be transferred to a federal state. The sovereignty of a nation is founded upon its state territory, and the rights of the individual that are based on this sovereignty are not transferable. At the same time – precisely in view of the legacy of Renner and Bauer – the question of national minorities and nationalities and the question of nations that have not yet achieved their own statehood require separate discussion.

Joan Estruch

The social construction of national identities: the case of Catalonia as a nation in the Spanish state

According to William Thomas' principle (1919), what is defined as real is real in its consequences. This is probably not a bad starting point to try to understand the peculiar situation of Catalonia as a European nation officially belonging to the Spanish state (and in part to the French state as well). For, however strongly I might wish to stress that I am a Catalan and not a Spaniard, you could ask me obviously to show the identity card which I carry in my pocket, or ask me where I pay my taxes, or in which army I underwent military service. I would even have to confess that, as a university professor in Barcelona, my official status is that of a civil servant of the Spanish state. However strongly I may want to maintain that 'Spain' is in fact a mere fantasy, a pseudonym rather than a reality, what definitely counts is its definition as real and its perception as such, which means that the consequences of this definition are also appallingly real.

A Catalan sociologist has put it in the following terms:

For Catalans with a national conscience, to visit a foreign country is a totally different experience from that of most Europeans, owing to the fact that our national conflict attacks the very roots of our collective identity. It is an experience which easily leads to a state of anxiety: in the case of the Catalan, because he simply does not want to be taken for a Spaniard, since he feels that this would hide and blur his true identity; in the case of the foreigner who receives him, because in his mental diagram regarding the way the world is distributed, he does not usually find a spot named Catalonia, and therefore rather suspects the other of being a little crazy. Thus what should have been an immediate and almost mechanical identification is transformed into a laborious event requiring long explanations in order to make sure that both parts have come to an understanding. We must not forget that present-ations and first meetings are formal rituals and as such should have the automatic character of a stereotype.[131]

[131] Antoni Estradé, 'Intellectuals, nacionalisme i universalitat,' El Nacionalisme Català a la fi del Segle XX (Barcelona: La Magrana and Edicions 62, 1989), 162.

Thus the first problem which the citizens of a stateless nation have to face is a problem of typification; or more precisely, the problem of the incoherence resulting from the typification in terms of which they are viewed for themselves by others, set against the identity which they have constructed for themselves. 'The social reality of everyday life is apprehended in a continuum of typifications,' write Berger and Luckmann;[132] even in a face-to-face situation, perception takes place through a series of typifications. However, given that these typifications are reciprocal, they enter into an ongoing 'negotiation' in the face-to-face situation, as a result of which they may be modified. They are in this sense relatively 'vulnerable,' in any case much more so than in 'remoter' forms of interaction.[133]

Thus, in a face-to-face situation, it would not be at all difficult to 'negotiate' various ways of understanding between a Catalan and persons from other countries. With a Slovene, for instance, we would soon reach agreement about the meaning of the peripheral situation of a region economically more developed than the state to which it is ascribed; a region culturally much more oriented toward the heart of Europe than toward the territory to which it officially belongs; and we would possibly celebrate the success of our negotiation by exchanging jokes about the inefficiency of the bureaucrats in Belgrade and Madrid, and even discovering, perhaps, that some of the jokes are identical.

In this same perspective of North-South relationships, it would be relatively easy to make a Lombard from Milan see the bother it is for a Catalan to depend in all political and economical matters on decisions taken by state agencies in which he scarcely has a word to say, controlled by persons who live in the center but come from the deep South. A Latvian would immediately realize the impact in Catalonia of successive migration waves systematically encouraged for many years by the Franco regime, as a result of which about 50 percent of the inhabitants of Catalonia are nowadays of non-Catalan origin. A Welsh or Scottish rugby fan would sympathize completely with the Catalan complaint about not being allowed to have a national team; they would understand equally well his dream of witnessing a severe defeat of the Spanish team at the hands of the Catalan team. In order to make them fully understand the situation,

---

[132] Peter Berger and Thomas Luckmann, *The Social Construction of Reality* (New York: Doubleday-Anchor Books, 1966), 33.
[133] *Ibid.*, 30 ff.

we would only have to point out the difference between the British Isles and Spain, making clear that in the latter there is no equivalent of the notion of Great Britain as distinct from England. Lastly, a Fleming from Antwerp would understand without great difficulty the linguistic problem if we explained to him that the situation which some time ago used to be valid for Belgium – every Fleming having to learn French and no Walloon wanting to speak Flemish – has been consecrated in Spain as a victory for democracy and post-Franquist liberties: the Constitution of 1978 lays down that everybody has the right and the duty to know Spanish, while Catalans have the right to speak their own language within the territorial limits of Catalonia.

A Catalan writer, Quim Monzó, synthesizes the question as follows:

Fed up with having to explain everywhere that I was a Catalan, from Catalonia, a nation occupied by Spain and France, and fed up with invariably receiving the reply: 'Oh, I see . . . so what are you? Spanish or French?' I resolved some time ago to say firmly: 'I'm from Andorra, a country that's between Spain and France.
Oh, I see . . .
Yes . . . As a matter of fact, Andorra is a much bigger country than it appears on the map . . . Andorra stretches as far as Alacant and includes the Balearic Islands.
The Balearic Islands, too?
Yes, yes; that's all Andorra. But only a small part of Andorra is independent. The rest isn't. I, for one, come from that less fortunate part. From Barcelona, a city of that not yet independent part of Andorra . . .
Well, now I see . . . Just like Ireland, with only one half of the country independent; Southern Ireland . . .
You got it, baby . . .'
Explaining it this way, I have never had any problem of making myself understood.
Be that as it may, the problem remains that the citizens of stateless nations always have to look for some way of explaining this so that their fellowmen can understand: in other words, their reality is never a 'taken-for-granted reality.[134]

On the other hand, the very idea of a stateless nation, though analytically useful, nonetheless hides a series of divergences which may turn out to be of no small importance. Thus, for example, Bavaria – which is not only a German *Land*, but even *der Freistaat Bayern*, the 'Free state of Bavaria' – might be considered from one point of view a stateless nation, yet there can be no doubt about the

[134] *Ibid.*; Quim Monozó, *El Día del Senyor* (Barcelona: Quaderns Crema, 1984).

Bavarians' feeling fully-fledged *Bundesdeutsche* – in this sense they do not feel 'stateless' as a Catalan does. In a Bavarian survey it would not seem reasonable at all to ask a question like that included in a recent poll carried out in Catalonia:[135] A representative sample of 2,100 was asked whether they considered themselves 'Catalans living in Catalonia,' 'Catalans living in Spain,' 'Spaniards living in Catalonia,' or 'Spaniards living in Spain.' Independently of the results, which are given in Table 1, the very plausibility of the question is interesting in itself: it was understood and answered by 97 percent of Catalan-born people (considering as such all individuals born in Catalonia of Catalan parents), and by 93 percent of those not of Catalan origin (not born in Catalonia, or else born in Catalonia but with one or both parents born elsewhere).

Table 1

Self-appraisal as: (N=878) (%)	Catalan origin (N=1,222) (%)	Non-Catalan origin (N=2,100) (%)	Total
Catalan living in Catalonia	79.4	35.7	54.0
Catalan living in Spain	13.8	12.8	13.2
Spaniard living in Catalonia	3.5	33.3	20.8
Spaniard living in Spain	0.3	11.0	6.6
No answer	3.0	7.2	5.4

In fact, the plausibility of the question in different contexts would probably be a good indicator of the diversity of situations theoretically covered by the one all-inclusive formula 'stateless nation.' The question certainly makes no sense in the Bavarian/German context. I am not really sure it would make sense in the context of Alsace/France, or in the context of Slovakia/Czechoslovakia, either, though for different reasons. Yet it is a perfectly plausible question in the context of Lithuania/Soviet Union, and in the context of Catalonia/Spain.

In other words:

1 There are nations without a state of their own which feel integrated in the state to which they belong (Bavaria, for instance).

---

[135] Antoni Estradé and Montserrat Treserra, *Catalunya Independent?* (Barcelona: Fundació Jaume Bofill, 1990), 59.

2   There are those which have lost the notion of being a nation, or where this notion is at most preserved by a very small minority (the case of Alsace, perhaps).

3   Other nations, though their delimitation does not coincide with that of the state, are constitutive of it to such a degree that without them the state itself would not exist (Belgium, for example, or Czechoslovakia, where in spite of the Czechs probably being 'more state' than the Slovaks the latter at least furnish half of the country's name).

4   But there are other nations – occupied, or colonized, or submitted nations, whichever you prefer – that owing to their history, language and culture do not identify with the state to which they belong in accordance with the official definition of the situation. They are 'nations without a state,' stateless nations, but in their case this does not only mean that they lack a state of their own: it implies furthermore that they have a state against them.

In cases like this the resort to violence, apart from other possible functions, and apart from its tragic consequences, has the effect of opposing to the official definition of reality an alternative definition: besides demonstrating something that Weber (1922) had already pointed out – namely that it is the state that retains the monopoly of legitimate violence – it makes one's own national identity seem real (in the European context, we have the obvious examples of Euskadi, i.e., the Basque Country, and Ireland). In the same way, the recent independence declaration proclaimed by Lithuania had the effect on public opinion of opposing a new definition of reality against the hitherto official definition.

The case of Catalonia is peculiar because:

1   It is not a nation identified with the state to which it belongs: the so-called 'unity of Spain,' symptomatically quite often called 'sacred unity,' has only been brought about by destroying the liberty of the nations of the peninsula, with the sole exception of Portugal.

2   It has never lost its consciousness of being a nation. At best, this has signified political – and at worst, military – defeats, that have generated at the same time an attitude of resistance expressed above all in the defense of its language and cultural identity.

3   It has never succeeded in joining a common Spanish political project: having tried on various occasions, it has always been rebuffed. The current formula, i.e., the so-called 'state of Autonomies,' has led in fact to an absolute trivialization of the

problem of national diversity by smothering the claims of the historic nations as the result of the adoption of a model of decentralization with 17 'autonomous communities,' all possessing their own institutions and symbols – anthems and flags – which first had to be invented in most cases. The paradoxical consequence has been a reinforcement of the Spanish nationalist project.

4 While Catalonia has definitely not opted for the recourse to violence and armed struggle, neither has it declared (nor does it seem set on that road) its independence from the Spanish state.

Everything considered, the result is an extremely precarious reality. On the one hand, according to the recent poll discussed earlier, if a referendum were to be conducted 'in order to gradually initiate a process leading to the independence of Catalonia,' the results would be as in Table 2:

Table 2

	Catalan origin (%)	Non-Catalan origin (%)	Total (%)
Yes	60.5	33.0	44.5
No	14.9	34.6	26.4
Would leave blank	2.5	3.6	3.1
Would not vote	6.5	11.8	9.6
No answer	15.6	17.0	16.4

In their comments the authors point out that the results are highly significant considering that the whole pressure of the mass media runs counter to these opinions, and that none of the bigger political forces explicitly subscribes to a hypothetical 'yes' vote.[136] For the benefit of those who profoundly mistrust the results of all opinion polls, whether they correspond or not to their own personal preferences, I would like to add two possible indicators that can easily be verified in any European country. In Catalonia there is a football team known throughout Europe (Barcelona F.C.) which plays a series of matches in a European competition shown on TV every year (the team represents Spain, of course: remember what we said about official definitions having real effects). Each time you can observe how the stadium is filled with Catalan flags – you won't see any Spanish flags! A second example: almost two-thirds of the Spanish private cars circulating on European roads during the

[136] *Ibid.*, 108 ff.

summer months are Catalan. Most of them can be identified by the 'B' standing for Barcelona on their registration plates; and 80–90 percent deliberately drive without the prescribed letter 'E' indicating the state on the back of the trunk.

Yet, on the other hand, all this hinges on definitions of reality that are not the official ones. And it creates problems not only at the moment of interaction in face-to-face situations when one is confronted with the typifications that are used in order to perceive the members of a stateless nation, as discussed at the beginning of this chapter, but also causes considerable problems with regard to what Berger and Luckmann call 'the maintenance of subjective reality.'[137]

The citizen of a stateless nation like Catalonia in fact is usually assailed by two kinds of reasoning that threaten this maintenance of subjective reality. In the first place, individuals will point out to him the futility of talking about independence at the present time, considering that the outstanding feature of the contemporary world is precisely growing interdependence on a world-wide scale. To this three replies may be made: first, nobody today can reasonably confound independence with autarky. Second, the stateless nations are not the only ones to lack independence in this sense: the states themselves, at least in their great majority, are in the same situation; neither 'proud' Spain, nor France with its dreams of 'grandeur' is now independent, just as the 'splendid isolation' of the British also belongs to the past. And third, independence today means not complete liberty, but at the least a certain ability to choose the interdependencies one considers more desirable.

The second type of argument tends to associate contemporary nationalist phenomena with certain forms of particularism, provincialism, and *esprit de clocher*. This argument is fallacious for two reasons: first, because it directs its accusation exclusively against a certain kind of nationalism, i.e., that which is not supported by the power of the state apparatus, thereby forgetting that the states, too, are nationalist. It is understandable, for example, that from an official perspective the Soviet Union may speak of the perils of nationalism (whether Armenian, Ukrainian or Baltic); but quite as obviously, from the Armenian point of view, the only really dangerous nationalism is that of the Soviets. In the same way, in Catalan eyes the nationalism that is dangerous as well as provincial

---

[137] Berger and Luckmann, *op. cit.*, 147 ff.

and ridiculous is Spanish nationalism. In the second place, the argument is fallacious because it is sociologically evident that an opening to the world and an access to universality can never be attained out of a void or nothingness, but only on the basis of an identity that is both socially constructed and personally internalized.

The fraud of which those who brand nationalism as particularistic are guilty lies in the fact that ultimately they pretend to substitute for the identity which the individual has internalized a different identity which they seek to impose coercively.

Precisely in situations where a national identity needs to be imposed by coercion, it is tempting to use the adjective 'sacred' which I mentioned earlier, i.e., the *sacred* unity of a state or of a *patrie*, employing the term in a sense not so different from the one Durkheim meant to give it and furthermore in a context closely related to the new 'divinities,' the birth of which he very likely wished to favor, as set out in the concluding chapter of his *Les Formes Élémentaires de la Vie Religieuse*.[138]

In effect, recourse to the notion of 'sacred' in this context (a recourse that Spain has used and abused) signifies nothing but the denial of the idea that national identities are social constructions. To recognize the socially constructed character of a national reality implies acknowledgment of the fact that things are what they are, but that at the same time, being human products, they might be different. On the contrary, to confer on it a 'sacred' character is equivalent to denying it this quality of human product: from acceptance of the objectivity of social facts one proceeds to their reification.

I would suggest that the political area is at present one of the areas where under the pretext of realism and objectivity we encounter the most reification. Since I am neither a politician nor a political scientist, you will perhaps allow me to conclude by saying that at least as far as the European context is concerned, though the aim of many may be to arrive at a kind of United States of Europe, that utopia – a reality that does not exist, but for the existence of which it is worth our while to strive – consists in the unity of its basic historical entities, even if they are not defined officially as such: i.e., the unity of peoples, of communities, of nations – not sacred, just slowly and painfully constructed by men and women who start from their own precarious and fragile collective identity.

[138] Émile Durkheim, *Les Formes Élémentaires de la Vie Religieuse* (Paris: PUF, 1967, originally published in 1912).

Richard Parry

State and nation in the United Kingdom

The circumstances of the United Kingdom make it a very appropriate case for the examination of the Renner/Bauer thesis that a multi-national state can provide a vehicle for political stabilization that reconciles the top-down needs of the state with the bottom-up pressures from the nation.

At the beginning of the 20th century, the British and Austro–Hungarian empires had certain parallels, especially in the nostalgic idea of a family of peoples under a monarchy. By extension, they sought a political system that defused the sharper conflicts of class and nation and whose attractions were as much a matter of mood as of substance. When Italian Foreign Minister Gianni de Michelis, promoter of the Pentagonale 'club' of Austria, Hungary, Czechoslovakia, Italy and Slovenia, speaks of the need to recover a ' "world behind the nations", which not only represented a form but a political style,'[139] he is very close to the sense of civilizing mission found in the British Empire. In the macro-historical map of Europe, both the catholic–baroque mentality of Austria and the modern liberal protestantism of Britain are counterweights to the over-logical centralizing states of France and Germany.

Before one presses the British/Austrian analogy too far, however, it should be said that the Renner/Bauer approach, and indeed the whole Austrian Marxist school, have attracted relatively little academic or political attention in Britain. The works of Karl Renner and Otto Bauer are mostly untranslated, and the differences between them and the evolution of their positions over time are not well understood. Rather, their prescriptions are seen as part of the

[139] Edward Steen, 'In Search of the Centre that Could not Hold,' *Independent on Sunday Review*, October 7, 1990, 8.

scrapheap of history, overtaken by World War I and its aftermath. In the words of A. J. P. Taylor (1905–1990) in his classic *The Habsburg Monarchy*, 'The conflict between a super-national dynastic state and the national principle had to be fought to a finish; and so, too, had the conflict between master and subject nations.'[140] Writing in 1979 about the Labour Party and Scottish Nationalism, Michael Keating and David Bleiman discussed Bauer's *Die Nationalitätenfrage und die Sozialdemokratie* but were skeptical about whether his logic could ever replace the psychological näiveté of most nationalist movements.[141] Hugh Seton-Watson's *Nations and States* regards the opposition of Lenin as the deathknell of the idea but suggests it might have offered a solution to the problem of multi-tribal states in post-colonial Africa.[142]

E. J. Hobsbawm's recent *Nations and Nationalism since 1780* speaks of the 'programmatic mythology' in Renner's idea of how 'peoples, having silently matured throughout the centuries, emerge from the world of passive existence.'[143] Hobsbawm, the old-fashioned Marxist, proclaims the primacy of class variables when he asserts that 'Problems of power, status, politics and ideology and not of communication or even culture, lie at the heart of the nationalism of language.'[144] He notes Renner's attempts to rescue nationalist emergence from right-wing xenophobia, but suggests that 'The socialists of the period (1870–1918) who rarely used the word 'nationalism' without the prefix 'petty-bourgeois' knew what they were talking about.'[145]

Moreover, to the extent that the Renner–Bauer model might have involved the entrenchment of German minority rights in parts of the empire outside the German-speaking heartland, it was unlikely to win much British sympathy. Bauer's and Renner's willingness to consider a German–Austrian *Anschluss* could be interpreted as a pan-German political manifesto and as a threat to the fragile identity of the nation-states that emerged from World War I. Much of the

---

[140] A. J. P. Taylor, *The Hapsburg Monarchy* (Peregine ed., Harmondsworth: Penguin, 1964), 9.

[141] Michael Keating and David Bleiman, *Labour and Scottish Nationalism* (London: Macmillan, 1979), 5–6.

[142] Hugh Seton-Watson, *Nations and States* (London: Methuen, 1977), 470.

[143] E. J. Hobsbawm, *Nations and Nationalism since 1780* (Cambridge: Cambridge University Press, 1990), 101.

[144] *Ibid.*, 110.

[145] *Ibid.*, 117.

subtlety, and the socialist credentials, of Renner–Bauer failed to travel beyond their place and time. The activities of British sympathizers of Central and Eastern European nationalism (R. W. Seton-Watson after World War I and Timothy Garton Ash in 1989) had a romantic aspect which was very skeptical of devices that might seem to lock the submerged nationalities into a German or Russian orbit.

From the British perspective there is something strange about the notion of a forced ethnic or national choice, of accepting a fixed identity for constitutional purposes as happened, for instance, in the Moravian compromise of 1905 between Czech and German speakers. It has too many echoes of South African racial policies or internal passports in the U.S.S.R. It is only with reluctance that for the first time in the 1991 census the British census asks about ethnic group identification as well as place of birth. Ambivalence about ethnic identification – Scottish + British, Welsh + British, perhaps even Austrian + British in the case of the political refugees of 1938 – is at the heart of British territorial politics. An approach like Renner–Bauer which applies a logical solution based on an ascription of national status seems alien, in the same way as monetary union in the European Community is rejected by the present British government in favor of an ambivalent coexistence of national currencies with a European currency unit.

However, even if Britain is not fertile ground for a schematic policy like Renner–Bauer, there remains the attraction of the 'Austro–Hungarian' style and the dream that national identity might be secured without demarcated state structures. Here, the United Kingdom has relevant experience to offer, especially in the way that its non-English parts – Scotland, Wales and Northern Ireland – have been incorporated. This involves a detachment of the political and economic system from civil society. In the latter, education and culture are allowed full national expression: the clearest example, and one that is far from trivial, is the separate football teams. But, crucially, language is not the demarcator; English is the predominant language throughout the British Isles, and the effective linguistic frontiers of Welsh, Gaelic (in their Scottish and Irish forms) and formerly Cornish are distinct but lie within national frontiers. Nationality based upon language cannot serve as a political criterion in the same way as it did in the Austro–Hungarian empire. The search for points of contact between British circumstances and the Renner–Bauer debate is hence elusive, but there may be insights from the United Kingdom's territorial formation, degree of national homogeneity, and recent attempts to manage its national problems in Scotland, Wales and Ireland.

The territorial formation of the United Kingdom

Uniquely in Western Europe, the United Kingdom has a territory without frontiers, and no constraint of geographical contiguity to inform its relations with other polities. Its only land frontier, that with the Republic of Ireland, is less than 60 years old, is economically and culturally arbitrary, and reflects the unique circumstances of Northern Ireland. Traditional British usages of 'Europe' and 'the Continent' to refer to mainland Western Europe reflect this distancing from direct contact with other states. The British national identity was dispersed world-wide through the empire, and bound together by allegiance to the British monarchy. British nationality law is complex and inconsistent: the existence of the common-wealth, the voluntary association of former British possessions, gives millions of people throughout the world the status of British subjects without any right of residence in the mother country. There is no tradition of administrative law in Britain, and so much of the con-tinental European debate on the status of the citizen and the rights of collectivities seems strange; Britain has been a reluctant partner in the European Community in large part because it cannot understand its logic.

Moreover, the United Kingdom itself is a multinational state. The three non-English nations were incorporated relatively late in its history – Wales in 1536, Scotland in 1707 and Ireland in 1801 – and the U.K.'s present boundaries date only from 1922, when the 26 counties of Southern Ireland were given their independence. Scotland, Wales and Northern Ireland retained or have acquired distinctive institutions and a position in the mental configuration of the United Kingdom out of proportion to their size. England's share of the total population has increased from 53 percent in 1801 to 83 percent today, but the political salience of the 'Celtic fringe' has not diminished. The traditional motive for this attention was security – the danger of having disaffected areas so close to the heartland of the empire (another Austro–Hungarian motif). It was this that prompted the conquest of Wales, the Union of England and Scotland (without any *Ausgleich*-type federal structure) in 1707, and especially the attempts to find a stable political settlement for Ireland. Irish circumstances were unique and involved a degree of religious and economic discrimination that might not have been soluble within the United Kingdom. But proposals for Irish home rule from 1886 onwards prompted similar interest in Scotland and Wales, and in the 20th century the growth of nationalist movements in the two nations, fuelled by economic weakness and with intermittent electoral success, maintained the salience of the constitutional issue.

Scotland and Wales were granted distinctive institutions, especially their own departments of central government (the Scottish Office in 1885, the Welsh Office not until 1964) to administer on a territorial basis domestic functions spread over many departments in England. The separate Scottish legal system (guaranteed in 1707) necessitates separate legislation in the United Kingdom Parliament, and sometimes Wales receives separate treatment in English legislation. Devolved assemblies were enacted for the two nations in 1978, the Scottish to have legislative powers in most of the functions administered by the Scottish Office, the Welsh with executive powers only, but the assemblies were not established after referendums in 1979 failed to provide a sufficient majority (though 52 percent voted in favor in Scotland, against only 20 percent in Wales). The six counties of Northern Ireland, which remained in the United Kingdom after the rest of Ireland was granted independence, had a devolved legislature from 1921 to 1972, and then briefly in 1974; attempts were made through assembly elections in 1982 and the Anglo–Irish agreement in 1985 to revive it, but have proved abortive. In contrast, England has no elected intermediate government and a patchwork of regional agencies without consistent boundaries.

This amounts to a policy of exceptionalism, i.e., the granting of differential autonomy to particular areas within the overall polity. As well as their historical inheritance, Scots and Welsh have been able to draw political strength from a sense of dual identity – both Scottish/Welsh and British. Opinion surveys show that a little over one-third of people in Britain see themselves as 'British,' but over one-half as respectively 'English,' 'Scottish,' and 'Welsh.' The 'British' identification is at a remarkably similar level – 38 percent in England, 35 percent in Wales and 33 percent in Scotland.[146] The

[146] Richard Rose, *Understanding the United Kingdom* (London: Longman, 1982), Table 1.1.

'English' political identification has little political salience and obscures regional identities within England, which in some places like the Northeast and Southwest are strong; the Scottish and Welsh identities reinforce pressure for distinctive local institutions.

Outside England, in the non-political sphere, the distinct profile of the Scottish, Welsh and Irish identities and the lack of resonance of British as a description are quite striking. I am Welsh (though long resident in Scotland), dislike being regarded as English, and would find British a rather empty description. Here international sport is important as a focus for loyalty. The British invented football (soccer) and organized themselves as four nations (now five, counting both the Irelands) which uniquely have separate representation in international competitions like the World Cup. Similar arrangements apply in rugby football, though here there is an all-Ireland team, one of a number of civil society institutions (including the churches) which survived partition. Distinct cultural traditions, mostly in the English language, are further reinforcements. Such sentiment is important, as is personal status: the fact that this is written by a Welshman long resident in Scotland and hence having an ambivalent identity must affect the character of the analysis. But when we search for ways that they might be used to devise political systems, the matter is less clear.

Data on national characteristics within the United Kingdom

For a national choice to be expressed within a multinational political system, relevant criteria include: the homogeneity by birth of the inhabitants of the territory of a nation; the extent of the 'diaspora' (those born in the nation but since emigrated); and the use of language. On all of these the British scene has complications. On homogeneity, Table 1 shows a substantial identity, except in the case of Wales, where the main lines of communication are east–west to England rather than north–south within Wales; in the 1980s the 'non-native' proportion has risen to over 20 percent. This has led nationalist parties to adopt a fairly relaxed attitude to the granting of nationality in their putative independent state, extending it to residents as well as native-born. National boundaries within Great Britain have been firm for centuries, again with the exception of Wales: the southeastern county of Gwent (formerly Mon-mouthshire) was confirmed as fully Welsh rather than English only in 1974. We may conclude that the nations of the United Kingdom are reasonably homogeneous and that the question is whether the inhabitants within them are prepared to accept the national identity that their residence and birth implies.

Table 1 *Population born in nation as percentage of its total population*[147]

	1951	1961	1971	1981	Change
1. Northern Ireland	90.3	90.5	90.1	92.0	+ 1.7
2. Scotland	92.1	91.8	91.0	90.3	− 0.8
3. England	92.2	91.1	89.7	89.8	− 2.4
4. Wales	82.8	82.8	81.2	79.5	− 3.2

On mobility, Table 2 identifies the problem that a substantial minority of Welsh, Scots and Northern Irish – 21 percent, 15 percent, and 15 percent – lives elsewhere in the United Kingdom. Regional economic imbalances may promote emigration without lessening devotion to the cultural artefacts of the home country. The clearest example is Ireland, where massive migration to Britain and the United States meant that in the early years of the century little short of half of Irish-born people lived abroad and came to form distinctive religious and political blocs. Today, 700,000 people born in the Irish Republic (whose population is less than 3.5 million) live in the United Kingdom. But within Britain cross-national movement tends to work in favor of unitary political structures that endorse this mobility. Welsh Labour Party politicians have been particularly prominent among the opponents of devolution, among them Aneurin Bevan (1897–1960) and Neil Kinnock, the present leader of the party, whose strong opposition to the 1978 proposals has now – some say reluctantly – been moderated.

Language (see Table 3) confuses rather than clarifies national differences within the British Isles. Virtually everyone understands English; the main exceptions are in Asian immigrant communities. The most substantial linguistic minority areas are in Wales: in the northwest county of Gwynedd, where nearly two-thirds speak Welsh and it is the language of everyday communication, and in Dyfed in the southwest. Controversy often emerges over the status of Welsh as a teaching medium, especially when education authorities

[147] Richard Rose and Ian McAllister, *United Kingdom Facts* (London: Macmillan, 1980), Table 9.4 (A); *Census 1981: Great Britain* (London: HMSO), Country of Birth Tables: Table 2 and *Northern Ireland Summary Report* (Belfast: HMSO), Table 7.

try to preserve Welsh-only schools in areas with English immigrant families. In Scotland, Gaelic is spoken by less than two percent

Table 2 *Percentage of those born in each nation now living in another part of the United Kingdom*[148]

	1951	1961	1971*	1981*	Change
1. Wales	23.5	22.7	23.3	21.1	− 2.4
2. Northern Ireland	12.6	14.8	15.2	15.3	+ 2.7
3. Scotland	11.4	12.4	14.0	14.2	+ 2.8
4. England	1.6	1.6	1.7	1.8	+ 0.2

* excluding migration to Northern Ireland, which is no longer separately identified but is likely to be small.

overall and is heavily concentrated in the Western Isles (where 80 percent have a knowledge of it); despite symbolic displays such as bilingual slogans at the conferences of the Scottish National Party, there has been no serious attempt to promote it as the national language of Scotland. English spoken in a Scots dialect (sometimes known as 'Lallans') has in its broadest form a vocabulary and pronunciation not easily understood by outsiders, but it has been eclipsed by standard English and survives in written form only in poetry.

Table 3 *Percentage speaking Welsh*[149]

	1951	1961	1971	1981	Change
1. Gwynedd	70.3	67.8	61.3	61.2	− 9.1
2. Dyfed	60.4	44.4	40.6	46.3	− 14.1
Wales total	27.5	24.8	19.8	18.9	− 7.6

It is interesting to speculate about the fate of the minority languages if they had been the official medium of an autonomous nation. Welsh has received much encouragement, especially with a television channel since 1982 (Sianel 4 Cymru) subsidized by the rest of British broadcasting. With this help, the decline in the proportion of Welsh-speakers was arrested in the 1970s. Fear of domination by

[148] Rose and McAllister, 1980, Table 9.4 (B); *Census 1981: Great Britain* (London: HMSO), Country of Birth Tables: Table 2 and *Northern Ireland Summary Report* (Belfast: HMSO), Table 7.

[149] Rose and McAllister, 1980, Table 9.5; *Digest of Welsh Statistics* 1989 (Cardiff: HMSO), Table 2.70.

a bilingual élite was a prominent theme of the massive rejection of devolution by English-speaking Wales in 1979. But the example of the Irish Republic is not encouraging to promoters of the native language. Decades of encouragement, including compulsory teaching in schools and, until the 1970s, obligatory qualifications for university entrants and civil servants, have failed to arrest the decline of Irish to the medium of communication of less than one percent of the population. The widespread familiarity with it and its use in official documents is something of a museum piece, far removed from the notion of language as a life-spirit propounded by the Gaelic League before World War I.

The British data suggest relatively infertile ground for the Renner-Bauer solution. There is no replication of the Czech/German problem of Bohemia and Moravia; nations are fairly homogeneous (Scotland more than Wales) and emigration if anything promotes the unitariness of the United Kingdom; language is an intra-national issue, often a source of tension, and does not in itself ascribe a national identity. The notion of a political registration of Welshness or Scottishness which could be carried throughout the state does not make sense in British terms; these are personal emotions and they can be asserted politically only within the territorial boundaries of the nation.

The British political response

Even if they do not think on Renner-Bauer lines, British political parties have had to produce a response to the demands of Irish, Scottish and Welsh nationalism. But they have been unsystematic in their approach. Broadly, the Conservatives have been the party of 'the Union' and of a homogeneous territorial élite. For a time in the 1970s they supported the idea of a devolved Scottish assembly as part of the United Kingdom legislative process, and in recent years have resisted the closer integration of Northern Ireland, but these should be seen as exceptions to their unitary, anglocentric emotions. The Labour Party started out with a 'Home Rule' tradition, but this was suppressed under what seemed the need to promote economic development and win a U.K. parliamentary majority. The Liberal Party has consistently been in favor of a federal system throughout the United Kingdom. The nationalists (the Scottish National Party, and Plaid Cymru in Wales) have been pro-independence since the

1930s, but the degree of 'separatism' has sometimes been equivocal, given the existence of the British Commonwealth and later the European Community.

Within all parties is found the spirit described by Jones and Keating when they speak of the way that 'British Socialism acquired a pragmatism in its dealings with the state.'[150] In the Labour Party's case this involved two sharp reversals of its stance on devolution. From the foundation of the Scottish Labour Party by Keir Hardie in 1888 until 1924 Labour was firmly in favor of 'Home Rule.' This was downplayed during the interwar years and rejected in 1958.[151] When the Scottish National Party increased in strength in the 1960s the issue at first was evaded by setting up a Commission on the Constitution, but when it was later faced, the result was a political calculation in 1974 that the promise of an assembly had to be conceded. A referendum to approve this received an insufficient majority in 1979 (some leading Labour politicians were opposed), but the party's commitment to Scottish devolution has since intensified. In 1989 it agreed to participate in an unofficial Scottish Constitutional Convention together with other political and social interests, although the convention was boycotted by the Scottish National and Conservative parties. The convention's reports called for a strong version of devolution rooted in a notion of popular sovereignty.

The Conservative Party engaged in the ultimate pragmatic compromise when, in coalition with Lloyd George's Liberals, it allowed Ireland to be divided into two sectarian states: the Catholic Irish Free State (later the Republic of Ireland) and Protestant Northern Ireland (an autonomous province within the United Kingdom). For the Conservatives, cutting Ireland loose was a means of safeguarding their English heartland, and in recent years the party has been concentrated within it: in the 1987 general election, 357 out of the 375 Conservative MPs were from England, whereas the non-English 18 faced 107 from other parties. Four out of six Labour Party election victories since 1945 would have been reversed if England alone had voted.

The Irish solution resembles that addressed by Renner-Bauer, since both states contained substantial minorities of the other

[150] Barry Jones and Michael Keating, *Labour and the British State* (Oxford: Clarendon Press, 1985), 23.
[151] Keating and Bleiman, *op. cit.*, 60–1, 146–7.

confession that might have welcomed the chance to opt for a governmental body that safeguarded their cultural interests. In fact, both minorities suffered: southern Protestants had to live in a state where Catholic moral teaching was codified into law and the teaching of Irish made compulsory; northern Catholics were discriminated against in public life and found the Irish-Gaelic cultural heritage neglected (though Catholic schools receive state support). It was only in the 1970s that the concept of 'power-sharing' in the North sought to recognize both cultural identities, but the attempts to engineer a political coalition of unionist and nationalist parties failed. In the South, two referenda in the 1980s wrote a prohibition of abortion into the constitution and reaffirmed the constitutional ban on divorce. In both parts of Ireland, the national majority within each state rejected the Renner-Bauer approach in what represented its sharpest British Isles test.

The European Community dimension

The closest that present-day Britain comes to a Renner-Bauer dichotomy is in its attitude to the European Community. Here we find the dichotomy between the state as a political instrument for necessary functions and the nation as a vehicle for collective identity. Contrary to the intentions of the E.C.'s founders, in Britain the emotive aspect attaches to the nation and the instrumental one to the community. This is clearest in the notion of a 'Europe of regions' promoted by the Scottish National Party and Plaid Cymru. Their position is that the effective unit for economic and security policy is much larger than the traditional nation-state, whereas the appropriate unit for cultural and social organization is much smaller; hence the nation-state that seeks to combine both can be rejected as obsolete, yet the 'separatist' unsolidaristic aspects of nationalism are made safe. In Scotland, the electoral approval of the slogan 'independence in the European Community,' adopted by the Scottish National Party in 1988, is evident from the opinion polls: it enabled the party to abandon its anti-E.C. stance ('no entry on anybody else's terms') and seem forward-looking in its European policy. The response of the Labour Party was the slogan 'independence in the U.K.,' implying something much closer to self-government than to devolution as hitherto understood.

The indubitable historical reality of Scotland as a once-independent nation, which, however much coerced, chose to merge with England, leaves it as a 'lost state.' Its national expression can be insisted upon (and, most would agree, should be conceded in the interest of political stability), but its political identity may well be adequately safeguarded as a devolved part of a 19th-century state. Comparable examples are Catalonia in Spain, Bavaria in Germany, Sicily in Italy, Slovenia in Yugoslavia and Quebec in Canada. In the latter the idea of a 'moment of independence' has been advocated, whereby once *de jure* independence is granted and the point made, the nation rejoins the larger entity. This proposal would not appeal to nationalists whose whole intellectual rationale is based on the identity of nation and state, but it might have elements of a 'first-best' solution.

The same proposal might work for Scotland, but it does not address the case of Wales, where the frontier has been compromised by centuries of permeation. We observe the high degree of cross-migration, the unhelpful nature of the language issue and the lack of consent to increased political distinctiveness. A Renner-Bauer approach sounds plausible until we recognize that in Wales the language element (and thus education) is a divisive rather than a unifying voice and might lead to an insistence on English-medium education by immigrants to Welsh-speaking areas. It is much more comfortable to go no further than the symbolic representation of nationality in a hotel register, football match or opinion poll. The British political system is usually quite skilled at the defusing of such susceptibilities, to the despair of many nationalists. For instance, the British royal family, with its considerable Scottish ancestry, has been careful not to emphasize an English identity (echoing Otto von Habsburg's reply, 'who were we playing?' when asked if he had watched the Austria–Hungary football match), and politicians also learn the protocol of not saying 'English' when they mean 'British.' In such ways has the British polity consistently evaded the logic of nation and state which Renner and Bauer sought to systematize.

Conclusion

The tragedy of social democracy is that it must deny the full political expression of the nationalist impulses that often inspire its sup-porters. The Renner-Bauer vision was of a nationalism defused so that the class-based international political and economic system could occupy its proper place. Democratic socialism in Britain has tended to wish that nationalism were out of the way, but has failed to come up with means to secure this end; generally it lives in hope that nationalist parties will not secure a majority, and in Scotland and Wales it has so far been successful. The Conservative Party has deferred to cultural differences within the United Kingdom and not tried to assimilate them, yet it has always sought to manage the periphery in the interest of the security of its English heartland. What we are left with is a plurality of individual choice in which citizens are free to regard themselves as British and/or English/Welsh/Scottish/ Irish and/or a subregional identity as long as they are not making a contentious or political statement or asserting national rights.

British politics neglects national and cultural variables within the state and makes a pragmatic and usually inconsistent response when territorial stability seems to be in doubt. When this style works, it can be an admirable form of political management; when it does not, as in Ireland, it can lead to a tragic repetition of errors and misunderstandings. The Renner-Bauer approach would always have seemed hopelessly oversystematic to British eyes, but its attempt at a logical resolution of conflict has a certain strength which the circumstances of 20th-century European history have never allowed to be tested.

Berel Rodal[152]

The Canadian conundrum: two concepts of nationhood

Canada is undergoing deep political change. Quebec is now formally debating its constitutional future, in a remarkably calm, systematic, and comprehensive way. There is, among élites in any event, increasing realization in English-speaking Canada[153] that the country has entered into a process, it would seem irreversible, of self-redefinition. It has been said for some time that Canadians are the only people who regularly pull themselves up by their roots to see if they are still alive. The current debate in Canada, however, is different, in tone, context, and in the appreciation of what is at issue.

State and nation in Canada

The debate in Canada, historically and in particularly sharpened form since 1960, has fundamentally ways of thinking about 'state and nation,' very much along the lines treated by Renner/Bauer. I have in mind both the themes of 'consociationalism' – power-sharing and accommodation among the elites of competing ethnic groups – and the de-territorialization of ethnicity developed in various versions and with different emphases by Karl Renner and Otto Bauer. If it is of value to explore or determine how something like the approach advocated by Renner/Bauer might work in practice somewhere today, I believe that Canada affords certain lessons. The

---

[152] The views expressed by the author are his own and are not necessarily those of the government of Canada.

[153] A serviceable enough though awkward and incomplete term to denote 'Canada other than Quebec.' There is much discomfort in the domestic debate about the terms to be used to refer to this Canada: 'English-Canada' is dated, misleading, and gives offence to the very large numbers of Canadians of other ethnic and national origins (as discussed later in this paper). No one today would use the term 'French-Canada' to denote Quebec.

Canadian experience concerns a minority ethnic group which, once able to become a local majority and given a real choice between equality, language and cultural rights in an overarching multi-ethnic state, and majority status and control of its own state and territory, prefers territorial control. The question is whether Canada's circumstances are so particular, so *sui generis*, that the apparent conclusion might not be so widely applicable. God, and the devil, are in details, as Mies van der Rohe observed.

As it happens, the present crisis came upon the country almost unexpectedly, an instance of what Uri Ra'anan so accurately portrays in his chapter as the received wisdom that 'modernization and democratization somehow would cause ethnic self-assertion to fade away,' that the development of supranational forms of organization would advance the integration of groups and peoples into larger, functional units geared to economic growth. Separatism was written off only a year or two ago: yet today, as a result of the failed attempt to gain Quebec's full and formal assent to the 1982 Constitution Act, Quebec nationalism and the demands for forms of self-rule on the part of aboriginal peoples dominate the Canadian national agenda. I should add at this point that this chapter does not treat, except tangentially, aboriginal peoples' demands for self-government. Even though aboriginal peoples constitute less than four percent of the population of Canada, the issues involved are important ones, and related to those of 'state and nation,' nationalism and ethnicity, but different enough categorically to warrant not including them in this forum.

The puzzling thing for many is why there should be talk of the country's being at breaking point, when in fact so little is at issue. There is no clamor for civil rights, no outrage at discrimination and disadvantage (again, with the qualification of the special case of aboriginal peoples). The Canadian policy universe is a quiet one. Canada stands as a model, though an expensive one, of a federation which has managed to combine a high degree of decentralization with harmonized national arrangements governing social policy (health care, income security, and unemployment insurance, for example), financial equalization, and legal rights. Social programs are universally accessible, and portable. Francophone Canadians have been accommodated: their linguistic rights have not only been expanded with the Official Languages Act and bilingualism policies, but up to 50 percent of younger Canadian children in the major centers of English-speaking Canada are enrolled in French-immersion schools.[154] The French language has majority status in Quebec, equal status in New Brunswick, special status in Ontario and minority status in most other provinces. Quebec legislation bans English from signs and storefronts, to assert and protect the status of the French language.

Federal policies to bring French-speaking Canadians into the upper reaches of Canadian government and enterprise, policies introduced by Prime Minister Lester Pearson and further developed by Pierre Trudeau, and continued by every succeeding Prime Minister, have been highly successful. French-speaking Canadians have held every critical portfolio in cabinet in recent years, occupy almost one-third of all cabinet posts, and head important Crown Corporations, state enterprises, and national cultural institutions. It is virtually unthinkable today that a Canadian Prime Minister would not be bilingual; indeed, the Prime Minister of Canada has come from Quebec in 30 of the past 42 years.

There is no suppression of Quebec. There is no food, energy, trade, or faith grievance. I am from Montreal myself, and this gives me something of a vantage point from which to view the mounting paradox of Quebec. From 1960, Québécois have experienced a growing self-consciousness as a people, and success as a polity. Why is it that when Québécois, at the height of their self-confidence and enjoying perhaps the highest standing of any community in Canada, and at the height of their role and participation in the Canadian state, when they have coalesced linguistically, culturally, economically, and politically, when there is a drive by English-speaking Canadians to acquire French as second language, when protections for French-Canadian minorities outside Quebec are in place, when Québécois have achieved all the spiritual and material things sought since World War II, and when there is acceptance of French-Canadians not as a minority, but as one of the country's majorities and as the majority in Quebec, that the upsurge of separatist and sovereignist feeling should be at its height, with a clear majority seemingly prepared to opt for some form of sovereignty for Quebec?

'Canada' used to designate something fairly clear. One gathers that in Eastern Europe in the 1940s and 1950s, and sometimes in

---

[154] For statistical data on relative numbers of English-speakers and French-speakers in Quebec and other Canadian provinces, as well as in Canada as a whole, see Figures 1–5 and Tables 1–2, pp. 169–74.

Poland today, the word for 'great' in the sense of 'wonderful' or 'capital,' was 'Canada.' As Professor Ra'anan reminds us, 'nation-building,' where it has been successful, as it largely has been in the United States, has been based on the 'voluntary confluence of separate ethnic and cultural mainstreams.' This description also characterizes English-speaking Canada, which has come to see the nation and the state in highly pluralistic terms – in terms of 10 provinces of disparate size, population and wealth, each marked by a distinct resource endowment and economic base and ethnic and linguistic composition. While there has been a very rapid acculturation to the mainstream English-American commonwealth culture, there is no sense of a cultural or ethnic majority, dominant or otherwise. Canada outside of Quebec is an immigrant society. The proportion of Canadians born outside the country is considerably higher than in the United States. The 'British,' those tracing their ancestry to the British Isles, were less than 40 percent of the Canadian population in the 1981 census, and this proportion would be lower today. In the four Western provinces (Manitoba, Saskatchewan, Alberta, and British Columbia), those of other than British or French descent outnumber those of British and French combined. The principal source of stress has been seen as economic regionalism, amplified by the imbalance between center and periphery.

The Québécois, however, did not and do not now see themselves as part of the 'voluntary confluence of separate ethnic and cultural mainstreams' making up Canada. They long saw themselves as the only real Canadians, denied both partnership in the colonization and westward expansion of the country, and their communal/cultural rights outside their heartland in Quebec. Quebec's evolution since 1960, the year of the 'Quiet Revolution,' has been truly radical. It is a remarkable story of a society's transformation from a defensive minority sheltering in a linguistic and cultural enclave to a self-confident majority and, in its own terms, a distinctive 'nation' ready if it wishes to assume control of its own national state (viewed as the 'expression and instrument of its rebirth.)[155]

---

[155] Thomas J. Courchene, submission to Quebec's La Commission sur l'Avenir Politique et Constitutionnel du Québec. I am indebted in what follows on the chronology of developments in Quebec after 1960 to Professor Courchene's work, among other sources.

The Québécois: evolution of a *Staatsvolk*

The present-day French-speaking majority in Quebec – about 83 percent of the population of the province – are the descendants of the roughly 60,000 French settlers in New France at the time of the British conquest in 1760. The French/Catholics (Canadiens, and then Québécois) protected their cultural distinctness by jealous maintenance of their autonomy, for nearly two centuries sheltering from the English and North American mainstream, which they saw as secular, materialistic, superficial, and corrupting. The 1774 Quebec Act and Confederation in 1867 confirmed and strengthened the French/Catholic community's authority to order those activities critical to the maintenance of societal and cultural distinctness – a different regime for education, marriage and family law, social welfare, land tenure and inheritance, and so on. Lord Durham in fact warned in 1839 of the dangers being stored for the future, of 'two nations warring in the bosom of a single state,' and advocated a policy of assimilation – advice which was not taken.

The French-Canadian mission was *la survivance*, based in some measure on belief in a morally superior special vocation. In the words of a Bishop Pâquet in 1902:

As for those of us who believe in God, in a wise, good, and powerful God, we know how this goodness, wisdom, and power are revealed in the government of nations; how the Maker of All Things has created different races with varied tastes and aptitudes; and also how, within the hierarchy of societies and empires, He has assigned to each one of these races a distinct role of its own . . . not only is there a vocation for peoples but in addition some of these peoples have the honour of being called to a kind of priesthood . . . we have the privilege of being entrusted with this social priesthood granted only to select peoples . . . this religious and civilizing mission is the true vocation and the special vocation of the French race in America . . . . Our mission is less to handle capital than to stimulate ideas; less to light the furnaces of factories than to maintain and spread the glowing fires of religion and thought, and to help them cast their light into the distance.[156]

A host of other influences on French Canada however grew increasingly important. There was large-scale migration to New England, and to other parts of Canada. The World War II industrial effort brought large numbers of French-Canadians from rural areas

---

[156] Monseigneur L.-A. Pâquet, 'A Sermon on the Vocation of the French Race in America' (1902), in Ramsay Cook, *French Canadian Nationalism* (Toronto: 1969), 153–4; cited in Peter M. Leslie, *Ethnonationalism in a Federal State: The Case of Canada* (Kingston, Ontario: 1988), 14–15.

into Montreal, into industry, and into closer contact with the worlds of commerce and English. Political corruption and the sense of economic deprivation, greater ease to travel and study abroad, decolonization and the creation of new states, notably the state of Israel and francophone states in Africa, television,[157] all contributed to the decline of the old régime. The 1960 election of a reforming Liberal Party broke the mold.

The new Quebec government saw itself as having to build in a short time and in a coordinated way much that had been built up gradually and incrementally over many years in other provinces and societies. It saw its role not as that of local administration, but the transformation of Québécois society. The period – marked by the Kennedy presidency in the United States – was one of belief in activism and in social progress under state and political auspices. Modernization began with secularization. The Church had been the matrix of social institutions in French-speaking Quebec. Education, family law, social affairs, hospitals, savings institutions, and trade unions had been ordered under confessional auspices. State institutions were strengthened or created to assume responsibilities in these areas, which brought the social and educational institutions of non-French-speaking and non-Catholic populations under the purview of the state and French-Canadians for the first time.

The Quebec state, which recruited the best and brightest to politics and government to build the new Quebec, became extremely active in the policy, regulatory, and entrepreneurial domains. The slogan and rhetoric was that of '*maître chez nous.*' The view was that economic circumstances and imperatives powerfully shaped one's way of living and thinking; that French-Canadians, at the bottom of the economic heap, had little control of their economic destiny; and that remaining in an economically inert cultural enclave out of phase with conditions outside the community's boundaries would accelerate rather than protect French-Canadians from enfeeblement and assimilation. Nationalization of Quebec's hydroelectric power utilities gave French-Canadians the opportunity to manage and

[157] The role of television is worthy of detailed analysis. Radio-Canada – the French-language service of the Canadian Broadcasting Corporation – has played a central and continuing role in developing and communicating a distinctive and specific Québécois identity, spirit, culture – and politics. Seventy percent of francophones in Quebec watch French-language television programming; the audience for Radio-Canada programming outside Quebec is under 5 percent at any given time.

direct major enterprises. Hydro remains a critical element to this day: Lavalin and S.N.C, Quebec engineering firms operating internationally, were created by and remain direct beneficiaries of Hydro policies and activities.

The Quebec government opted out of several major federal programs, preferring to develop its own. Quebec developed mandates, expertise, appetites, and capacities in areas much broader than in other provinces. Canada developed a public contributory pension system: Quebec created its own, investing the funds in the Caisse de Dépôt,[158] which became Quebec's state capital fund and an engine for the creation of a distinct Québécois financial and corporate structure and élite.

The 'Quiet Revolution' led in 1963 to the creation of the Royal Commission on Bilingualism and Biculturalism (the 'B&B' Commission), which warned that Canada, unconscious of the fact, was in crisis, and proposed that if Quebec were to be challenged, Canada needed to become a more credible 'national center' for French-Canadians. The commissioners advocated wider recognition of 'cultural dualism' and a vastly expanded acceptance of and space for French-Canadians in Canada at large – in concrete terms, the acceptance and institutionalization of equal partnership and full participation of French-Canadians in political and economic decision-making in Canada; policies for the protection of the French language and culture; and bilingualism.

Canadian federalism: the personal principle versus territorial imperative

Pierre Trudeau strongly opposed the focus on the Quebec state while a law professor and activist intellectual in Montreal, rejecting the link between ethnicity and territoriality, a link which he saw as leading to illiberalism. The ideal was the multinational, pluralist state.[159] As Prime Minister of Canada after 1968, he forcefully

---

[158] The Caisse de Dépôt et Placement du Québec invests various Quebec public pension and insurance funds. It is one of the largest financial institutions in North America with assets of the order of Can$40 billion.

[159] In a striking, oft-quoted statement of Trudeau's:
'Or l'histoire de la civilisation, c'est l'histoire de la subordination du 'nationalisme' tribal à des appartenances plus larges . . . la nation n'est pas une réalité 'biologique,' je veux dire une communauté qui découlerait de la nature même de l'homme . . . la petite parcelle de l'histoire qui est marquée par l'émergence des Etats-nations, est aussi celle des guerres les plus dévastatrices, des atrocités les plus nombreuses et des haines

articulated a stance and policy which went beyond the removal of discrimination and irritants and the containment and accommodation of Quebec's demands for increased autonomy. Trudeau's policy was specifically to depoliticize ethnicity, to separate the concepts of the ethnically determined 'nation,' and 'state,' and to strengthen the Canadian state as a liberal, secular, pluralistic polity better able to serve the interests of justice for all citizens, ensure equitable prosperity, and provide the space and scope needed to preserve French-speaking Canadians' language and culture.

Trudeau's dominance on the federal scene, in large measure due to the forcefulness, clarity, and consistency of his vision and approach, made the debate in Canada a dramatically clear conflict of alternative visions of the state and ethnicity, though the terms may have been obscured by the stresses of Canadian regionalism over the same period and the waxing and waning of the intensity of nationalism within the Québécois population. Trudeau amplified and sharpened the focal points of conflict with Québécois nationalism. In Professor Ra'anan's schema, Trudeau's was the 'Western' territorial approach, where it is the state which is at the base of the nation, and where nationality is a matter of citizenship and residence. For the Québécois, it is the nation that is at the base of the state, though citizenship would remain a matter of territoriality and residence in the Quebec state in which the Québécois are the *Staatsvolk*, the

---

collectives les plus dégradantes de toute l'épopée humaine . . . les nationalistes – même de gauche – sont politiquement réactionnaires parce qu'en donnant une très grande importance à l'idée de nation dans leur échelle de valeurs politiques, ils sont infailliblement amenés à définir le bien commun en fonction du groupe ethnique plutôt qu'en fonction de l'ensemble des citoyens, sans acception (sic) de personne. C'est pour cela qu'un gouvernement nationaliste est par essence intolérant, discriminatoire et en fin de compte totalitaire.' ('La Nouvelle Trahison des Clercs,' 165, 166, 178, 188; originally published in *Cité Libre* (1962), republished in *Le Fédéralisme et la Société Canadienne-Française* (Montréal 1967). Trudeau himself quotes Lord Acton (*op. cit.*, 188): A great democracy must either sacrifice self-government to unity or preserve it by federalism . . . the coexistence of several nations under the same State is a test, as well as the best security of its freedom. It is also one of the chief instruments of civilisation . . . the combination of different nations in one State is as necessary a condition of civilised life as the combination of men in society . . . where political and national boundaries coincide, society ceases to advance, and nations relapse into a condition corresponding to that of men who renounce intercourse with their fellow-men . . . a State which is incompetent to satisfy different races condemns itself; a State which labours to neutralize, to absorb, or to expel them, destroys its own vitality; a State which does not include them is destitute of the chief basis of self-government. The theory of nationality, therefore, is a retrograde step in history.'

ethnic group that defines the state, constitutes its core, and provides its elite and culture. The centerpiece of Trudeau's vision and political arrangement was citizenship, individual rights, and uniform entitlements across Canada, a regime in which no one should be subjected to territorial majority rule and relegated to dependent minority status with respect to basic political and cultural rights. The French-English dualism of Trudeau's conception followed the logic of Renner-Bauer's 'personal principle.' The French-English dualism of Quebec's conception was that of Quebec and the rest of Canada, and the essence of Quebec's quest was control of a Québécois state.

Quebec for its part meanwhile proceeded with the transformation and 'francization' of Quebec society. Bill 101 made French the language of work in Quebec, and opened enterprise, in particular its upper reaches, to francophones and the products of Quebec's new educational and managerial system. The rise of a successful middle class under the auspices of the state has been a development of central importance. The best and brightest were now attracted to business schools (and engineering, with the growth of Hydro and related enterprises), in place of the previously traditional careers in the clergy, law, and public administration. With the defeat of Quebec's 1980 referendum on sovereignty,[160] the focus shifted sharply to the economic sphere, with the objective of completing the building of a distinct and independent Quebec economy, one which would advance the reality of autonomy and reduce the population's fear of sovereignty. This post-referendum agenda[161] was happily congruent with the climate of the 1980s. There was concerted action to build a much stronger Québécois corporate base, to put Quebec's fiscal house in order, to strengthen Quebec's self-sustaining network of financial institutions (the base of which were the *caisses populaires*,[162] and the Caisse de Dépôt); and to decrease dependency on, and economic ties with, Ottawa and the rest of Canada, a development greatly helped by negotiation of the Canada–U.S. Free Trade Agreement, of which Quebec was the strongest provincial proponent.

[160] The government sought a mandate for 'sovereignty-association,' i.e., political sovereignty in economic association with Canada: the 'No' side prevailed by a 60–40 margin. Eighty-five percent of those eligible to vote participated. There continues to be disagreement whether there was a majority in favor amongst francophones.

[161] Courchene, *op. cit.*

[162] Indigenous Québécois savings and loan cooperatives. Assets are Can$49 billion; membership is in the order of Can$5 million.

The strategic aim was long-term viability based on an internationally competitive, Québécois-owned and -run outward-looking private sector, helped by the state. Observers have commented on how Japan-like the process of state-building has been, a process marked by a high degree of concertation and commonality between business and government. The nominally federalist Quebec Liberals continued in this vein when they replaced the Parti Québécois in office in 1985. Comprehensive, ambitious blueprints for Quebec's economic future were commissioned. In the view of particularly knowledgeable observers, the sum of these reports on privatization, the role of government and the delivery of socioeconomic programs, and on deregulation 'represents . . . the most comprehensive market-oriented yet equity-conscious approach to socio-economic policy ever promulgated by any government in the western world.'[163] A special, privileged regime was put in place for Quebec's indigenous financial institutions.

The combination of this process of transformation with English Canada's rejection or lack of comprehension of Quebec's concept of duality appears to have created a consensus on sovereignty in Quebec,[164] though not one on its content, means to achieve it, and willingness to absorb the costs which may be involved in bringing it about.

The paradox, again, is that Quebec has managed to achieve all that it has under the existing constitution, and under the aegis of a supple, accommodating federalism. Why the thrust to sovereignty, whether defined as 'renewed federalism' or full independence?

The key element is Quebec's sense of distinctiveness, buttressed by the creation of a successful and autonomous society, and allied to a sense of historical grievance, the memory of subordinate status and insults; demographic strength and vulnerability; the sense that on the larger issues, Quebec thinks and feels differently from English Canada; and the attrition of over 25 years of discussion of constitutional change. What is seen as English Canada's refusal, in the rejection last year of the Meech Lake Accord,[165] to acknowledge

---

[163] Courchene, *op. cit.*, 10.

[164] Current polls suggest a majority in the order of 75 percent for some form of sovereignty.

[165] The intergovernmental agreement to secure Quebec's full and formal assent to the 1982 Constitution Act. In fact, the Accord was ratified by the Parliament of Canada and by the legislatures of 8 of Canada's 10 provinces, representing some 91.5 percent of the population.

even the basic proposition that Quebec is indeed a distinct society has clearly, for the present at least, served to fuse these elements in the minds of the majority of Québécois.

Quebec distinctiveness seems all too obvious to Québécois, whether comparing English Canada's and Quebec's legal systems, municipal and provincial institutions, *corps intermédiaires*, arts, literature, educational systems, social and health care networks, religious institutions, financial institutions, language, or political culture. To Québécois, Canadian provinces seem in all or most essential respects like U.S. states – except for Quebec. Charles Taylor, former Chichele Professor of Political Theory at Oxford, in his recent submission to the Commission on Quebec's Constitutional Future, began by framing Quebec's reality as follows: 'Le Québec est une société distincte, l'expression politique d'une nation, dont la grande majorité vit à l'intérieur de ses frontières; ... le Québec est le foyer principal de cette nation, dont des branches se sont établies ailleurs en Amérique du Nord, et principalement au Canada.'[166]

The general sense in Quebec is very much one of an internal process, one in which Quebec is as it were communing with itself. There is little knowledge or cognizance of an 'English-Canada' seen as at once amorphous, yet rejecting and culturally and demographically threatening. In the new circumstances, there is renewed, perhaps deepened opposition to the 1982 Constitution Act and the values it enshrines – to strengthen an encompassing pan-Canadian citizenship and political identity, a non-provincial/regional sense of Canada, embodied in the reform and the provisions of the Charter of Rights and Freedoms.

The concerns are both material and symbolic. Québécois are concerned about the declining weight and therefore weakening influence of both Quebec and French-Canadians in Canada.[167] French Canadians are now about 25 percent of Canada's population, concentrated nearly 90 percent in Quebec, where they constitute 83 percent of the population. The highest French-Canadian share in another province is some 30 percent in New Brunswick (numbering some 217,000), the highest number, 330,000

---

[166] Charles Taylor, *Les Enjeux de la Réforme Constitutionelle*, Mémoire soumis à la Commission sur l'Avenir Politique et Constitutionnel du Québec, 26 November 1990.

[167] See Figure 5 and Tables 1–2, pp. 172–4.

in Ontario (under 4 percent of Ontario's population).[168] There are fewer French-speaking Canadians than 'allophones' (persons of a mother tongue other than English or French) in every province but Nova Scotia and tiny Prince Edward Island.

There is an acute sense of a precarious status as a French-speaking island and culture in an English-speaking sea. The Québécois view has been that without the application of state power, special protection and unilingualism, the reality would be domination by those speaking English. There is alarm that secularization and modernization have reduced Quebec's birthrate from one of the highest in the world to the lowest in Canada, and that 51 percent of children in the Montreal school system are today 'allophones,' with a clear and strong preference for adaptation to the North American continental, English-speaking mainstream. Eighty-five percent of immigrants assimilate into the English-speaking community. Québécois appear unwilling 'To tolerate a conception of Canada where they become "citizens" by virtue of a set of rights adjudicated by a national Supreme Court where any "collective rights" legislation must rely on the notwithstanding clause which is then open to criticism from the rest of Canada.'[169]

The preference as things are would appear to be one in favor of 'our own laws, our own gallows,' in Peter Berger's felicitous phrase, citing the preference of the citizens of the Canton of Basel.

Bilingualism and *le rayonnement du français*, promoted as pan-Canadian, may well have changed English-Canada more than French-Canada. While it created acceptance for the 'French fact' across Canada, and to a certain degree has become part of English Canada's sense of national identity, it has been minimized in Quebec to the extent it was seen as an aspect of a policy which involves denial of special status for Quebec and the legitimacy of the Québécois approach to 'state' and 'nation.'

Canada, then, is at a defining moment in its history, one turning on the potency of symbols and interests, but also on the meanings to attach to terms, and the consequences which attach to such meanings. With the evolution of opinion following the collapse of the Meech Lake Accord, both Quebec parties are territorial and 'sovereignist.' The Parti Québécois, currently ahead in the opinion polls, is for classical independence. The governing Liberal Party,

---

[168] See Figure 4, p. 172.
[169] Courchene, *op. cit.*, 22.

traditionally though conditionally federalist, is presently committed to the achievement of political autonomy, involving the 'exclusive, discretionary, and total control' of most areas of governmental activity. Canada represents a partnership to be reformed 'on the basis of free and voluntary association of the participating states,' in the language of the Report of the Liberal Party's Committee on the Constitution. Quebec would assume exclusive jurisdictional authority in a very wide range of areas of activity, including powers germane to its 'national economic development,' including investment, industrial policy, R&D, and corporations. Responsibility for foreign relations would be allocated on the basis of which government held jurisdictional authority for the field in question domestically. Quebec would obtain jurisdiction in any field not specifically allocated, as it would in the great majority of fields allocated. The federal government, at least as regards Quebec, would have exclusive powers in only four areas – currency, customs, defense, and financial equalization – with new rules to determine how Quebec participates in formulating policy and arriving at decisions federally in these areas. The Charter of Rights would be limited in its application to Quebec, and decisions of the Quebec courts could not be appealed in the Canadian Supreme Court. English-speaking Canada does not recognize federalism or indeed a country in any of this.

Conclusion

Canada, then, is something of a battlefield on which Renner-Bauer's ideas have been and continue to be tested in fairly clear form. The Québécois preference has been to achieve, retain, and expand their control of their own territorial state, and not to be satisfied with equality, language and cultural rights in an overarching multi-ethnic state. The hope is that the consequence of the developments of the last few years, particularly of the last 30 years, will not be the fragmentation of Canada into two or more independent states, but new arrangements which will accommodate the existence and needs of the 'distinct societies' cohabiting in the Canadian community without enfeebling pluralism and the Canadian state itself. While there is preparedness in English-speaking Canada to contemplate and undertake significant reform, including forms of decentralization, to accommodate regional diversity, there is also a growing sense, or realization, that accommodating two majorities is one thing, but two concepts of nationality and statehood quite another.

There are of course also considerable interests at issue, interests which, it is hoped, will induce compromise. Confederation is nearly 125 years old, and Canada is the world's eighth largest economy. There is no legal or constitutional process for the dismantling of confederation, and breakup of the country would not be a simple matter. The choices to be made in the next two years or so are likely to provide a still more decisive test of the relative power on the one hand of prudential judgment and Renner-Bauer's ideas put into practice, and on the other hand the appeal of nationalism.

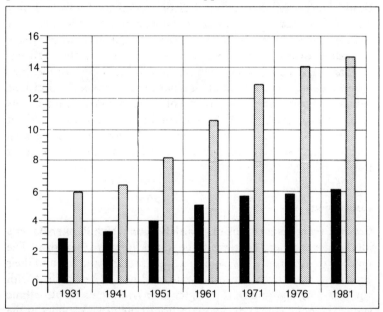

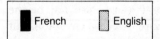

Figure 1   Two official language communities in Canada, 1931–81
(millions)

	1931	1941	1951	1961	1971	1976	1981
French	2.8	3.3	4.0	5.1	5.7	5.8	6.1
English	5.9	6.4	8.2	10.6	12.9	14.1	14.7

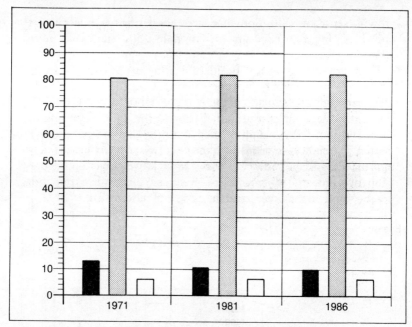

Figure 2 Linguistic profile of Quebec, 1971–86

	1971	1981	1986
English	13.10	11.00	10.40
French	80.70	82.40	82.80
Other	6.20	6.60	6.80

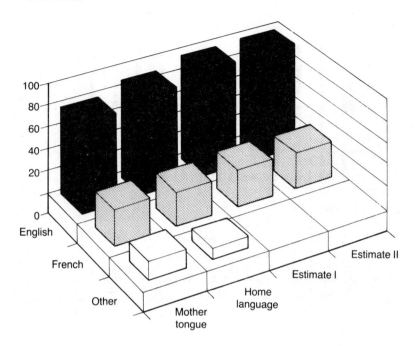

Figure 3 Linguistic composition of Canada by official language (%)

	English	French	Other
Mother tongue	62.07	25.11	12.82
Home language	68.94	24.04	7.02
Estimate I	73.93	26.07	
Estimate II	74.75	25.25	

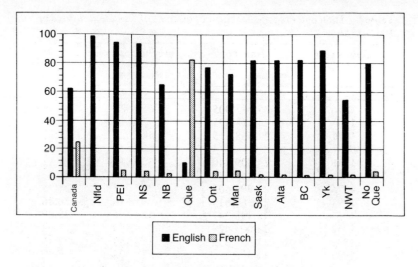

Figure 4   Distribution of population of Canada by mother tongue, 1986 (%)

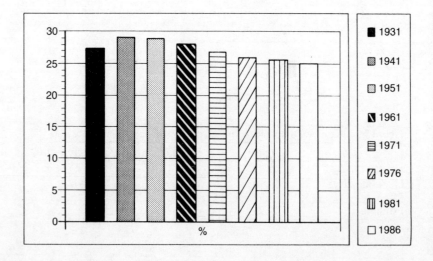

Figure 5   French-speaking shares (mother tongue), population of Canada, 1931–86 (%)

Table 1 *Total and French-speaking populations of Canada, censuses of 1931–1986*

Census year	Total pop.	French-speaking	
		Number	% of total
By home language			
1986	25,022,005	6,015,680	24.04
1981	24,083,495	5,923,010	24.59
1971	21,568,315	5,546,025	25.71
By mother tongue			
1986	25,309,340	6,354,840	25.11
1981	24,343,180	6,249,095	25.67
1976	22,992,605	5,966,707	25.95
1971	21,568,315	5,793,650	26.86
1961	18,238,247	5,123,151	28.09
1951	14,009,429	4,068,850	29.04
1941	11,506,655	3,354,753	29.15
1931	10,376,786	2,832,298	27.29

Table 2 *Population, income, ethnic origins and language by province*

Province ('000)	Population income	Per capita income index	Ethnic origin (%) British	Ethnic origin (%) French	Ethnic origin (%) Other	Home language English	Home language French	Home language Other
Atlantic Region								
Newfoundland	564	65.3	92.0	3.0	5.0	99.3	0.3	0.4
PEI	121	68.0	77.0	12.0	11.0	96.6	3.0	0.3
Nova Scotia	840	79.0	72.0	8.0	19.0	96.1	2.9	1.0
New Brunswick	689	71.8	54.0	36.0	10.0	68.0	31.4	0.6
Subtotal	2214	72.5	72.0	16.0	12.0	88.2	11.1	0.7
Central Region								
Quebec	6369	92.5	8.0	80.0	12.0	12.7	82.5	4.8
Ontario	8534	107.5	53.0	8.0	40.0	86.0	3.9	10.1
Subtotal	14903	101.1	33.0	39.0	28.0	54.7	37.5	7.8
Western Region								
Manitoba	1014	93.8	37.0	7.0	56.0	86.0	3.1	10.9
Saskatchewan	956	100.5	38.0	5.0	57.0	92.8	1.1	6.2
Alberta	2214	110.9	43.0	5.0	51.0	91.7	1.3	7.0
British Columbia	2714	108.8	51.0	3.0	46.0	91.7	0.6	7.8
Subtotal	68987	106.1	45.0	5.0	51.0	91.0	1.2	7.7
Territories	68	102.4	30.0	4.0	66.0	74.5	1.2	24.2
Canada	24083	100.0	40.0	27.0	33.0	68.2	24.6	7.2

Sources: Statistics Canada/National Accounts; 1981 Census of Canada

Lawrence Schlemmer

Between race, class and culture: social divisions in South Africa's political transition and their policy implications

Introduction

South Africa is currently in a phase of negotiated transition to inclusive rule after nearly three centuries of exclusive or near-exclusive government by a white minority of European settler origin. Over this period South Africa achieved the dubious distinction of producing the internationally notorious policy of apartheid. In its latter stages apartheid was officially known in South Africa as 'separate development.' Separate development, among its various nuances, had two major characteristics. One was the very wide and pervasive socioeconomic and power inequality between white and 'non-white' communities which it helped to establish and maintain. The second major aspect were the official attempts to promote and develop the greatest possible degree of political autonomy for whites on the one hand, and for twelve other 'groups' of different language of origin or race among the 'non-white' population on the other hand.

After so long a period of ethnic domination by one part of the population and ethnic 'engineering' imposed on others, the current stage of transition in South Africa obviously raises a number of interesting issues relating to the mutability or persistence of ethnicity in times of political change. On the one hand, there is widespread commitment among intellectuals to the eradication of old social divisions and a sense of the impetus and inevitability of social change. As the former leader of the opposition in South Africa's parliament, Van Zyl Slabbert, put it, 'The seventies saw the collapse of the partition state, the eighties saw the shift to the integrated state, the nineties will see the battle for the non-racial democratic state.'[170]

[170] Ronal Scheffer, 'The Battle for a Non-Racial State,' *Democracy in Action* July 1989, 16.

On the other hand, as world history has shown, social forms and patterns have a remarkable capacity to survive political change and even revolution.

In some ways, South Africa appears to represent a classic case of identity conflict very similar to other divided and conflict-ridden societies like, say, Sri-Lanka, Northern Ireland, Indonesia, Israel (within the wider setting of the mobilization of Palestinians), Cyprus and Lebanon. It shares some major indicators: a ruling group racially and culturally distinguishable from the remainder of the population, which constitutes a majority hitherto excluded from political participation; a strongly formed 'sub-national' identity among Afrikaans-speaking whites whose history has been characterized by successive attempts to establish an autonomous nation-state; opposition groupings like the Pan African Congress (P.A.C.) and the Azanian Peoples Organization (Azapo) which in part are mobilized on the basis of a racial and sociocultural identity (Africanness or blackness) in contrast to the identity of the ruling group of whites.

Accordingly, a number of analysts have recommended solutions to the conflict in South Africa which conform to a model of inter-ethnic power accommodation or 'consociationalism.' These views take the sociocultural identities as both the major problem to be resolved and the building-blocks of a solution based on interethnic power sharing. One of the best-known examples of this approach is that of Arend Lÿphart (1985).

An approach to solutions in South Africa within this conceptual framework runs, however, into a very large number of difficulties. The present assessment will attempt to show that while the view of South Africa as a society of ethnic conflict is not invalid, it is strongly contested in South Africa and perhaps too limited to encompass other very powerful aspects of the South African problem, including very pervasive features of South African political culture. It is argued further that solutions to South Africa's problems are made simpler in some respects and much more difficult in others by the complexity of ways in which conflicting interests and identities in South Africa have taken shape and are articulated. It is suggested that 'solutions' to political conflict in South Africa need to be more subtle than in societies in which ethnic conflict per se is the dominant and generally recognized problem.

Conceptual views on conflict in South Africa

A major difficulty in analyzing ethnicity in South Africa is that the ethnic perspective has been widely challenged in the internal debate in the country. One needs to review these challenges very briefly. Horowitz notes correctly that 'ranked' as opposed to 'unranked' systems of ethnic division lead to significant differences in the way the divisions are interpreted.[171] If South Africa's ethnic categories had a rough equality of incomes, occupational status, educational attainment and technological sophistication, there would be little argument about the kind of society it is. It would be commonly accepted as a society of divided nationality and a social identity arising out of historical conquest, i.e., a 'plural society' as defined by Kuper and Smith and earlier by Furnivall.[172]

However, South Africa's 'ranked' divisions are associated with contrasts of pigmentation and with large material inequalities and occupational status differences. This has created a furious debate which has raged since the 1940s among the social scientists analyzing South Africa. Furthermore, this debate in stereotyped form has penetrated the interpretations of political activists, who in turn have communicated it in even more oversimplified form to their politicized constituencies and even beyond. In the 1980s prepubertal children in the black townships have been heard chanting 'viva communism,' prepubertal children of right-wing white activists carry banners proclaiming the right of an Afrikaner people to a '*Boerestaat*,' while the equally young children of politically active white liberals are quite capable of extolling the virtues of 'non-racial' peace and harmony.

Academic explanations of South African conflict at times have been so polarized that they might almost have been analyzing different societies. One emphasis has certainly been on the conflict of national identities or nationalisms, largely informed by the emergence among white Afrikaners of a politicized concern with the survival of a language (first Dutch, then Afrikaans) and later by the development of a more comprehensive definition of an Afrikaans heritage, religious and cultural world view, and political destiny.

---

[171] Donald Horowitz, *Ethnic Groups in Conflict* (Berkeley: University of California Press, 1985).
[172] J. S. Furnivall, *Colonial Policy and Practice* (London: Cambridge University Press, 1948); L. Kuper and M. G. Smith, eds. *Pluralism in Africa* (Los Angeles: University of California Press, 1971).

This was the Afrikaans 'Christian National' orthodoxy, well analyzed by Moodie, and Adam and Giliomee,[173] among many others. The contrast between what Moodie describes as the Afrikaner 'civil religion' and the aspirations and identities of the mass of non-Afrikaans and particularly black South Africans is an obvious basis for concluding that South Africa is a society of divided national commitments.

Another interpretation has been based on the framework derived from Furnival and developed by M. G. Smith that was referred to earlier. The divided political commitments and the socioeconomic correlates of ethnic group identity are combined into a comprehensive conceptualization of South Africa as 'a *structurally plural* society characterized by differential incorporation of various corporate *groups* and corporate *categories* which are not composed simply or only of "racial" or "cultural" differences.'[174] The basic pattern is established by 'the rigorous and pervasive . . . differential distribution of civil and political rights and the economic, social and other opportunities which these permit or enjoin.'[175] In one sense this kind of depiction says nothing more than that divided national identities in South Africa have become pervasively institutionalized. There might be a little more to this theory, however, as I will argue presently.

Yet another approach has typified Afrikaners as culturally archaic or deviant. The formative period of the modern Afrikaans 'ideology' was redolent of references to a divinely inspired calling for the Afrikaner people and of invidious comparisons between what was seen as the social discipline, moral character and racial integrity of Afrikaners and whites as compared with black South Africans.[176] This world view, substantially influenced by German racial theory of the thirties, was in sharp contrast to the secular urban political culture of English-speaking industrial interest groups. Given this tension, a liberal critique of Afrikaner nationalism and its civil religion emerged which depicted Afrikaner commitments at the time

---

[173] H. Adam and H. B. Giliomee, *The Rise and Crisis of Afrikaner Power* (Cape Town: David Philip, 1979); T. D. Moodie, *The Rise of Afrikanerdom* (Berkeley: University of California Press, 1975).
[174] A. Leftwich, ed. *South Africa: Economic Growth and Political Change* (London: The Anchor Press, 1974), 128.
[175] L. Kuper and M. G. Smith, *op. cit.* (1971), 430.
[176] G. Cronjé, *n Tuiste vir die Nageslag* (Johannesburg: Publicite Handelsreklamediens, 1945).

as premodern, parochial and irrational in the light of modern economic needs.[177] Broadly compatible with this view was that of van den Berghe describing South Africa as a racial 'caste' system.[178] This view in sociology and political science was essentially similar to the views of psychologists and social psychologists who described South Africa as a system of organized race prejudice and discrimination.[179]

This view of the nature of apartheid is perpetuated in much popular writing, which to a lesser or greater extent ascribes it to a chauvinistic, authoritarian or antiquated traditionalist Afrikaner mentality. A recent example tending in this direction is Sparks.[180]

The approaches mentioned above all have been strongly contested by what has been the most cohesive and energetically pursued school of explanation of South African society: the neo-marxist so-called 'revisionist' approach. Rex argues that South Africa represents a '*kind* of class struggle' in which 'the classes are groups of varying histories and ethnic origins who enter the modern society with varying rights and degrees of rightlessness according to the kind of conquest and unfreedom which was imposed on them in an earlier period.' He has written that controls on labor in an earlier South Africa were the 'theoretically most perfect system of labor exploitation yet devised.'[181]

The issue of the control of and measures taken to ensure the availability and 'reproduction' of black labor power has been the central aspect of neo-Marxist writing in South Africa. Through institutions directly and indirectly defining the conditions of black labor, apartheid is seen to have promoted and perpetuated capitalist exploitation of the poor and the powerless.[182] Obviously these

---

[177] R. Horwitz, *Expand or Explode: Apartheid's Threat to South African Industry* (Cape Town: Business Bookman, 1957).

[178] Van den Berghe, *South Africa: A Study in Conflict* (Berkeley: University of California Press, 1967).

[179] I. D. MacCrone, *Race Attitudes in South Africa* (Johannesburg: University of the Witwatersrand Press, 1957); H. Lever, *South African Society* (Johannesburg: Jonathan Ball, 1978).

[180] A. Sparks, *The Mind of South Africa: The Story of the Rise and Fall of Apartheid* (London: Heinemann, 1990).

[181] John Rex, 'The Plural Society: The South African Case,' *Race* vol. 12 (1970–71), 401–13.

[182] See, for example, F. Johnstone, 'White Supremacy and White Prosperity in South Africa,' *African Affairs* vol. 69 (1970), 124–40; M. Legassick, 'South Africa: Capital Accumulation and Violence,' *Economy and Society* vol. 3, no. 3 (1974),

authors extend their analyses beyond labor institutions, since their work covers the full ramifications of a capitalist political economy. As Posel put it, however, the approach 'imposed a functionalist and reductionist perspective . . . the South African 'social formation' has been treated as if a functionally integrated whole, its racist political and ideological superstructive [sic] wholly serving the interests of the capitalist base which determines it.'[182] Elements of race consciousness, ethnic commitments and political ideologies in South Africa tend to be seen by the neo-Marxists as ways in which base interests, through the *social* relations of production, manipulate or influence the political economy to respond appropriately (the notion of 'false consciousness' is obviously relevant). While writers of this conceptual school have become noticeably more cautious since the collapse of communist orthodoxies in Eastern Europe, powerful strands of this type of analysis persist. Leninist scientific socialism is being replaced by an emphasis on a yet to be discovered democratic communism.

A significant development in South Africa since the forties is the fact that the premier 'liberation' movement, the African National Congress, has absorbed large aspects of the Marxist and neo-Marxist view of the society. This has occurred because of the determined penetration of communists into the top echelons of the A.N.C. from the twenties onwards, but particularly from the time of the Congress Alliance in the fifties, and because of the fairly universal tendency of progressive academics and intellectuals to assist or declare sympathy for underdog organizations, as the A.N.C. was over the entire period of its prohibition from 1960 to 1990.

The A.N.C.'s journal *Sechaba* of May 1979, for example, contained the following quotation: 'Socialism and nationalism could not develop separately from each other in South Africa . . . . The burning issues of national grievances, national oppression and national assertiveness and aspirations came to be understood as inseparably linked to class-exploitation.' The same issue of *Sechaba* went on to say, 'To end the barbarism of white domination we must destroy its foundations – the capitalist system.' Today the most senior and most prominent intellectual on the A.N.C. National

253–91; H. Wolpe, 'Capitalism and Cheap Labour Power in South Africa,' *Economy and Society* vol. 1, no. 4 (1972), 425–58.

[183] Debbie Posel, 'Rethinking the Race-Class Debate in South African Historiography,' *Social Dynamics* vol. 9, no. 1 (1983), 50–65.

Executive Committee, Mr Joe Slovo, explains his view in the following words: 'The concept of national domination is not a mystification to divert us [the A.N.C.?] from class approaches; *it infects every level of class exploitation* . . . The winning of the objectives of the national democratic revolution will in turn lay the basis for a steady advance in the direction of deepening our national unity on all fronts . . . and towards a socialist transformation.'[184] The conceptions of ethnicity held by Slovo and many of his colleagues have been limited in the past to the Leninist approach to the problem of nationalities in the U.S.S.R. More generally, however, A.N.C. and South African Communist Party policy is to disavow and indeed to act against any tendencies which could be argued to be associated with race separation or race divisions. It is easy to extend this rejection to ethnic aspirations of all kinds.

There are many more nuances of interpretation of the South African problem than those presented above, but those discussed will suffice to show that the nature of South Africa's divided society is deeply in contest. One cannot debate the topic of state and nation in South Africa's multi-ethnic society without recognizing that large constituencies of intellectuals, writers, journalists and political activists see ethnicity as a side issue – a distraction or diversion from the essence of the conflict, which is seen as either 'pathological' race consciousness or class exploitation.

For these reasons this analysis cannot proceed from the straightforward assumption of an ethnic problem. To avoid endless conceptual debate, however, some empirical indicators of how ordinary South Africans see the problems of the society will be adduced. On that basis some conclusions may be drawn about state, nation and identity in a changing South Africa. At the same time these indicators will help place in perspective the various theoretical perspectives outlined above.

Some empirical indicators

Attention will be focused mainly on whites, since as the minority on which all governments of modern South Africa have been based their interests have obviously been critical in shaping the fundamentals of

---

[184] Joseph Slovo, 'The South African Working Class, and the National Democratic Revolution,' *Umsebenzi, Discussion Pamphlet*, South African Communist Party (1988), 4, 36.

the system. Since the present elected white government is also a 'gatekeeper' to a future system, white interests are very salient. A great deal of evidence extending over a long period is available, but space permits only a brief review of fairly recent data. One is aware of the fact that in presenting survey data one will immediately face the rejoinder that the attitudes and sentiments represent 'false consciousness' or manipulated consciousness of some sort or another. These considerations will be addressed in due course.

In May 1990 this author conducted an attitude survey among 1,311 white adult voters on the nationwide postal panel of Market and Opinion Surveys, (Pty) Ltd.[185] The panel is composed on the basis of a stratified probability sample of all whites, urban and rural. The panel is subject to a 33.3 percent random replacement every year to counter the effects of respondent 'socialization.' One advantage of the panel is that familiarity with the research organization encourages great frankness of answers. It should be noted, however, that on the basis of a comparison between political party choices in the sample and the results of the last general election, the sample has a slight *liberal* bias (27 percent of the sample support the Conservative Party as opposed to a level of support among whites of 31 percent in the September 1989 election).

The respondents, all of whom were obviously aware of their government's current intention to negotiate a new political system with the representatives of the non-enfranchised majority, were asked the following question: 'In future negotiation, which of the following forms of protection for the white minority are absolutely essential – in other words *non-negotiable?*' The alternatives presented to the respondents and the percentage endorsement by various subcategories in the sample are given in Table 1.

Another question to which a response was sought was 'the government intends to negotiate with the A.N.C. and other political groups . . . (about) a parliament representing all people, blacks included, with a lesser or greater degree of protection for whites and other minorities . . .' The results appear in Table 2.

A further question was: 'As far as the policy of any political party is concerned, which of the following is most important and second most important to you?' In Table 3 the percentages relating to first and second choices are averaged in order to simplify presentation.

[185] Source for Tables 1–4 (following): Market and Opinion Surveys, *Survey Report No. 3, 1990* (Durbanville: Cape, 1990).

Table 1 White interests considered to be essential/non-negotiable: percentage of sample selecting each of a range of interests

Paraphrased alternatives	n1311 All whites	n788 Afrikaans-speaking	n524 English-speaking	n229 Afrikaans income Low	n140 Afrikaans income High	n83 English income Low	n135 English income High
Full control of all own political affairs	63	72	50	88	48	63	36
Afrikaans as one offical language	54	72	27	84	48	32	13
Protection of property rights against confiscation or nationalization	93	94	91	96	92	89	97
Parents' right to define school admissions	68	79	49	89	68	63	41
Rights to decide composition of own area	61	73	43	88	51	55	33
Protection of individuals against discrimination by religion, political expression and social background	94	93	95	96	91	89	99
Equal political decision-making rights for whites as a political group (relative to blacks)	73	73	73	81	67	65	65

Notes: 1. Percentages sum to more than 100 because each item could be endorsed independently.
2. Low income <R2500 per month, high income >R6000 per month.
3. Sample sizes are standard for subsequent tables.

Table 2 *White responses to the prospect of an inclusive parliamentary franchise (%)*

Response	All whites	Afrikaans-speaking	English-speaking	Afrikaans income		English income	
				Low	*High*	*Low*	*High*
Would welcome new system	17	11	28	2	24	10	39
Would accept new system	25	24	26	16	30	23	36
Depends on how much power whites as a group retain	35	37	32	41	28	46	21
Oppose/reject new system	22	28	15	41	17	21	2

Table 3 *Priorities attached to various party-political policies by whites: percentages for first and second selection of priorities averaged*

Party Policy	All Whites	Afrikaans-speaking	English-speaking
Future general security of whites	22	25	17
Fairness to all races	28	25	33
Moral standards	10	12	9
Maintaining white political power	11	13	7
Economic welfare of whites	5	5	6
Interest of own cultural group	6	8	2
Protecting whites' work and occupations	4	4	4
Political opportunities for blacks	17	15	21
Economic welfare for as many as possible	21	17	27

Finally, the white respondents were asked a question from this range of questions that possibly penetrated most deeply as far as the issue under consideration is concerned: 'Which of the following would you regard as the most likely change which would take place if blacks were to rule South Africa?' We should note that given that blacks constitute 65 percent of the total adult population, a black-dominated government is a plausible prospect in an unqualified, numerically based democratic voting system. The results are given in Table 4.

No attempt will be made to comment on each table individually, since the pattern of results emerges most clearly if the responses to different items are interrelated. What may appear to be contradictions in these results are fairly easily explained. The results make it clear that a majority of both Afrikaans' and English-speaking whites appear to accept a need for an extension of political participation to all adult members of the population. This is

Table 4 White perceptions of the most likely change that would occur if blacks were to rule South Africa in terms of options presented to respondents

Anticipated change	All whites	Afrikaans-speaking	English-speaking	Afrikaans income		English income	
				Low	High	Low	High
No serious or permanent change	7	5	10	2	9	5	15
Order and physical safety would be threatened	46	55	33	63	41	40	32
White occupational security would be threatened	9	8	9	14	2	21	7
White incomes and standards of living would decline	18	19	15	19	25	16	17
Afrikaans language and culture would be threatened	6	4	11	6	2	8	11
White living habits would have to change	7	6	7	3	12	10	6
Standards of public administration would fall	16	14	19	12	12	15	15

supported by data not presented above showing that only 13 percent of whites (16 percent of Afrikaans speakers and eight percent of English speakers) considered that it was feasible to attempt a division of territory so as to avoid black participation indefinitely. Some 61 percent of whites (52 percent of Afrikaans speakers and 77 percent of English speakers) accepted that negotiations with either the A.N.C. or other black political groupings about black entry into the political system were inevitable and necessary. In Table 3 above these views are evident from the high percentage of endorsement of policies of fairness to all groups, of providing political opportunities for blacks and striving for general economic welfare. It would appear that a fairly clear majority of whites in both language groups has accepted the principle of a common (political) citizenship for South Africa.

This acceptance, however, is very clearly qualified by what appears to be a roughly equal insistence by a majority of whites that whites, as a mobilized or politically identifiable group, should retain a significant share of decision-making in a new system. Some seven out of ten English- and Afrikaans-speaking whites see a roughly equal power division between whites and blacks as non-negotiable. Even among English speakers, a majority of whom has not voted in the past for the present government, some five out of ten insist on what has been the government policy until recently, namely full community power over the community's 'own' affairs. It appears from the results, therefore, that while power-sharing is accepted in principle the degree of power to be retained by whites will determine whether the outcome of current negotiation is to be endorsed or not.

The motivations which appear to underlie this insistence on a power balance (see Table 4) appear to consist mainly in concerns about generalized security, law and order, and physical safety. Related to this there is also a fear of a fall in standards of public administration should whites lose all influence. Probably also related to the general concern about an orderly society is a fear that standards of living and incomes will fall. Even among Afrikaans speakers these general concerns about public order and standards eclipse concerns about Afrikaans culture and language. This is also evident in the support for various policies of political parties (see Table 3). In response to likely changes under black rule, it would appear that specific economic and occupational interests are overshadowed by generalized concerns about security (and the need for social justice and fairness, which can be seen as a basis for longer-term security for minorities).

These results are supported by other studies. A September 1990 poll conducted by the same organization (Market and Opinion Surveys (Pty) Ltd) reflected the levels of fear of a range of consequences of negotiations shown in Table 5.

Table 5 *Perceived consequences of negotiations (%)*

	All whites	Afrikaans speakers	English speakers
Political domination/ discrimination (by blacks)	29	31	26
Anarchy, civil war, chaos	22	19	27
A.N.C. not trusted to honor agreements	9	9	7
Economic degeneration	14	15	12

In a 1987 survey among whites (published 1989), the Human Sciences Research Council found that only 37 percent of whites (24 percent of Afrikaans speakers and 54 percent of English speakers) considered that blacks and whites had 'sufficient common values and principles to jointly draw up a democratic constitution for South Africa.'

The range of results discussed above tends to suggest that Afrikaners are more fearful and pessimistic than English speakers about the consequences of a majority rule dispensation, but *not* because they are particularly concerned about their own ethnic identity. Their fears are more generalized than that – even specific economic concerns are eclipsed by the more pervasive concern about public order and physical safety of all whites.

In the tables presented earlier there was evidence of variations in attitudes by income depending on Afrikaans or English ethnicity. The general pattern is for Afrikaners to be more concerned about threats to security than English speakers. Once again, one must emphasize that it does not appear that the threats are experienced in relation to Afrikaans interests in particular, rather that Afrikaners are more sensitive to perceived threats to wider 'white' interests. As is clear from the tables, the difference between Afrikaans and English responses is not reduced when one controls for income levels. Irrespective of income, Afrikaners tend to be more cautious or conservative than their English-speaking fellow whites. It is interesting, however, that an exception to this pattern appears in regard to the perceived need for *equal* power-sharing between blacks and whites (see Table 1). In this respect English' and Afrikaans-speaking respondents appear to be essentially similar in orientation.

These empirical results are difficult to reconcile with some of the very clearly etched theoretical views about the dynamics of conflict in South Africa. For example, there is no clearly discernible 'primordial' attachment to cultural interests among most Afrikaners (according to the polls discussed earlier) and, given the concerns with social justice, political fairness and general welfare, there is little evidence of strong hostility toward out-groups, or of a desire to keep black South Africans in an inferior position.

The evidence presented above as well as a mass of impressions from day-to-day interaction in the society itself is that the white minority at rank-and-file level is not a captive of any of the cultural or economic élites which might prescribe political or cultural autonomy for whites or social engineering aimed specifically at creating an environment friendly for business. For example, in a large 1988 survey by Marketing and Media Research, more than four out of ten Afrikaners felt that there should be more state control over business.[186] This is hardly the corporate agenda.

The evidence of the surveys above is not incompatible with the theory that South Africa is a society of divided 'corporate groups.' However, this terminology is perhaps redundant, i.e., white institutional leaders in a range of sectors and institutions have a broad everyday value-consensus, are organized and mobilized as a political constituency, have a shared awareness of popular socioeconomic interests and concerns, but are rational enough to know that they cannot expect a system which excludes the black majority to endure in perpetuity.

The white minority has a self-conscious view of itself as an offshoot of a first-world or European sociocultural tradition. Its patriotism is indigenous, but its norms and expectations regarding public administration, schools, amenities and lifestyles are attuned to what the developed West has achieved. Whites are a 'fragment' of Europe in Africa, a phenomenon described by the historian Louis

---

[186] Marketing and Media Research, *Opinion Poll*, June 1988, Johannesburg, 1988.

Hartz in his *Founding of New Societies.*[187]

In view of this broad self-definition, South African whites fear that the third-world realities of South Africa will usurp their indigenized settler lifestyle and social order. They are sufficiently well-informed to know that conditions among the majority of the population, including conditions that minority rule has created, are at odds with their popular lifestyle concerns. They fear the mass expectations of a third-world population and mistrust its leadership's ability to maintain the standards to which they are accustomed.

The group interests of whites are described above in a particular way. Perhaps others with greater economy of words will describe these interests as middle-class privilege. Some will mystify them by ascribing some allegedly deeply imbued cultural meaning to their concerns. It is neither privilege nor primordial identity – it is simply clean sidewalks, safe streets, predictable politicians, and the luxury of leaving public administration to competent professionals. In a sense it is what is privilege in Africa, but normal in Europe, which white South Africans tend to take as a normative reference.

Since the empirical evidence referred to above was gathered, a wave of violence has engulfed South Africa's black townships. In the first ten months of 1990, 3,035 people died in what was mainly interfactional conflict between the A.N.C., Inkatha and P.A.C. groups in black areas, allegedly encouraged in some instances by right-wing groups or perhaps policemen with agendas of their own (in 1990 over 80 policemen were killed and nearly 2,000 had their homes attacked by township militants – arguably and understandably the police are therefore not neutral). This kind of turmoil can be expected at a time of heightened political competition and of raised expectations during a period of political transition. Such instability is likely to continue. The typical concerns of whites reflected in the poll findings will hardly be assuaged in months to come. South Africa will enter its new phase of majority political participation with popular white fears thoroughly aroused by day-to-day events. The white conservative opposition parties, which gained 31 percent of the white vote in the September 1989 election and since then have increased their support to some 35 to 40 percent

[187] L. Hartz, *The Founding of New Societies* (New York: Harcourt Brace and World, 1964).

of whites,[188] will see to it that the issue of white security is well aired in the public debate and becomes a major issue in the political negotiations.

Brief observations on ethnicity among blacks

Because the policy of separate development aimed to establish autonomous ministates ('homelands') for each of the country's black linguistic-ethnic categories, and presented this policy as an alternative to black participation in the central government of the area of the country controlled by whites, considerable ideological and political resistance to ethnicity as an element in politics has developed in black movements. This has been reinforced by the non-racial idealism espoused by the A.N.C. and white and Indian liberal and socialist intellectuals over the years of strong political opposition to apartheid. Theodor Hanf depicts the A.N.C.'s strategy as 'clearly Jacobinistic,' reflecting a concept that he describes as 'Europe's leading political export, usually sold as "Nation-building." The less homogeneous the social realities in a country, the greater the attraction of a crusade against tribalism, parochialism, particularism and secularism.'[189] Since Hanf wrote this some members of the A.N.C. have moved to a more flexible position in regard to ethnicity and minority rights,[190] but the major emphasis on a popular cultural unity remains.

The A.N.C. has a particular reason to adopt a strictly non-racial, non-ethnic approach in politics. It is well-known that its top levels of leadership are dominated by Xhosa-speaking people (Mandela, Tambo, Hani, Mbeki (Sr. and Jr.), and many others). If one adds the substantial number of socialist whites and Indians at these levels of the organization, it is apparent that Zulu, South Sotho, Pedi, and other ethnic-linguistic divisions are markedly under-represented. In the rhetorical interchanges of competitive politics which lie ahead, the fact that a party primarily aimed at the general black

---

[188] Lawrence Schlemmer, L. Stack and C. Berkow, 'Transition and the White Grassroots,' in *Transition to Democracy: Policy Perspectives*, eds. R.H. Lee and L. Schlemmer (Cape Town: Oxford University Press, 1991), 159–74.

[189] Theodor Hanf, 'The Prospects of Accommodation in Plural Societies: a Comparative Study,' in H. Giliomee and Lawrence Schlemmer, *Negotiating South Africa's Future* (Johannesburg: Southern, 1989), 89–113.

[190] Albie Sachs, *The Future Constitutional Position of White South Africans: Some Initial Ideas* (London: Institute of Commonwealth Studies, 1990).

constituency is so dominated by one black ethnic group and by 'non-Africans' is bound to emerge as an image liability. The best defense against this is to deny or deflect the problem by emphasizing the ideal of unity and non-racism.

More broadly, however, there is something akin to a popular passion against ethnicity in all black political movements. The communally oriented movements like the P.A.C. and Azapo focus on black unity on the one side of the racial divide. Even a party like the Inkatha Freedom Party, which manifestly has a primary base among Zulu people, has traditionally insisted that it is non-ethnic and non-racial. Consequently, the mobilizing political institutions among blacks in South Africa with minor exceptions are all formally committed to interethnic unity across or within broader race categories. The ethnic characteristics of parties have to be detected in unadvertised associations between a party and its supporters' ethnic characteristics. Yet ethnicity appears to be powerfully latent, pervading the system of political mobilization. It becomes evident particularly at times of stress and conflict.

An example would be the interfactional black violence referred to earlier. Whether egged on by *agents provocateurs* or not, it reveals just how readily ethnic solidarity and militant sectional passions can become aroused. One may accept that the causes of the violence are multiple[191] but what is significant is that interparty competition, job shortages at a time of recession and a host of other stresses in the black communities *so readily* take the form of structured violence between Zulus and Xhosas, or in one instance between Sothos and Xhosas.

The same phenomenon was encountered in an extensive study of interfactional violence among mineworkers, which in 1986-87 had become so frequent as to create enormous problems for mine management.[192] Despite overt commitments to interethnic solidarity, changes in recruitment patterns, conflicts over women and even supposedly shared worker grievances very readily led to a crystallization of identities and to militant ethnic solidarity.

In earlier attitude surveys, given in Tables 6 and 7, this author

[191] Lawrence Schlemmer, 'Factional Violence and Democracy in South Africa,' *S.A. Foundation Review* vol. 16, no. 6 (1990), 1–2; Lawrence Schlemmer, 'The Current Violence,' *S.A. Foundation Executive Briefing*, no. 2 (1990), 1–2.
[192] J. K. McNamara, and Lawrence Schlemmer, *Black Employees Attitudes to Inter-Group Violence on Gold Mines* (Mimeo) 1988.

attempted to penetrate beyond superficial attitudes of black unity to the ethnic dimension by framing particular questions asked of representative samples of black people.[193]

Table 6 *Ethnic self-definition (1981 study)*

'One person says – I am a (name of tribal group) before anything else. Another says – I am first a Black person of South Africa, then (a group). Another says – I am only a Black person of South Africa. Which one of these people would be talking for you?'

Responses
Percentages considering themselves to be tribal before anything else:

Soweto* Zulu	5	(n 300)
Other groups in Soweto	4	(n 200)
Natal: KwaZulu urban	18	(n 280)
KwaZulu rural	25	(n 250)
Zulu migrants	21	(n 200)
Squatters: Durban	43	(n 150)
Inkatha members	33	(n 200)

* Soweto is a metropolitan suburb with a population exceeding one million.

'If all Black people voted together in South Africa, people of (name of group) would be small in numbers and other groups would have more power in government. Would people like you feel weak and insecure, or because Blacks are all one people, would it not matter at all?'

Table 7 *Forced choice question (1979 and 1981 studies)*

Percentage ethnic defensive: i.e., would feel weak and insecure:

City Xhosa	24	(n 100)
Soweto Zulu	21	(n 300)
Soweto Pedi	35	(n 75)
Ciskei urban	34	(n 199)
Eastern Cape	50	(n 417)
Ciskei rural	44	(n 100)
Migrant workers	46	(n 83)
Natal urban	32	(n 280, 1981)
Zulu rural	47	(n 250, 1981)
Zulu migrants, Tvl	64	(n 100, 1981)

These figures show that particularly among squatters, migrant workers and rural black people the tribal or ethnic dimension of

[193] Source for Tables 6–7 (following): Lawrence Schlemmer, 'Data Collection among Black People in South Africa,' in *Truth Be in the Field: Social Science Research in South Africa*, ed. P. Hugo (Pretoria: University of South Africa Press, 1990).

consciousness is fairly easily elicited.

The survey of white political opinions cited earlier showed that, among Afrikaners who were not overtly ethnic in their motivation, ethnic identity appears to have a latent effect in aggravating fears of political change. The observations for blacks reveal that the same latent strong ethnic consciousness exists outside of the fully urbanized communities.

Some broad conclusions: nationality and ethnicity in a future South Africa

It seems clear that South Africa is not a case of political conflict dominantly structured in ethnic terms. The country may have all the objective conditions for ethnically based articulation of political interests and goals, but this dimension is confused, obscured, or weakened by a number of factors: a general awareness of the fact that territorial interpretation and a thoroughly integrated economy impose objective requirements for mutual accommodation that transcend the ethnic group; political movements mobilized around ideologies that consistently deny the relevance of ethnic consciousness (i.e., socialism, communism, interethnic black consciousness and, among the whites, a unified commitment to 'European' standards and norms); socioeconomic inequalities and lifestyle differences primarily structured in terms of race and class rather than ethnic allegiance; a reaction to earlier apartheid, popularly depicted as having used ethnicity to justify white racial domination; and black popular mobilization occurring mainly in urban areas, where blacks experience their conditions as a race-class rather than as ethnic groups.

Another major factor perhaps deserves mention, i.e., middle-class bias in South African politics. The National Party and the Democratic Party among whites are today dominantly middle- to upper-middle class in composition. The leadership of majority-based movements is packed with lawyers, social workers, academics, churchmen, economists and graduates of all kinds. Non-graduates tend to be trade unionists whose occupations require cross-ethnic solidarity. Hence the articulators and formulators of political positions in South Africa are generally a culturally 'secularized' category. Ethnic leadership as such is in a minority. Chief Buthelezi of Inkatha is a keynote exception since, although also a graduate, he is a traditional aristocrat among the Zulus. Middle-class graduate leaders are inclined to take cautious positions on race and ethnicity. This is very clearly seen in the government's current negotiating strategy under which it is retreating very rapidly from any overt references to white group rights or Afrikaner rights, emphasizing instead minority rights, balance, and quality in government.[194] South African middle-class graduates are also exposed to the international Western middle-class political culture, which tends to abjure social goals that are not universalistic and anti-parochial.[195]

All these factors have led to a political culture in which ethnicity is veiled and interacts with race distinctions. Both ethnicity and race are qualified in different ways by different popular ideologies and by practical political imperatives in the transition to inclusive rule. However, a few major conclusions stand out. First, the most powerful group consciousness (aside from small minorities like Indians) is that of whites. This consciousness is in a sense a quasi-ethnicity, since it is based partly on race and partly on a perception of European identity. It is a sense of category rather than a coherent nationalism. For this reason white group motivations are not likely to extend to an insistence on autonomy or self-determination. Nevertheless, since they are built around perceived threats emanating from a much larger third-world majority with high expectations, they will include an insistence on reliable safeguards. Such reliability can only be ensured by whites' retaining a substantial share of power. White 'ethnicity,' unlike ethnic consciousness, say, in parts of Eastern Europe, does not make positive claims to territory and national symbols. It is a powerful group consciousness, but essentially defensive.

Secondly, ethnic consciousness among rural and marginal urban black populations is not mobilized (with the possible exception of the rural Zulus under Inkatha). It is strongly present in latent form, however, and could be readily mobilized in future in the arena of competitive politics. It is then likely to take the form of regional movements contesting the power of the center – a well-known phenomenon in Africa.

Thirdly, in the urban industrial complexes, the mobilization for political competition will be dominantly on what is termed 'race-

[194] G. Viljoen, 'Motivations for Minority Participation,' *RSA Policy Review* vol. 3, no. 6 (1990), 59, 3–20.
[195] R. Lewis, *Anti Racism: A Manica Exposed* (London: Quartet Books, 1988).

class' lines, with the A.N.C. and its alliances giving more emphasis to class, and the P.A.C. and associated groups placing emphasis on race. This kind of mobilization will tend to reinforce the white quasi-ethnicity referred to earlier.

Given this mix of elements, it seems clear that South Africa does not conform to the requirements of a 'concordance' or 'consociational' solution, i.e., one in which two or more social identities of equivalent form and status reach a mutual accommodation. A *grand ethnic coalition* of white and black representatives acknowledging each other's right to communal autonomy and symbols simply does not fit South Africa's situation.

On the other hand, an open numbers-based democracy will offer too few safeguards to address the needs of the powerful white quasi-community and of potentially antagonistic regional ethnic groups. If they are true, current allegations of white right-wing complicity in black factional violence suggest how readily dissenting whites and black regional groups could combine against a majority in power at the center. Furthermore, black-white income inequality, black unemployment (currently well over 20 percent) and a host of related socioeconomic differences will make class-based politics extremely militant. South Africa's Gini coefficient of inequality is the highest in the world among countries which publish reliable income data.[196]

These features and others that it was not possible to discuss here suggest that the form of political resolution attainable in South Africa will be an untidy mix of elements. Because the major white political party is the only political agency able to exercise legitimate authority over South Africa's large public bureaucracy and security agencies, it will have to be included in executive government. There will have to be substantial devolution of powers to provinces or regions as a basis for retaining the compliance of strong regional ethnic formations like the rural Zulus. Powerful and effective agencies will also have to be established by the constitution in order to resolve civic and class conflict in the industrial core areas of the country.

There is no existing constitutional system in the world suited to South Africa. The system which emerges in South Africa will be born in turmoil and will satisfy nobody. It will never be taken as a model

[196] F. Wilson and M. Ramphaele, *Uprooting Poverty: The South African Challenge* (Cape Town: David Philip, 1989).

constitution by any textbook of political science. Middle-class Western observers will find its peculiarities distasteful. It might, however, just keep together one of the most problematic societies in the world.

Robert W. Hefner

State, nation, and ethnicity in modern Indonesia

In the 1950s and early 1960s, the problem of national integration –
the processes by which the inhabitants of a territory are transformed
from mere co-residents to citizens influenced by cultural ideas of
what the nation is and should become – moved to the center of
attention in the human sciences. Throughout Africa and Asia,
European colonies were coming to independence, and their passage
was often not an easy one. The departure of European colonials gave
rise to such severe competition among native groupings for control
of government that it put the survival of some nations in question.
Viewing this turmoil, many Western observers came to the realization that successful development is not simply a matter of technical fine-tuning or infrastructural change, but a deeply cultural and
political process as well. An integral part of a nation's development,
it seemed, is a people's coming to agreement on a national identity
and procedures for the management of state.

Few countries seemed to be as unlikely a candidate for success in
this effort as the newly independent nation of Indonesia. Graced
with only the most primitive transport and communications
infrastructure, the country lay scattered across an archipelago as
broad as the United States, with some 13,000 islands (half of them
inhabited), a population of almost one hundred million people, more
than three hundred ethnic groups and languages, two distinct racial
groups, and a total of four world religions as well as dozens of tribal
faiths. At a time when 'primordial' ties of territory, race, ethnicity,
and religion seemed to present serious obstacles to national
integration,[197] the former colony of the Dutch East Indies struck

---

[197] Clifford Geertz, 'The Integrative Revolution: Primordial Sentiments and Civil
Politics in the New States,' in *Basic Interpretation of Cultures* (New York: Basic

many observers, including the American Central Intelligence Agency, as one of the new states least likely to succeed.

Though in the 1950s and 1960s Indonesia experienced powerful threats to its national integrity, it somehow survived this turmoil. Today Indonesia is, in cultural terms, more of a nation than it was in the early years of independence. Though problems of political succession and democratic participation promise further instability in coming years, there can be little doubt that Indonesia has developed the rudiments of a national culture quite unlike anything seen in the colonial era. The government has succeeded in bringing standardized education to even the most remote territories. At the same time, it has managed to introduce the majority of the population to the national language, *Bahasa Indonesia*, an achievement which ranks as the most successful program of national-language development in the Third World. Finally, during this same period, Indonesian media, markets, and transportation have introduced much of the population to national images and lifestyles, undermining received ideas of consumption and well-being.[198] Given Indonesia's continental proportions, these achievements represent one of the most successful examples of national self-creation in the entire developing world.

In this chapter, I would like to examine briefly the history of Indonesian national culture from the late colonial era to the present day. I also want to address the question whether the Renner-Bauer model of a multinational state might provide, or might have provided, a fairer and more effective vehicle for political stabilization by separating the political–economic exigencies of the state from the cultural demands of ethnic nationalism. To anticipate my conclusion, let me say that my answer to this question in the Indonesian context will be a qualified negative. Though elements of the model might be incorporated into its system of government, Indonesia's history has militated against such an idea of multinational federation.

Books, 1973); Edward Shils, 'Political Development in the New States,' *Comparative Studies in Society and History* 2, 265–92, 370–411.

[198] John R. Bowen, 'On the Political Construction of Tradition: *Gotong Royong* in Indonesia,' *The Journal of Asian Studies* 45 (1986) 545–61; Robert W. Hefner, 'The Problem of Preference: Ritual and Economic Change in Highland Java,' *Man* (n.s.)18 (1983), 669–89; Robert W. Hefner, *The Political Economy of Mountain Java: An Interpretive History* (Berkeley: University of California Press, 1990).

The reasons the Renner-Bauer model seems unhelpful in the Indonesian context are both historical and conceptual. As in some other multi-ethnic societies, ethnic and national culture in Indonesia have diverged, in the sense that national identity has not been built on the deeply sedimented heritage of any particular ethnic group. National communications and political–economic development have heightened popular awareness of ethnic differences and sometimes exacerbated communal tensions. But they have also set contrary processes in motion, spurring the development of a new and genuinely transethnic national culture. Modern Indonesia thus presents us with an example of a country in which national culture has a dynamism distinct from ethnic communalism. This development makes the Renner-Bauer model, with its implicit emphasis on the equivalence of ethnicity and nation, of questionable utility for Indonesian affairs.

In addition to these historical issues, the Indonesian example raises general theoretical questions concerning the concepts of ethnicity and nationalism implicit in the Renner-Bauer model. In particular, I will suggest that the model is constructed on a model of ethnicity that does not accord with the realities of ethnicity in Indonesia and at least some other developing countries. This severely limits its utility for the formulation of policies in these multi-ethnic countries.

The nation conceived: from colonialism to nationalism

Having first arrived in the region in the final years of the 16th century, Dutch Europeans came to rule small portions of the East Indies in the early 17th century. With the exception of a few areas of estate settlement in Sumatra, Java and the spice islands of eastern Indonesia, however, it was only in the 19th and early 20th centuries that the Dutch intervened in all the territories of the archipelago and reorganized politics and production along systematic, centrally coordinated lines. European rule and culture came to most of the Indies' hinterland, therefore, rather late in the colonial era. This meant that when the Japanese arrived in early 1942 to expel the Europeans and establish an Asian Co-Prosperity Zone, Dutch influence throughout the archipelago was still uneven and in some places superficial.

In some areas of the Indies like the east coast of Sumatra or inland

Central Java, colonial economic programs had totally transformed indigenous patterns of politics and production. In these territories, the 19th-century colonial state had abolished traditional law, mobilized masses of labor in forced cultivation schemes, and integrated traditional rulers into a thoroughly rationalized, bureaucratic system of governance. In the 20th century, under the liberal-minded reforms of the 'Ethical Policy,' public education was also established in these same regions, drawing a significant (though rarely majority) proportion of the male population into the modernizing exercises of literacy and general education.

In other parts of the archipelago, however, particularly those which lacked the human or natural resources to which Dutch colonialism was attracted, European intervention in local affairs was extremely limited. The Dutch had governed these territories through a system of native rule only loosely integrated into the larger Indies bureaucracy. In these regions, then, the departure of the Dutch in 1942 had only a small impact on local society, leaving largely traditional social structures in place.

When the Dutch returned to the Indies after World War II, intending to reappropriate their colony, they hoped to use this cultural diversity to their advantage in their effort to suppress the fierce republican insurgency which arose in the aftermath of the Japanese surrender in August 1945. Indonesian nationalists called for an independent Republic of Indonesia with a unitary constitution, a national language, and a centrally controlled government, military, and school system. Recognizing that they could not entirely suppress Indonesian aspirations for independence, the Dutch called for the creation of a multinational federation, to be organized along territorial and ethnic lines. The colonialists' hope was that with such a plan they could isolate most of the archipelago from the strongholds of republicanism on Sumatra, Madura and Java. The Dutch would recognize republican sovereignty on these islands where the pro-independence insurgency was already well advanced, but preserve European rule elsewhere. With the islands of the archipelago segregated in this fashion, the Dutch would then establish a Netherlands–Indonesia union in which Dutch dominance would be guaranteed.

In 1948 the Dutch moved forward with their plan to create a federal United States of Indonesia. However, fierce republican resistance and pressures from the United States (which was providing postwar aid to the Netherlands) ultimately resulted in the plan's failure. In late 1949 a compromise was reached between the Indonesian Republic and the Netherlands. But the federated government which was supposed to result from this agreement broke down in the months following the settlement. By 1950 the Dutch-negotiated United States of Indonesia gave way to a united and administratively centralized Republic of Indonesia.[199]

Consequently, in the end the strength of Indonesian nationalism militated against the success of the colonial plan for multinational federation. In years to come any such proposal for multinational federation would be regarded as a sure formula for Indonesia's demise.

Had history turned out otherwise, the East Indies might perhaps have been an ideal candidate for such a federationist arrangement. The unevenness of socioeconomic integration throughout the archipelago ensured that even in 1950 large areas of the country preserved a traditional social organization. In these areas, at least, ethnic and regional allegiances remained vital social forces. Unfortunately for devotees of the multinational solution, however, the Indies' most populous islands, in particular Java and Sumatra, where about three-fourths of the Indies' population resided, were the same regions that had experienced the most far-reaching transformations of their social structures. Sumatra had seen large-scale estate development, the commercialization of small-scale agriculture, aggressive movements for Muslim reform (sparked in part by antipathy for the Dutch), and, in its non-Muslim highlands, mass conversion to Christianity. Though daily dress, marriage customs, and some aspects of local government preserved a traditional pattern, most of Sumatra was well on its way to becoming a post-traditional society, sufficiently well integrated into the surrounding society to aspire to membership in a more overarching political community.

Circumstances in Java were even more thoroughly detraditionalized. A formal and rather decrepit remnant of Central Java's indigenous sultanates had been preserved even after the final Dutch assault on these principalities in the Java war of 1825–30.[200] From

[199] M. C. Ricklefs, *A History of Modern Indonesia* (Bloomington: Indiana University Press, 1981), 200–21; Anthony Reid, *The Indonesian National Revolution, 1940–1950* (Hawthorn: Longman, 1974).

[200] Peter B. R. Carey 'Aspects of Javanese History in the Nineteenth Century,' *The Development of Indonesian Society: From the Coming of Islam to the Present Day*, ed. Harry Aveling (St. Lucia: University of Queensland Press, 1979), 45–105.

1830–70, however, the sultanates were used to provide cover for what was colonial Asia's most aggressive program of forced agricultural cultivation, the famous *Cultuurstelsel* or Cultivation System.[201] Though popular society preserved a strong sense of Javaneseness, the collaboration of indigenous authorities with the Dutch caused them to lose their legitimacy in the eyes of many Javanese. As a result, many rural people looked to rural religious teachers, many with millenarian ideas, as an alternative to the discredited native courts.[202] In the early 20th century these nativist movements were themselves displaced by more formally organized political associations organized along Muslim, nationalist, and communist lines. Though appeals to ethnic pride continued to have some influence, most of these modernist organizations were committed to the idea of a unitary Indonesian republic. In other words, from early on Indonesian nationalism was dedicated to transethnic ideals.

In these heartland territories, colonialism had rewrought local society so thoroughly that Dutch appeals to ethnic and regional pride fell on deaf ears. Indeed, even in more peripheral areas of the archipelago, the Dutch had undermined their case for a federationist solution earlier by drawing local leaders into a system of national education and administration. Native elites recruited into this structure were taken to the Indies capital of Batavia. As Benedict Anderson has argued,[203] government schools created a kind of functionary 'pilgrimage,' socializing people of diverse ethnic background into a common political vocabulary and sense of shared community. Though recruited into a European-run civil service, these native officials were barred from positions of real authority, no matter how good their education or how complete their mastery of European ways. They were 'natives' (*inlanders*), not Europeans, and in enforcing this distinction with arbitrary tyranny the Dutch unwittingly drove much of the native civil service into the ranks of the nationalist community. Even among the elite of the Indies' remote territories the idea of transethnic nationalism took hold, ultimately undercutting Dutch appeals to ethnicity and territory as

---

[201] Clifford Geertz, *Agricultural Involution: The Process of Ecological Change in Indonesia* (Berkeley: University of California Press, 1963); Hefner, 1990, *op. cit.*

[202] Sartono Kartodirdjo, *Protest Movements in Rural Java* (Kuala Lumpur: Oxford University Press, 1973).

[203] Benedict R. Anderson, *Imagined Communities: Reflections on the Origin and Spread of Nationalism* (London: Verso, 1983).

the basis for political federation.

Nation and culture in the Sukarno era, 1950–1965

Circumstances during the first period of Indonesian independence from 1950 to 1965 only served to reinforce hostility to the ideal of multinational federation or similar proposals for reorganizing politics along ethnic lines. The first seven years of Indonesian independence, from 1950 to 1957, were characterized by intensifying competition among political parties within a free democratic parliamentary system. During the first three years of the Republic, politics was essentially confined to a small circle of leaders in the capital city of Jakarta, and though ideologically polarized, remained relatively civil.[204] This changed dramatically, however, in 1954 as political parties geared up for the nation's first general elections in 1955. Though traditionalist Muslims and the communist party had established a rudimentary organization in the countryside prior to this time, from 1954 to 1957 all the major political parties scrambled wildly to establish chapters in rural areas.

As party organizations penetrated the countryside, they established themselves along pre-existing lines of religion, culture and class. In Java, the nationalist party (P.N.I.) and the communist party (P.K.I.) drew the bulk of their support from the ranks of poor peasants and 'Javanists,' i.e., that portion of the population which though nominally Muslim was devoted to Javanese forms of ritual, etiquette, and mysticism.[205] The two most important rivals to the nationalists and communists were the party of modernist Muslims, known as Masyumi, and the party of neotraditional Muslim clerics, known as Nahdatul Ulama. Though Masyumi enjoyed broad support in Muslim territories outside Java, on Java itself its primary support lay among urban, affluent and better educated Muslims. Nahdatul Ulama's base lay in the traditional bastions of Islam along the northern and eastern coasts of the islands. Consequently above

[204] Herbert Feith, *The Indonesian Elections of 1955*, Interim Report Series, Modern Indonesia Project (Ithaca: Cornell University, Southeast Asia Program, 1957).
[205] Clifford Geertz, *The Religion of Java* (New York: Free Press, 1960); Robert R. Jay, *Religion and Politics in Rural Central Java*, Cultural Report Series No. 12 (New Haven: Yale University, Program in Southeast Asian Studies, 1963); Robert W. Hefner, 'Islamizing Java? Religion and Politics in Rural East Java,' *The Journal of Asian Studies* 46 (1987).

all in Java, modern party politics conformed to previously established cleavages of religion and social organization.

However, the political contests of the 1950s were not just old wine in new bottles. Party factionalism supercharged animosities at the local level, providing both the ideological motivation and institutional organization needed to raise rural tensions to new heights. Anthropological accounts of village life in Java at this time captured this tension brilliantly.[206] Whereas in earlier years orthodox and 'Javanist' Muslims had argued more or less quietly over religious issues, in the mid-1950s their disagreements exploded. With the aid of communist and nationalist sympathizers, some in the Javanist community campaigned openly for the rejection of Islam and a return to 'the original religion of Java,' a putative mix of Javanism, Hinduism and Islam.[207] Reacting against this apostasy – the most serious of sins in Islam – militants in the Muslim community demanded the abolition of Javanist rituals and the establishment of an Islamic state. Muslim leaders outside Java saw the exponential growth of the communist party in Java as confirmation of their worst fears and joined with devout Javanese Muslims to demand the imposition of Muslim law. Secretly, however, many Muslims outside Java were convinced that Java was lost and that outer-island Muslims would be doomed to the tyranny of godless communism if they remained in the republic. Hence some began to ponder seceding from the republic.

The elections of 1955 provided no solution to this impasse. The 39 million votes cast were evenly split between Muslim parties on the one hand and nationalists and communists on the other.[208] These results only fuelled secessionist fires outside Java. Having established an organization in the early 1950s, Muslim militants associated with the fundamentalist Darul Islam now called openly for secession from the republic and the establishment of an Islamic state. Their forces began operations in the hinterlands of Aceh (north Sumatra), West Java, and South Sulawesi. In December 1956 they were joined by disaffected members of the military stationed in their territories; the rebellion was formalized in March 1957 with the declaration of the 'Universal Struggle Charter.'

Responding to these challenges to central authority, President

[206] Geertz, *ibid.* and Jay, *ibid.*
[207] Geertz, *op. cit.*, 112–18, and Hefner, 1987, *op. cit.*
[208] Feith, *op. cit.*

Sukarno initiated his program of 'Guided Democracy.' He outlawed the parties of his most intransigent foes, greatly reduced the influence of the parliament, and over the course of the next few years drew closer to the Indonesian communist party. The communists made impressive gains in the elections for provincial councils held in late 1957, establishing themselves as the premier party in Java. Sukarno's flirtation with the communists, however, only served to alienate the other major player on the national scene, the military. The armed forces were expanding their political influence at this time because of their pivotal role in the suppression of regional rebellions. Equally important, the military gained independent access to vital economic resources as a result of the nationalization of Dutch enterprises after 1957; agricultural estates and much of the oil industry were turned over to regional military commanders. The military leadership was united in its hostility to ethnic separatism and Islamic fundamentalism. They blamed both for the secessionist rebellions, and were determined to hold the country together at all costs.[209]

In this manner the lines were slowly drawn for the conflict which would climax in the great conflagration of 1965–66. The open parliamentary contests of the early 1950s gave way to an era of 'Guided Democracy' in which the operations of political parties were severely restricted. The national scene was dominated by a four-sided rivalry between Sukarno, the military, Muslims, and the communist party. By the early 1960s, the Indonesian Communist Party had become the largest outside the communist world. It pressed its campaign to mobilize Java's rural poor, so as to provide itself with the muscle needed for whatever showdown with Muslims and the military might lie ahead.

In late 1963 the communists launched a series of 'unilateral actions' designed to carry out the land-reform laws of 1959–60, implementation of which had been impeded by a combination of administrative lethargy and landowner resistance.[210] Wracked by hyperinflation, the deteriorating national economy made the idea of land reform all the more appealing to Java's landless poor. As communist villagers began seizing land, however, they encountered unexpectedly fierce resistance on the part of landlords, army officers, village leaders, and, most critically, Muslims. The intensity of the

[209] Ricklefs, *op. cit.*
[210] Rex Mortimer, *Indonesian Communism under Sukarno: Ideology and Politics, 1959–1965* (Ithaca: Cornell University Press, 1974).

anticommunist response, and the communist party's own inability to control the actions of its followers, ultimately led the party to call for a slowdown in the rural campaign.

The die had been cast, however, for the bloody events soon to come. On the night of September 30, 1965 there was a left-wing officers' coup in the capital of Jakarta. Junior officers launched the initiative apparently fearing that Sukarno's health was failing and that conservative generals were about to launch a pre-emptive strike. The leftist coup collapsed, but not before providing anticommunist officers with the ammunition they needed to launch joint Muslim and military assaults on the powerful communist party. Over the months that followed, several hundred thousand communists were massacred. The communist party itself was outlawed and its organization annihilated. Equally important, President Sukarno was slowly stripped of his power. By late 1966, power rested in the hands of a small group of military officers determined to establish a 'New Order' government that would pursue a new program of nation-state consolidation.

The politics of culture in 'new order' Indonesia

Though the military-dominated government that took power in the wake of the Sukarno regime quickly embarked on a pro-Western and pro-Japanese path of economic development, its political ideas still bore the distinctive imprint of Indonesian nationalism. Most of the military leadership had first come on the national scene during the independence war of 1945–49. They had witnessed firsthand Dutch efforts to organize a multinational federation, and had come to view such proposals as a sure formula for Indonesia's dissolution. Though politically conservative or moderate, these military men were still strongly committed to the idea of a unitary Indonesia. For them, the events of 1945–1965 had only confirmed their view that centralized control of military, economic, and cultural life was necessary for Indonesia's survival.

The political and cultural policies promoted by the new leadership were consistent with these views. The leaders vehemently rejected the idea of legalizing any left-wing party for fear of resuscitating what had been their most virulent enemy. Hence they retained the ban on the Indonesian Communist Party and all other mass-based leftist organizations, and kept a watchful eye on unions, universities, and the press. As a result of government repression and the declining status of international communism, most of what might be regarded as the Indonesian 'left' came by the late 1970s to rally around Western democratic ideals of constitutional law, freedom of expression, and human rights.

The events of the 1950s and the 1960s had also hardened the military's attitude to its other rival from the pre-1965 era, Islamic fundamentalism. Having relied upon Muslim militants to provide much of the organizational power for the bloodletting of 1965–66, most in government felt obliged to deal with their Muslim rivals more gently than with the Indonesian left. Nonetheless by the early 1970s Indonesia's military leaders had effectively consolidated their hold on government, and it soon became apparent that the power-sharing arrangements Muslims had expected as reward for their cooperation in the anticommunist campaign would not be forthcoming. The government declared, for example, that it had no intention of lifting its ban on Masyumi, the influential party of modernist Muslims, originally outlawed in 1958. Worse yet, in the aftermath of the 1971 elections the government compelled all Muslim parties to unite under a single party structure. Having grouped Muslims into this umbrella organization, the government then manipulated party congresses to ensure the election of a leadership sympathetic to government views. Its emasculation of Muslim (and all other) parties was completed by the imposition of draconian restrictions on political activity in the countryside. Not coincidentally, this restriction did not apply to the recently organized party of government functionaries, *Golkar*, which all government officials from the cabinet level down to village government were obliged to join. Deemed a 'non-political' or 'functional' association, *Golkar* operated freely throughout the countryside.[211]

Government efforts to undercut Muslim organizations took a new turn in the 1980s. Having already achieved behind-the-scenes influence in Muslim party congresses, in the mid-1980s the government sought to impose new ideological restrictions on all Muslim associations. It announced that it would require all such organiza-

[211] Harold Crouch, *The Army and Politics in Indonesia* (Ithaca: Cornell University Press, 1978); B. B. Hering and G. A. Willis, *The Indonesian General Election of 1973* (Brussels: Centre d'Etude du Sud-Est Asiatique et de l'Extréme Orient, 1973); Ken Ward, *The 1971 Elections in Indonesia: An East Java Case Study*, Papers on Southeast Asia No. 2 (Clayton: Monash University, Centre of Southeast Asian Studies, 1974).

tions to renounce any intent of working for the establishment of a
Muslim state and to accept the government's own charter principles,
Pancasila ('The Five Principles'), as a condition for legal association.
The government's demand caused great consternation in Muslim
circles. Though the first four principles of the *Pancasila* consisted of
innocuous declarations of nationalism, humanitarianism, social
justice, and democracy, the fifth *sila* affirms that all Indonesians must
believe in a supreme and monotheistic God. Like the other *sila*, this
principle of religious profession goes back to the original Indonesian
Constitution of 1945, a compromise arrangement formulated by the
nationalist leaders Sukarno and Muhammad Yamir.[212] Though
details of its formulation are disputed by historians (and by
Indonesian politicians), it is clear that the declaration was originally
designed to strike a balance between Muslims, on the one hand, who
wanted to make the new republic an Islamic state, and on the other,
secularly oriented nationalists, who insisted that the nation should
be nonconfessional. The compromise expressed in the fifth principle
of the *Pancasila* declares that Indonesia is a state based on religion.
But it deliberately eschews any commitment to a particular religion,
notably Islam.

In actual practice, this rather ambiguous formula has been interpreted to mean that all Indonesian citizens must adhere to a monotheistic religion officially recognized by the Indonesian government.
Since 1962 the list of such nationally sanctioned religions has
included Islam, Catholicism, Protestantism, and nominally monotheistic variants of Buddhism and Hinduism.[213] To work within
Indonesia, organizations associated with these religions must
develop standardized rituals, doctrines, and textbooks that conform
to national criteria for official religion.

By insisting that Muslim organizations acknowledge the fifth principle of the *Pancasila*, the government perpetuated an arrangement
worked out in 1945 between Muslims and secular nationalists. This
disappointed Muslims who had hoped that the post-1965 regime
would implement at least some principles of Islamic governance.
Even worse as far as Muslims were concerned, the government now
required that Muslims introduce this same troubling principle into

[212] B. J. Boland, *The Struggle of Islam in Modern Indonesia* (The Hague: Martinus
Nijhoff, 1982), 17–23.
[213] Boland, *ibid.*, and Hefner, 1987, *op. cit.*

their organizational charters. The regime's intent in all this was clear: It was determined to create a new framework for Indonesian politics, one which would eliminate once and for all both atheistic communism and Islamic fundamentalism as options for political consideration. For Muslims, acceptance of the fifth *sila* meant giving up one of their most cherished political projects, the idea of working for the establishment of an Islamic state. For many, such a project was the only legitimate rationale for their organizational existence.

Despite widespread Muslim opposition, in the end the government got its way and succeeded in pushing through acceptance of the government policy in the Muslim party congress. In doing so, the government appeared to win yet another in a series of victories in its effort to define the meaning and evolution of Indonesian political culture. Its primary rival in national elections, the Muslim-dominated P.P.P. ('Party of Unity and Development'), was thrown into crisis when its leadership caved in to the government's demand. Much of the party's mass following was so thoroughly disgusted with its leadership's capitulation that it gave up on the party entirely. The Muslim party has subsequently seen its share of the vote in national elections decline precipitously. For the near future, the legally enfranchised Muslim opposition – the last center of popularly based opposition to the 'New Order' government – seems destined to play a diminished role in national politics.

Like much social action, however, the government's policies have had unintended effects. In its campaign against atheism, communism, individualism, and other forms of Western spiritual contamination, the 'New Order' government has supported the expansion of the Department of Religion. Dominated by devout Muslims, and with bureaus in every district of the country, the Department's programs of mosque construction and religious education have heightened religious orthodoxy throughout Indonesia. In areas inhabited by the non-Muslim 12 percent of the population, the department gladly accedes to the wishes of local people and encourages the strengthening of Christian, Hindu, or Buddhist orthodoxy. Even in these cases, however, the department requires congregations to use nationally standardized religious texts.[214] In areas where the local population is Muslim, the department has self-consciously promoted Islamic orthodoxy. In Java, in particular,

---

[214] Boland, *ibid.*, and Hefner, 1987, *op. cit.*

where much of the rural population was long opposed to formalistic Islam, its programs have sought (successfully, much evidence suggests) to heighten popular commitment to Muslim orthodoxy.[215] Paradoxically, the government's campaign against *political* Islam has been accompanied by its support of programs which have decisively enhanced the *cultural* appeal of Islam among the populace. This paradox only underscores the fact that, contrary to some portrayals of the 'New Order' regime, the government is far from unitary, particularly in its attitudes toward religion. While some members of the highest echelons of government seem more inclined to Javanese mysticism than Islamic orthodoxy,[216] it is clear that others are not. At the very least, devout Muslims in the Department of Religion have achieved a greater measure of social influence than monolithic characterizations of 'New Order' government suggest.

Not coincidentally, the government's drive for cultural standardization has occurred at precisely the same time that communications, markets, and government have penetrated even the most remote areas of the countryside. From this perspective, it is clear that the spread of official religion is not simply the result of the government's control of the national media. The wildfire diffusion of national religions has also been fuelled by a crisis of tradition that has swept Indonesia's hinterland. While the government has played a key role in the creation of new forms of religiosity, the diffusion of this religious culture has been aided by the integration of once remote peoples into a national network of communications and exchange, bringing with it the collapse of traditional institutions and moralities.

Throughout Indonesia, as in much of the developing world, premodern patterns of status, investment, and authority were predicated on inward-looking and locally controlled systems of meaning and authority. It would be a mistake to reify these premodern social orders as timeless 'tradition' and overlook how deeply involved many of them were in inter-regional affairs. Nonetheless, these social

---

[215] Hefner, 1987, *op. cit.*; Pierre Labrousse and Farida Soemargono, 'De l'Islam comme Morale du Développement: L'Action des Bureaux de Propagation de la Foi (Lembaga Dakwah),' in *L'Islam en Indonésie*, eds. M. Bonneff, H. Chambert-Loir, Denys Lombard, and Christian Pelras (Paris: Association Archipel, 1985), 219–28.

[216] Donald K. Emmerson, 'The Bureaucracy in Political Context: Weakness in Strength,' *Political Power and Communications in Indonesia*, eds. Karl D. Jackson and Lucian W. Pye (Berkeley: University of California Press, 1978), 82–136; Allan A. Samson, 'Army and Islam in Indonesia,' *Pacific Affairs* 44 (1971–72), 545–65.

orders were less comprehensively linked to the culture, commerce, and politics of the archipelago than are local communities in modern Indonesia. Today government bureaucracies, markets, and the media have penetrated even the most remote territories. *Bahasa Indonesia*, the national language, is intelligible to youths all over the archipelago, and makes the government's pronouncements on culture and identity readily accessible. Markets and consumer goods have introduced new forms of consumption and lifestyles more attuned to national trends than ancestral voices. In short, a national culture is taking shape, influenced but by no means exhaustively controlled by government policies. These developments have drawn even the most remote areas of the archipelago into the cultural life of the nation, and brought forth an unfinished but emerging national culture. Though drawing on diverse indigenous elements, this culture is not derivative of pre-existing ethnic traditions. Indonesia's national culture, and the political sensibility it informs, are modern creations, and ethnically catholic ones at that.

Ethnicity and nationalism in comparative perspective

What does this all too brief discussion imply about the nature of state, nation, and ethnicity in contemporary Indonesia? More generally, what comparative insights might it provide for analysis of the benefits of a governmental system built on parallel political structures, one statewide, territorial, and political–economic, and the other nonterritorial and concerned with cultural aspects of ethnic 'nationality?'

My overview of modern Indonesian politics was designed above all to explain the historical reasons why the idea of a multinational federation would be unappealing to modern Indonesia's leaders. Among the military and its civilian allies the lessons learned in combatting regional and religious secessions have reinforced a deep commitment to the idea of a centralized state and an ethnically unspecific national culture. The same experiences have convinced the leadership that government must play an active role in guiding the development of such a civic culture.

Though different in some respects, the leadership's vision of government and culture is not unlike that of leaders in much of the developing world. While embracing liberal economic policies based on capitalist ownership and market performance, Indonesia's leaders reject the Western idea that culture, religious, political, and economic, should be left to a free market of ideas. Though there are signs that capitalist development may undermine the government's ability to control popular culture, as in some other countries of East Asia, for the moment few Indonesian leaders would question the idea that the state has both a right and an obligation to nurture a national culture.

It may not be surprising that Indonesia's elite is unsympathetic to ideas of multinational federation and cultural self-determination for ethnic populations. It is noteworthy, however, that these same ideas have had little appeal among political leaders outside government. Although since the 1950s there have been several secessionist rebellions; with the exception of small movements in the Christian Moluccas and Irian Jaya, most were not cast in the idiom of ethnic nationalism. Though sometimes resentful of Javanese dominance in government, the most important secessionist movements were committed to ideas of Islamic modernism. Their goal was the establishment of a multi-ethnic state more Muslim in its policies than would have been acceptable to the existing central government. The same orientation informs the attitudes of the Muslim opposition today. Though ethnic tensions may influence their attitudes, none of their appeals is cast in the vocabulary of ethnic nationalism.

Some observers might find that there is little in this example that speaks to the problem of state and nation in multi-ethnic situations apart from Indonesia. I would suggest, however, that aspects of the Indonesian example speak to problems of ethnic pluralism in many other developing countries.

Clearly the Renner-Bauer model makes little sense in Muslim countries where the passage from ethnically fragmented agrarian societies to modern states has been facilitated by the growth of modernist Islam. In much of the Middle East, West Africa, South Asia, and island Southeast Asia, in particular, modernist Islam has provided a culture and organization for linking communities once separated by ethnic and political boundaries. Although Islam rarely succeeds in fully domesticating ethnic passions, as conflicts in Pakistan regularly remind us, it has served to undercut the legitimacy of political organizations grounded on narrow appeals to ethnic solidarity. Where modernist Islam has become a major player on the political scene, efforts to place the interests of ethnic community above those of the Islamic *ummat* are likely to be seen by Muslims as deeply offensive. Whatever its virtues, the Renner-Bauer model is premised on a largely Western or at the very least non-Muslim understanding of the relationship between politics, ethnicity, and religion. The model sanctions ethnic culture in a way that runs headlong into Muslim understandings that religious faith, not ethnicity, is the most suitable ground for political community.

The same difficulty arises even in religiously plural contexts such as neighboring Malaysia, where only part of the population is Muslim. In Malaysia the majority Malay population is Muslim, whereas the Chinese, the second largest ethnic group, are predominantly Christian or Buddhist. Given this social landscape, one might think that the Renner-Bauer formula would receive a sympathetic hearing. Under such a plan, each ethnic community would be given control of its cultural affairs, while jurisdiction over national political and economic issues would remain with the central government. I suspect that Chinese Malaysians would find such a plan quite acceptable; indeed, it corresponds in many ways to the kind of programs some in the Sino–Malaysian community have long promoted.

Again, however, the Renner-Bauer model is not culturally neutral, and Malay Muslims would likely have a very different reaction from that of their Chinese countrymen. First of all, as they have in the past, they would object to the idea that Chinese and Malay receive equal treatment in government and education. They would insist that such a policy only reinforces Chinese domination of business and industry, since the Chinese had a head start in acquiring educational and entrepreneurial skills. Hence, the argument goes, the government must commit additional resources to Malay education and welfare.

Many in the Malay community would have an additional objection to the Renner-Bauer plan. They would point out that the model requires that they renounce what all modernist Muslims must regard as a central principle of their faith, i.e., that they work for the realization of Islamic law in this world. Islam is not a religion exclusively concerned with the afterworld, they would insist, but a model for social life in this world. In view of their decidedly non-Western vision of the interconnection of religion and politics, modernist Muslims seem likely to give Renner-Bauer a cool reception.

The Indonesian example also provides a second lesson on politics and ethnicity. Modern Indonesia's history suggests that even in a richly plural society ethnicity can be far more malleable and far less disruptive than the Renner-Bauer model implies. The model makes sense only in cases where ethnicity is such a deeply rooted social reality that proposals to give each ethnic group a measure of cultural and political self-determination would have widespread appeal. But in countries like Indonesia ethnicity does not have such a far-reaching impact. At the same time, I am convinced that neither nationalism nor ethnicity are spent historical forces. Indeed, as I have emphasized on several occasions,[217] I believe that both modernization theory and Marxism were wrong to assume that modernization would render these forms of human solidarity obsolete.

In recognizing the enduring reality of ethnicity and nationalism, however, we are obliged to explain just what they are and why they are so powerful. In this regard the Renner-Bauer model takes too much for granted. It risks reinforcing a romantic view, popular in turn of the century (and contemporary) Central Europe, that sees nationalism as a product of deeply rooted and largely non-rational ethnic ties. As Ernest Gellner observed in 1983, however, there is far 'more' ethnicity in the world than there are movements for its realization in nation-state structures. This raises the difficult question why ethnicity becomes a strong political force in some countries, demanding representation in an independent state structure, while elsewhere it quietly submits to state structures predicated on non-ethnic nationalism? Indonesian and Philippino nationalism, I suggest, is largely of the latter sort, while Vietnamese and Thai nationalism more resembles the former.

Gellner provides one answer to this critical question. For Gellner, nationalism is not a deeply historical 'primordial' phenomenon, but a peculiarly modernist one. What nationalism involves, first and foremost, is the standardization of popular cultures where previously there was little lateral integration of local communities. The primary force behind the development of nationalism, Gellner argues, is not some 'unaccountable absolute import' attributed to an ineffable communal bond, as Clifford Geertz[218] once put it, but modern economics and government. Modern economies require mobile populations with generalized and standardized skills. Quite

[217] Robert W. Hefner, 'Politics and Social Identity: Introduction,' *The Journal of Asian Studies* 46 (1987), 491–3; and Hefner 1990, *op. cit.*

[218] Geertz, *op. cit.*, 259.

contrary to the pattern seen in pre-industrial societies, the state assumes responsibility for the inculcation of these standardized skills among the populace. In doing so, it obliterates the regional idio-syncrasies of folk culture and brings into being a standardized national culture. Despite the fact the folklorists and nationalists may convince the bearers of this newly standardized culture that it has deep historical roots, Gellner observes, nationalism is a distinctly modern invention.

As my brief discussion of Indonesian nationalism was intended to indicate, I believe that Gellner is correct to emphasize the role of modern education, literacy, and the state in the development of the standardized cultures that we identify with nationalism. However, like Benedict Anderson's[219] similarly modernist account, I believe Gellner's explanation of nationalism is unjustifiably unitary. Like many other social problems, what looks like a common pheno-menon – in this instance nationalism – is in fact the product of an assortment of influences, some near universal and others particular to specific histories and cultures. The modern state, mass education, and vernacular literacy, for example, appear to be of universal importance in the genesis of modern nationalism. But the nationalism of particular countries may be shaped by less universal influences. In some countries, ethnicity has provided a solid founda-tion for nationalism and given it a character quite unlike that of non-ethnic nationalism.

Evidence from some parts of the world would support Anderson and Gellner's modernist view of nationalism. Nigeria, Indonesia, the Philippines, and Brazil are all ethnically plural societies that have managed to develop a sense of nationalism above and beyond ethnic solidarity. Their historical experience indicates that modern nationalism does not need a specific premodern ethnic foundation in order to take hold. With the exception of Brazil, none of these nation-states had a political structure in earlier times corresponding to the territories of the modern state, and the national culture they have developed seems a peculiarly modern, non-ethnic construction.

When one turns to China, Japan, France, or Poland, however, the modernist view of nationalism seems less tenable or, more precisely, incomplete. Admittedly even in these examples the modern state has played a powerful role in standardizing language, education and

---

[219] Anderson, *op. cit.*

identity within modern territorial boundaries. Even prior to the development of a modern state structure, however, these countries displayed an important measure of cultural homogeneity, evident in everything from speech, dress and etiquette to religion and government. In the cases of China and Japan, the classical state and its associated cultural institutions played a central role in premodern standardization. Having achieved an institutional existence early in history, the state used ritual, literature, tax policies and other social media to aid the diffusion of a specific ethnic identity over broad social expanses. This ethnic sensibility then became a crucial political resource in its own right, and would play a role much later in the shaping of modern nationalism. Carol Gluck's masterful study of Meiji political culture demonstrates, I believe, a similar interplay of ethnic tradition and modern invention in the making of modern Japanese nationalism.[220] In both of these examples nationalism built on and transformed deeply rooted ethnic traditions.

My point is that what we call nationalism throughout the world is not a unitary phenomenon. In different settings it builds on different cultural and organizational foundations. In areas of Africa and Asia where there were few expansive political institutions in premodern times, nationalism is often woven from a distinctly modern thread, much as Anderson and Gellner claim. Elsewhere, as in Eastern Europe or, most spectacularly, East Asia, nationalism builds on institutions of considerable historical depth. No unitary model of nationalism can capture this diversity. Nor is it likely that a single policy formula, like that of Karl Renner and Otto Bauer, will be rich enough to deal with the complex challenge of ethnicity in all multi-ethnic countries. In particular, where nationalism is grounded on non-ethnic foundations, as in Indonesia, the Renner-Bauer proposal to reinstate ethnicity as a principle of political organization (even if only for 'non-political' affairs) risks undermining the impressive progress these nations have made toward developing a cohesive and ethnically catholic national culture.

The Renner-Bauer model might appear to make more sense in cases where ethnic organizations are already well entrenched on the national scene, as in Malaysia or Sri Lanka. A proposal to separate culture and politics in the manner proposed by Karl Renner and Otto

---

[220] Carol Gluck, *Japan's Modern Myths: Ideology in the Late Meiji Period* (Princeton University Press, 1985).

Bauer might have its intended effect of defusing ethnic passions by rechannelling their energy into 'non-political' cultural affairs. Even here, however, the model may be too simple in that it artificially separates culture from politics and economics.

In countries rife with ethnic strife such as Malaysia or Sri Lanka, one of the reasons that ethnicity continues to exercise much influence is that it does more than convey a deeply held sense of social identity; it also provides the skills and social networks necessary for success in certain practical endeavors. From this perspective, the power of ethnicity (where it possesses power) lies not so much in its ineffable and unconscious 'givenness,' as primordialist accounts sometimes suggest,[221] as in its ability to provide flexibly generalized values and organization for a changing array of social enterprises. However, ethnicity may lack such flexibility, and in such situations as Indonesia, religion or non-ethnic ideologies may respond more effectively to new social opportunities. Yet where ethnicity has long mediated political and economic relations, as in Malaysia, Sri Lanka, India, and much of Central Europe, its multifunctionality may give it a remarkable and disruptive durability.

In these cases in which ethnicity plays a prominent social role, it may also demand representation in government, or even a government all its own. In a multi-ethnic context like Malaysia or Sri Lanka, the danger is that granting too much cultural autonomy to ethnic communities may only reinforce the political and economic advantages that ethnic sodalities already give their members. Rather than defusing ethnic tensions, therefore, the kind of arrangement envisioned in the Renner-Bauer model may only exacerbate them by increasing rather than diminishing perceived social inequalities. I do not want to oversimplify a complex history, but this seems to be part of what has happened in Sri Lanka, where a once vital parliamentary democracy has degenerated into brutal ethnic violence.[222] One can envision the same tragedy unfolding in a future South Africa.

In other words, in many national contexts the Renner-Bauer proposal founders on a troubling paradox. Where ethnicity is already bound up with public life, governmental arrangements that heighten

[221] Geertz, *op. cit.*
[222] Stanley J. Tambiah, 'Ethnic Fratricide in Sri Lanka: An Update' in *Ethnicities and Nations: Processes of Interethnic Relations in Latin America, Southeast Asia and the Pacific*, eds. R. Guidieri, F. Pellizzi, and S. J. Tambiah (Austin: University of Texas Press, 1988), 283–319.

its public presence and increase its practical influence may only worsen ethnic tensions by perpetuating the uneven distribution of cultural skills needed for economic success. The best way to defuse such ethnic rivalries, therefore, may not be to grant it official representation at all, or at the least to confine it to a much narrower range of 'private' concerns than Renner-Bauer envisions.

Indeed, an economically liberal course might represent the safest, though by no means unfailingly successful, policy for neutralizing ethnic passions. Such a policy would require the government to ignore the realities of race, religion and ethnicity in most of its dealings. However, the government would in turn attempt to guarantee that at least in legal principle the cultural skills needed to succeed in political and economic markets are equally accessible to all segments of the population. On occasion, the latter policy may require the government to violate its own first principle of ethnic neutrality and to intervene to compensate for certain imbalances in the distribution of educational skills. But it would strenuously insist that its corrective programs are designed to level the playing field and guarantee its primary goal, i.e., to provide ethnically neutral equality of opportunity in the marketplaces of politics and economics.

In the end, I would suggest, it is only when ethnicity and other features of ascriptive status provide no institutionally salient impediment to social mobility that their corrosive threat to the integrity of the modern state will be neutralized. It is in countries where this ideal has come closest to realization, like Brazil and the United States, that ethnicity is a less divisive social force. Conversely, it is in countries where ethnicity corresponds to enduring inequalities of opportunity that we should expect it to acquire an explosive force. It is only when ethnicity does not correlate with systematic inequality of opportunity that we can expect a transethnic national culture to take hold.

On this last point I agree with Ernest Gellner's book published in 1983. When societal arrangements result in 'social dams' that disproportionately relegate a particular ethnic or other cultural minority to a subordinate status in a society, such policies will likely give rise to movements of mass protest that in seeking to correct perceived imbalances may threaten the integrity of the social order as a whole. There may be justifiable historical reasons for these social imbalances that have nothing to do with deliberate ethnic or cultural discrimination. As long as a social dam exists, however, the perception of inequality can have a powerful destabilizing effect.

Pronounced social imbalances of this kind would have posed no problem in traditional agrarian societies where inequality was an accepted fact of life. In the modern world in which capitalist industrialization has unleashed the aspiration for equal opportunity, however, the perception of unequal social access may give rise to a deep sense of injustice among subordinate populations. Ethnic antagonism is by no means an inevitable aspect of social relations in the modern state. It can be and in many cases has been neutralized by initiating once segregated populations into an ethnically catholic national culture that provides open access to the training and skills needed for economic success. Conversely, political arrangements, however well intended, that unwittingly segregate ethnic communities, like those proposed under the Renner-Bauer model, may only reinforce the appearance of ethnic inequality and inflame the passions they are intended to quell.

Coda

Elie Kedourie and George Urban

What's wrong with 'nationalism'? What's right with the 'balance of power'? A conversation

Dependence and independence

George Urban: Your best known contribution to the scholarly debate about national identity and nationalism may be summed up in the idea that humanity does not naturally divide into nations and that groups that claim to be 'nations' do not have an automatic right to be independent states. It is enough to speak these words to see hackles rising in many quarters of our planet – and not only in places where nationalism rides high. In the Soviet Union, in particular, your claim would have a stormy passage. Your Russian, Ukrainian, Latvian, Lithuanian, Georgian, Armenian and other critics would at once tell you that the dominant theme of our time is precisely that humanity is naturally divided into nations, and that the Soviet system carried the seeds of its own destruction from its birth in 1917 because Marxism–Leninism had failed to take account of this self-evident truth.

They would quote the fate of the Ottoman Empire, of the Austro–Hungarian Monarchy, of the British Empire, Woodrow Wilson's '14 Points,' Principle VIII of the Helsinki Final Act, and much else to show that nations have both a passive right not to be denied their identity, language, and cultural aspirations, and an active right to assert these in the framework of sovereign states, even if their material interests were better served if they remained members of a comprehensive multinational state such as an empire. How would you answer them?

Elie Kedourie: The various peoples that make up the Soviet Union were, of course, there under czarist rule and under conditions of comparable unfreedom. But not many thought of themselves as 'nations' and even fewer were seen to be such by the outside world.

The idea that nations, however defined, have a right to enjoy independence and a right to a separate state is a *new* idea with complicated roots in Western political thinking. It began with the French Revolution and then spread to the Ottoman and Hapsburg Empires, and eventually to all parts of the world.

Of the two great absurdities of our time – Marxism and nationalism – nationalism is, to be sure, the more attractive absurdity: yet, it *is* an absurdity and a dangerous one at that. Why do I say that?

There is nothing in human nature or in history to suggest that, because you are a Georgian or an Uzbek, you should risk life and limb, going to the very brink of extinction, in order to enjoy living in an independent state. When you look at the history of some of the new independent states or groups who advocate independence, you will find that in the past these groups were not aware of the need to have political independence, and that those that were independent at one time or another had the kind of independence that did not give them prosperity, or freedom, or anything else that makes life worth living. Today, the Lithuanians, Latvians, Estonians, Moldavians, Georgians, Armenians all want to be 'independent states.' But if they were to gain independence they would have to take on board the perils of conducting an independent foreign policy, assume the financial burdens of armed forces, and expect to be entangled in quarrels with their neighbors.

Moreover, it is anybody's guess whether these independent countries would survive for any length of time. The dependence of Tadzhiks and Uzbeks and Azeris on the central rule of Moscow is not due to Soviet power as such but to certain historical and geographical conditions, notably to the expansionism of the Grand Duchy of Moscow which swelled into an increasingly powerful Russia under the czars and swallowed up its weak neighbors. If the Soviet type of justification for Russian rule over these minority republics were to disappear – either because the Soviet system underwent thorough reform or because secessionist movements forced disintegration on the Union – a very powerful Russia would still remain at the heart of the Euro–Asian land mass, and it is more than likely that it would continue to make its power felt among its neighbors. 'National independence' for Armenians and Ukrainians would then prove to be an illusion.

Urban: International life, you suspect, is played out in a vast magnetic field, with one or two strong magnets exerting their influence on a large number of weak floaters. The precise quality of these magnets is irrelevant – it is their size that matters. The United States is, on this showing, one big magnet which tolerates no random behavior in Nicaragua or Panama, while the Soviet magnet is equally unforgiving *vis-à-vis* Lithuania or Azerbaijan. Yet all our declarations from the Atlantic Charter (1944) to the Helsinki Final Act (1975) run counter to these facts of history, if that is what they are. They renounce the notion of 'spheres of influence' and underline our support of self-determination and national independence. Are we caught in a dilemma to which there can be no solution?

Kedourie: Yes, we are. Nothing can erase the fact that Estonia, with a population of about one million, has to go on living side by side with Russia, counting 150 million; or that Eire is a neighbor of a much more powerful Britain. That does not make the dependence of small nations on large ones any more or less moral; but it is a fact of history we cannot ignore.

Urban: But you would surely agree that the current leaders of small nations have more than a little justice on their side when they accuse us of rank cynicism – seeing that we pick up their causes only when it suits our book, and not when justice and equity so demand? For example, the Baltic nations have a well-recognized right to secede from the Soviet Union, both on the strength of the Soviet Constitution and Principle VIII of the Helsinki Agreement. Yet we balance their claims to liberty on the scales of power-politics – or 'world stability,' as we like to call it in our Sunday sermons – ignoring our numerous declarations about self-determination. You will understand that, as one who has spent 30 years of his life talking to Soviet-dominated Eastern Europe about the Western commitment to national liberty, I am sensitive to charges of hypocrisy.

Kedourie: It would be absurd if I tried to judge which of the groups now constituting the Soviet Union have a claim to consider themselves 'nations' and which have not. Let me just say that government by foreigners has been the rule rather than the exception in world history, and the European – in this case the Russian – domination of parts of Asia is far from constituting a novelty. I am ready to concede that in the case of European peoples, such as the Baltic peoples and the Ukrainians, the idea of nationhood and independence has, over the last 200 years, been so powerfully transmitted from Western Europe that it has to be seriously reckoned with as a factor affecting the cohesion of the Soviet Empire and the world balance of power. I am not saying this is a bad thing . . . so long as national liberation is coterminous with the liberation of the individual and constitutional government.

But, as far as the Asian populations of the Soviet Union are concerned, it is far from obvious why they, too, should think that 'nationhood' and a national state will best promote their interests. Nation-states are not out of character with European history. They are rather an extension of the condition which, since the disappearance of the Roman Empire in the West, was customarily 'Europe,' with its feudal divisions, free cities, sovereign republics, and monarchies. But the typical Asian polity is the Chinese Empire, or the Empire of the Moguls, or the Ottoman Empire – large and varied areas administered by a *nomenklatura*, controlled by a single center. Nationalism and the idea of a sovereign nation-state is not something indigenous to Asia, nor is it an irresistible tendency of the human spirit, but rather an importation from Europe which does not fit. Almost any strand of Asian (and African) nationalism, considered as a program of action or a scheme of thought, suffers from artificiality, from being a laborious attempt to introduce outlandish standards and alien categories.

Urban: On a high level of historical generalization, this may well be the case. But don't the practical requirements of our time call for a different approach? It was 'only yesterday' that we saw the tyrannical Soviet Empire as the principal danger to the rest of the world, and we looked upon anything that might weaken that centralized tyranny – especially the spread of nationalism in the non-Russian parts of the empire – as deserving support. It was, we said, in the universal interests of freedom that we should recognize and promote these nationalisms. The risk that they might eventually get out of hand and follow the Mazzini- or Mickiewicz-type of 19th-century European nationalisms struck us as much smaller than the risk of allowing the Soviet system to continue.

Now that the Soviet Empire seems to be in danger of falling apart, we are increasingly confronted with two related and, in my view, surprising, arguments. Firstly, that almost any order is better than no order; and, secondly, that nation-states, especially 'new' ones, are not to be encouraged. Those who take these lines of reasoning seem to fear instability much more than they fear the absence of individual and national freedoms. In the nuclear age, I can understand some of our leaders' concern for world stability. But if 'natural justice' had any place in international affairs I would argue that those who now advocate the preservation of the Soviet state as a pillar of international stability have very short memories. They seem to forget that, until Gorbachev's arrival, the Soviet leaders never hesitated to subvert the French and British empires, undeterred by any thought that world disorder might follow. Indeed, it was world disorder, and a 'socialist' order to be built on its ruins, that they openly and proudly promoted.

Kedourie: If you want to stick to practical politics, I would say that encouraging nationalist movements in the Soviet Union is giving hostages to fortune; you may be starting something you cannot control. The rise of national forces and states is not necessarily benign. Take, for example, the fallout after the collapse of the Habsburg Empire. In 1918–19 there was a wave of enthusiasm for doing away with Austria–Hungary on the principle of self-determination as formulated in President Woodrow Wilson's '14 Points.' The Ottoman Empire too fell apart under comparable circumstances. But what resulted was *not* a group of states free from misrule, living side by side with each other as so many symbols of liberty – but a patchwork quilt of weak states which promoted, with the honorable exception of Czechoslovakia, neither individual freedom at home nor moderation abroad, and which were too feeble to resist either Hitler's or Stalin's aggression. The consequences of the breakup were much worse than the illnesses they were designed to cure.

In any case, we are quite powerless, so far as the Soviet Union is concerned, to prevent or to hasten its breakup. Support for Gorbachev – which seems to be current Western policy – may not ensure his survival; and if he does survive, it does not follow that he would be able or willing to continue the policies which have attracted support from Western governments. Nor is it the case that these policies will infallibly turn to Western advantage.

The right to self-determination?

Urban: But wouldn't you say that the wrongs committed by the Soviet system and the Soviet Empire are so much greater than anything we can associate with Austria–Hungary, or the Ottoman Empire, that to upset the kind of stability represented by the Soviet system is worth taking a few risks for, even the risk of unleashing a number of unguided nationalisms? None of us can really believe that another Mongol invasion of Europe is imminent and that the massed ranks of the Russian people are our best form of defense . . .

Kedourie: Well, what are the great wrongs the Soviet system expresses? They are Moscow's centralized despotism and the communist ideology – the two being really the same thing. These are, of course, great evils; and it was right that we should have opposed them. But what we can now observe is that these evils have been brought down by the weight of their own absurdity, and they no longer threaten us, for the time being at any rate.

Urban: Are you certain that they *have* indeed been brought down?

Kedourie: I feel that is not an unfair inference seeing the speed with which the system is unravelling. Whatever the results of Moscow's political infighting may be, I take it as read that the Kremlin is now unable to know, much less to control, what goes on in Turkmenistan or Kirghizia. Mackenzie Wallace, that eagle-eyed, late-19th-century observer of Russia, tells us in his book *Russia* (1877) that one day he appeared at a ferry station on the Volga hoping to cross the river as indicated in his timetable. But as no ferry appeared, he asked the local ferry-master why the delay. 'It says here that the boat should be leaving by now,' he told the official, brandishing his timetable. The Russian laughed at this Westerner's pitiful innocence. 'The more fool you, if you believe what is printed,' he said. I would say this applies to most things Soviet and Russian. *On paper*, Moscow may still be in control of its empire, but in reality it is no longer. Our own policies will, therefore, have to be reordered accordingly.

Urban: I am not persuaded that national ambitions in East/Central Europe, or in Asia, would respond to this argument. National self-determination (Principle VIII of the Helsinki Final Act) grows naturally out of the principle of individual human rights and fundamental freedoms (Principle VII). We can observe this in the history of the 1848 revolutions, when individual human rights and national rights were two sides of the same coin. 1848 is surely not lost on Asian nationalists; and even East and Central Europeans, who had their fingers severely burnt after the collapse of Austria–Hungary are, again, harking back to an age when it was thought that individual freedom is meaningless unless free men have the right to create free associations – that is to say, sovereign and independent nation-states.

My pessimistic reading of history, however, moves me to go along with your reasoning part of the way and to ask whether the African and Asian peoples aren't destined to go through the same miserable cycle as the Europeans have done, and, indeed, whether some of the East and Central European nations aren't themselves destined to repeat it before merging their identity, under the hammer-blows of the next round of troubles, in a broad European framework?

Kedourie: The national 'renewal' movements of the 19th century, such as Mazzini's 'Young Italy,' did indeed originally equate the idea of individual emancipation with national freedom. It was widely believed in 1848 that the two were indistinguishable, and that free nations composed of free individuals would create a free and equitable international order. But soon it was discovered that this was an illusion. The two were highly distinguishable! First, the states raised on the concept of 'the nation' embraced various forms of national Messianism and became internally oppressive and intolerant in their foreign policies. Second, it is impossible to redraw the map of the world in a way that would give us ethnically homogeneous states. This is particularly obvious in Central and Eastern Europe, where large pockets of Serbs live on Croatian territory, Hungarians in Slovakia and Romania, and so on. The tensions between the ideological obsessions of nationalism and what was politically and geographically possible under the Ottoman and Habsburg empires led to the destruction of our civilization in two World Wars.

There is now a new factor since the Soviet Union, which is a mere 73 years old, is itself the outcome of an ideological obsession. It tried to impose an ideological vision on the peoples it inherited from the wreckage of the Czarist Empire. It instituted a harsh and very oppressive regime; and I can well understand that, reacting to this oppression, the peoples under Soviet rule now tell us that they cannot be sure of their freedom unless they remove themselves from Moscow's central control and become 'independent nations.' This is a natural reaction, but I don't think it is a wise one. I am reminded of Lord Acton's praise of the Austro–Hungarian Empire. He saw its great virtue in that a large number of nationalities managed to live in it peacefully together. 'A state which is incompetent to satisfy different races condemns itself,' Lord Acton wrote in his essay on 'Nationality.' The tolerance of other races and religions, he said, was the absolute criterion of civilized politics; and so it is.

Urban: But, in the 1990s, how do you explain to a restive Lithuanian or Ukrainian that his now-burgeoning human rights should not include the right to sport his own national flag, the right not to be drafted into a foreign army, the right to control his own economy, the right to have his own national legislation and ultimately the right to full national independence? Isn't it asking too much of human nature to expect these people to heed, in the heady hour of their liberation, 'the lessons of history' or any other lessons?

Kedourie: Collective human rights do not automatically follow from the human rights of the individual – at least not to the extent that individual rights collectively asserted must lead to demands for national rights and nation-states. For an example: the United States is composed of a great mixture of peoples from all corners of the earth, and so long as one is an American citizen, one has certain constitutional rights and safeguards; but is anybody saying that one has to establish an 'independent Republic of Nebraska' in order to safeguard the rights of Nebraskans?

Urban: Margaret Thatcher, the former British Prime Minister, gave a similar reply to a Soviet questioner during a recent BBC 'phone-in' from Moscow. She was asked (by, I recall, a Georgian) whether she supported the rights of minority nations to become independent nations as part of *glasnost*, and *perestroika*. She responded cautiously by pointing to the U.S. where people of different backgrounds, language, and culture live together in peace and prosperity. I don't think her questioner was persuaded. To compare the American 'melting-pot' with the Soviet Empire or anything occurring in Central and Eastern Europe strikes me as difficult to sustain. In any case, I can, under certain conditions, well imagine a large American state such as California developing a 'Californian identity' and a Californian sense of nationhood, based on Ernest Renan's principle that a nation exists when so many people express the view that, by solidarity, sentiment, and 'a plebiscite of every day,' they are a nation.

Kedourie: Renan's analogy is striking. Two points, however, must be made. If a nation rests on a daily plebiscite, so then does the family, and the village community, and friendship, collegiality, social ties in general. So the image, suggestive as it may seem, tells us very little specifically about the nation. In the second place, a nation is not a state, and if we are talking about states, as we surely are here, then a plebiscite cannot possibly be the foundation or the organizing idea of a state. A plebiscite is a vote taken on a particular day. There is no inherent reason why the vote should not be repeated at intervals – but to ground a state on a vote which can change from time to time is manifestly impractical, indeed absurd. A plebiscite, again, can give no guidance about the organization of government, about the constitution, about the judiciary, about the administration. In all of these matters detail is of the essence, the kind of detail with which plebiscites cannot possibly deal.

Of culture and state power

Urban: You show in your book *Nationalism* (1960), much more persuasively than I have just done (apropos of the Helsinki Final Act), how the idea of human rights for the individual can turn into demands for national rights – how Kant's idea of individual self-determination became, in the hands of Fichte, a quest for national self-determination and national fanaticism. That you have been criticized for involving Kant in the pedigree of fanatical nationalism does not concern us here; but your emphasis on the great wrong that national self-assertion can inflict on the world (and has, we must concede, frequently inflicted on it) continues to worry me. Need we throw out the baby with the bathwater?

In a similar discussion some years ago, Hugh Seton-Watson made a sharp distinction between national consciousness, which he supported, and nationalism, which he did not:

If you say that Hitler was derived from the German national idea of the 19th century, Fichte for example, this is true up to a point. What you cannot say is that the national aspirations of Germans for unity, as they were worked out at the beginning of the 19th century under the first impact of Herder's wide influence, could only have ended in Hitler. They could have ended in many different ways. National consciousness does not *have* to lead to nationalist movements and conflict. National consciousness *may* lead to nationalism and conflict if it is frustrated. But even nationalist conflicts can end up as a beneficent force, provided that there is a statesmanship, wisdom and moderation.

It would, therefore, be very wrong to argue as follows: 'Nationalism is a destructive force, therefore let's suppress national consciousness.' That is what many governments have tried to do; they justify their repression of the national consciousness of their subjects on the grounds that they themselves stand for a higher civilization. Could there be anything wrong, they argue, in freeing these recalcitrant minorities from the beastly distemper of nationalism? Well, if history teaches us anything it is this, that the attempt to repress national consciousness is almost always self-defeating.[223]

I don't suppose you would disagree with that.

Kedourie: No, I would not, but I would qualify it further. The free expression of national consciousness can be most beneficial, and if (speaking in the Soviet context) it means the gradual retreat of Moscow's centralized despotism – who would shed tears for that? But, trying to look into the future, I cannot suppress a certain unease that history might *mutatis mutandis* repeat itself. Just as 1848 resulted, in the long run, in the disasters of unbridled nationalisms and two World Wars, so the liberating openings in the present might, unless a great deal of wisdom prevails, lead to highly undesirable consequences. In your conversation with Lord Dacre (Hugh Trevor-Roper)[224] we heard him repeatedly say that he is not afraid of German unification because the Germans have become democrats. He may be right, and I very much hope he is. But extrapolations from present trends are speculative. What we know from the historical evidence is that the kind of nationalist movements we can now see asserting themselves on the ruins of the Soviet Empire did lead, in their earlier incarnation between 1848 and 1945, to extremism, tyranny, and war.

You are familiar with L. B. Namier's work on the subject:

> With 1848 starts the German bid for power, for European pre-dominance, for world dominion: the national movement was the common denominator of the German revolution in 1848, and a mighty Germany, fit to give the law to other nations, its foremost aim. *Einheit, Freiheit und Macht* (Unity, Freedom and Power) was the slogan, with the emphasis on the first and third concepts.[225]

Namier called 1848 'the revolution of the intellectuals.' An ideological style of politics goes with intellectuals or intellectuals *manqués*. Hitler, I suppose, was one such intellectual *manqué*.

Urban: Let me try to approach the relationship between culture and national existence from a different angle. You show in your scholarly work that until the French Revolution the idea of 'nation' either did not exist or had wholly different connotations from the ones it has acquired in the last two centuries. At the University of Paris, you

[223] Hugh Seton-Watson and George R. Urban, 'The Fall of Multinational Empires in our Time' in *Communist Reformation*, ed. G.R. Urban (1979), 276–7.

[224] Hugh Trevor-Roper and George Urban, 'Aftermaths of Empire,' *Encounter*, December 1989.

[225] L.B. Namier, '1848: Seed-Plot of History,' *Avenues of History* (1952), 53.

remind us, the students were divided into four 'nations' – France, Picardy, Normandy, and Germany. The French 'nation' included the Italians and Spaniards; the German 'nation' were the English as well as the Germans living on the territory of Germany. Religions, empires, and dynasties, you tell us, were the centers of human allegiance and the springs of power.

Would you not agree, though, that so much of European culture – especially in the 'young' or reborn nations of Italy, Germany, Poland, Hungary – is centered on the idea of national rejuvenation that we would be losing something essential to our European identity if we disallowed its worth merely because it is 'tarred with the brush of nationalism?' Wouldn't we have to exclude, or elaborately 'explain,' some of the finest poetry and prose of the 19th century, to say nothing about the visual arts and music?

Kedourie: Far be it from me to disallow the value of 19th-century culture in any of its significant aspects. But we must distinguish between the cultural and the political, and this is a distinction that runs against the doctrine of nationalism which asserts that the two are inextricably mixed: if you have no political independence, you cannot have a national culture. This is absurd. Groups of people of every kind have and always have had their national culture without being politically sovereign. The idea that a country which rules another, or a group of people who rule another, should impose their language and mores on the ruled is a very recent development. It was certainly not the case in the Ottoman or the Habsburg empires; nor was it true in India under British rule. National culture can certainly exist in the absence of national independence – think of Belgium, or of Switzerland.

Urban: This may be true if a state grants all its citizens full cultural liberty as do the countries you mention – although Quebec's apparent quest for independence seems to weaken your case. But where this does not exist, it is difficult to see how the aspiration to cultural freedom can stop short of a demand for national liberation and ultimately independence. The cultural and linguistic russification of the Baltic states is one good example; the fate of the Hungarian minority under Ceausescu's (and now even Iliescu's) Romania is another.

Where a people's right to speak and be educated in its own language is denied, and its history, literature, and traditions are distorted to suit the ruling nation's *amour propre*, doesn't the cry not

only for cultural freedom but also for national independence rise
spontaneously (if irrationally) from the souls of the underprivileged
minority-nations? Can we, in the 1990s, expect Estonians or
Georgians to restrict their national aspirations to an Ottoman-style
millet system? Can we tell them with any hope of success to learn
from the dismemberment of the Austro–Hungarian Monarchy,
when their daily experience tells them that only by blowing the
Soviet Empire sky high can they hope to make a fresh start in their
own history?

Kedourie: The last thing I want to do is make excuses for
russification or romanianization. Where the majority-nation
indulges in such excesses it can, indeed, expect nothing but robust
resistance leading to demands for secession and independence. The
Soviet state must reform itself from the ground up, and so must
Romania. But arguments for separatism are, I insist, poorly based if
they are based on culture. Within the German-speaking world, for
example, there are vast differences between the culture of Bavaria,
the Rhineland, and Prussia. But should the unification of Germany of
1871 be reversed because these areas might qualify, on cultural
grounds, for separate statehood?

Or should the Bretons – or Provençals or Corsicans – qualify for
independent statehood because their culture and language are
different from French culture and language? Where does this argument end? I remember Sir Isaiah Berlin telling me many years ago
that in 1919, at the height of the agitation for 'self-determination,'
residents of a block of flats on Nevsky Prospekt in Petrograd
petitioned the authorities for self-determination. And why not? It is
absurd, but logical.

Urban: To deviate somewhat from the line of my own questioning,
there appears to be a 'law' of history which says: 'The greater your
self-determination the worse your oppressiveness.' No sooner did
the Lithuanians, in March 1990, declare their independence than
they decided to deny self-determination to the Poles in their midst.
The Abkhazians fared no better at the hands of the Georgians – to
say nothing about the fortunes of the Karabakh Armenian minority
in the republic of Azerbaijan. And, before we unduly idealize the
permissiveness of the Austro–Hungarian Monarchy, we might also
remember that Hungary's emancipation from Austrian tutelage in
1867 did not induce Budapest to pursue a liberal nationalities' policy
vis-à-vis Slovaks, Romanians, and Croats.

It ill becomes communist and 'socialist' critics to castigate the old Hungarian dual-state for its reactionary policies. It was none other than Friedrich Engels who derided, in 1848–49, the claims of the small Slavic races, and of the Romanians (a 'decayed nation') to independent statehood. He dismissed the Slovaks as 'a "nation" with absolutely no historical existence,' and doubted whether the South Slavs could 'botch together a powerful independent and viable nation out of these tattered rags? . . . If the 'eight million Slavs' had to allow the four million Magyars to impose their yoke on them for eight centuries this alone is sufficient proof that the few Magyars had more vitality and energy than the many Slavs.'[226]

Aren't you, by the logic of your argument, driven to embrace both the idea of an old-fashioned liberal imperialism as the smaller evil, *and* Marx's and Engels' presumption that 'the historic nations' enjoy more extensive rights than the smaller fry? In which case, wouldn't your strictures on nationalism indirectly assist the survival of the tyrannical Soviet Empire?

Kedourie: Not at all. What I am saying is that *small-nationhood* when it becomes small-statehood harbors certain great dangers of its own which the world can ill afford. When Woodrow Wilson's '14 Points' were translated into reality – to the extent that they were – in 1919, European instability ensued because the newly created states were too small to be defensible. It didn't really matter whether they had to face the expansionism of a *Nazi* Germany or a *Bolshevik* Russia – what mattered was that they were small states bordering on a mighty Germany and a mighty Russia. A great power like Russia will always be a source of danger to its small neighbors and so might an enlarged Germany, no matter how liberal and democratic its domestic institutions may be. Occasions will always arise when a big power bordering on an insignificant power will be tempted to dominate the smaller power. Thus, though the centralized Soviet state and its command economy does hide much inefficiency, disorder and corruption, it still wields very great power. It commands a very large and powerful army and a vast security network. We have seen in the Baltic republics with what unscrupulous brutality such power can be used. There have also been recent indications that in spite of the enormous upheavals of 1989 it may not be easy for East European countries to rid themselves of Soviet occupation troops.

[226] Friedrich Engels, *Neue Rheinische Zeitung*, Cologne (13 January, 15 February 1849).

Urban: You say: 'no matter how liberal and democratic its domestic institutions may be.' Doesn't this rather run counter to what we in the West have been saying since World War II about the foreign policy inclinations of dictatorships and democracies – namely, that governments which are aggressive and coercive *vis-à-vis* their own kinsmen are likely to be even more aggressive *vis-à-vis* foreign nations, and that, conversely, governments based on liberal-democratic principles are much less likely to be internationally aggressive? It was Vaclav Havel, the then newly elected Czecho-slovak President, who said in November 1989 that a unified Germany of 80 million people worried him no more than the Federal Republic of 60 million, so long as an enlarged Germany remained free and democratic.

Kedourie: First, that a country is liberal and democratic today is no guarantee that it will be so in succeeding generations. In the second place, Germany as a state is a big, productive, and vibrant entity. Because it weighs so much in the world balance of power it is bound to act as a magnet to others and to offer the holders of power in Bonn or Berlin – whoever they may be – the temptation to use that power. We need not assume that they would use it to barbaric ends as the Nazis did. We need not assume anything of the kind, but, speaking from the historical experience, we can assume that at some point Germany might decide that one mishap in a neighboring state might lead to another mishap in another and then to a third, until Germany would feel compelled to make some of these neighboring countries its satellites – if only to put a *cordon sanitaire* between itself and its large rival in the East. This is how great powers behave and how the balance of power is traditionally preserved.

Are wars inevitable?

Urban: But don't our incessant warnings about Germany, 45 years after the War, boil down to a form of racism – 'Once-a-German-always-a-German?' Some of our politicians talk as though there were some genetic flaw in the German national character (if, indeed, there is such a thing). I find this ignorant and insulting. Imagine the scandal if they said half as much about Negroes or about Jews.

Kedourie: No, I am certainly not implying that the Germans spring from corrupt seed or anything of the sort. What I'm saying is what reason should dictate to those of us who have any acquaintance with history. Here we have a big state and a highly energetic and gifted people placed in the middle of Europe – a state of this kind is in a position to throw its weight about. All I'm assuming is that the Germans, like the rest of us, are not angels – if they have great power, they will make use of it.

But to return to the balance of power; it seems to me the height of naiveté to assume, as the peacemakers of 1919 assumed, that one can establish an independent Polish state between Germany and Bolshevik Russia and exempt such a Poland from the inevitably conflicting interests of these two big states. It took only 20 years for German and Russian interests to reassert themselves and to destroy the independence of Poland. Without in any way assuming the return of a Stalin in Russia or a Hitler in Germany, I am bound to say that there will always be a Berlin and a Moscow, that these capitals are going to have foreign policy interests which may in some cases make them allies, and antagonists in others. In either case, Poland would be suspended between them, which is an uncomfortable and perilous position for any country to be in. It was, at best, an idealistic aberration, at worst the *hubris* of victory, that induced in 1919 the American, French, and British peacemakers to believe that Poland could survive the clash of great-power interests, or that the dismemberment of Hungary and the establishment of racially heterogeneous successor states could lead to lasting peace.

Urban: But isn't this rather picking up the language of power politics of an antiquated kind which those born after 1945 in Western Europe, in the U.S., and also the men in Mr. Gorbachev's leadership, have mercifully forgotten or deliberately turned their backs on? I find it most encouraging that so many Frenchmen, Germans, and Italians should think it inconceivable that a fratricidal war could once again erupt in Europe for whatever reason. And they think so, in my reading, not merely because there is a 'European Community,' nor merely because the nuclear factor would make any such war utterly suicidal, but because the spirit of our time – that indefinable *Zeitgeist* which Mikhail Gorbachev and Eduard Shevardnadze have captured so well – has ruled out war as a continuation of politics 'by other means.' Then-Foreign Minister Shevardnadze's words to the 28th Soviet Party Congress in July 1990 offer good evidence of how far the Gorbachev leadership had ceased to indulge in superpower posturing:

If we continue as we did before, spending a quarter of our budget on military expenditure, we shall ruin our country. We will then need no defense, just as a ruined country and an impoverished people do not need an army. There is no sense in protecting a system which has led us to economic and social ruin.

That political dinosaurs such as ex-Thatcher minister Nicholas Ridley on the fringes of Europe, and others on the fringes of Soviet political and military life, still cling to the notions and the vocabulary of yesterday's conflicts strikes me as requiring a psychological explanation.

Kedourie: These are fine sentiments, and let us hope that they may shape our future. But as an historian who has to consider the past, which is the only evidence he has, I must warn against mistaking the present peaceable pictures for the whole of reality. I am ready to agree that to your young Italian, or young German, it is inconceivable today that he should bear arms against his neighbor; but if you think of the mood of the people when they gather together and are addressed, not as individuals but as members of a crowd, your optimism will need correction. The behavior of a football mob is only the mildest manifestation of the irrationality of mass sentiment, although the mindless behavior of many English soccer supporters can hardly be described as mild.

Mass enthusiasms can grip any population. I can well understand why people demonstrated in East Berlin, in Leipzig, in Prague and Bucharest against wicked rulers; and it is admirable that, with the exception of Romania, they voiced their anger without bloodshed. But this can change with lightning speed. The Soviet reforms have unleashed passions not only against Moscow and its henchmen – they have also set Azeris against Armenians, Uzbeks against the Kirghiz, Ukrainians against Russians, with all the unabated intensity of earlier feuds. And if you remember the fate of the Armenians at the hands of the Turks in 1915 and a whole series of other genocidal attacks upon one racial group by another (not least in the Muslim parts of the world), then the virtue of national self-determination leading to separate statehood must be seriously questioned.

Urban: But what do you infer from these deplorable examples – that national aspirations should not be given their head in the age of human rights and self-determination?

Kedourie: All I am saying is that if a nation is to become a state, it has to consider the risks of statehood. 'Absolute independence' or total subjection to the rule of a centralized despotism are not the sole alternatives, moreover there can and should be a balance of power between states, because that is our only fully tested safeguard against international disorder.

Now, the balance of power is something for *states* to establish, not nations, because states alone have sovereignty. Once a state makes it clear which of its interests are negotiable in the pursuit of international stability and which of its interests are indispensable to its character and survival, a balance of power can be struck with other states making analogous stipulations. This is how international order was tolerably maintained up to 1914.

The small nations which are not states – your Armenians and Moldavians – will have to look very carefully at the perils of independent statehood and find ways and means of living peacefully together in some larger, confederative democratic state, perhaps on the model of the Habsburg Monarchy. This may not fully satisfy nationalist demands; but it might create, in Central Europe for example, a secure haven for several small nations which would, in the absence of such a structure, go on fighting one another, succumbing again and again to the power and influence of their mighty neighbors both in the East and the West. That a grouping of this kind is already under discussion, involving Yugoslavia, Austria, and Italy as well, is a hopeful sign for the future.

Urban: Kuwait – which is neither a separate nation nor of sufficient size to qualify for independent statehood – may have to be satisfied, on your showing, with a subordinate role assigned to it by a powerful Iraq. I am, of course, fairly certain you would not want to subscribe to this proposition, not least because Iraq is a highly undemocratic state which may treat the Kuwaitis no better than it has treated the Kurds. But that is the direction in which I'm led by your reasoning.

Earlier in this conversation (and in several of your books) you pointed out that the nation-state and even the concept of nationhood are alien imports to Asia: '. . . the typical Asian polity is the Chinese Empire, or the Empire of the Moguls, or the Ottoman Empire – large and varied areas administered by a nomenklatura controlled by a single center.' I would have thought Saddam Hussein's's Iraq, modelling itself, as it does, on the Akkadian Empire and Babylonia, would be the sort of state in which smaller peoples such as the Kuwaitis would have to be content to live in a state of dependency – if they accepted your argument.

Kedourie: Whether one likes Saddam's regime or not, it was in the cards that Kuwait and other sheikhdoms would be at the mercy of

Iraq – or of Iran – once British paramountcy disappeared. When it did, in 1971, there was much self-congratulation in Britain that it was to be replaced by a new and promising 'regional organization.' It was, or course, nothing of the kind – only a house of cards, which has now collapsed. British paramountcy, abandoned for ideological and frivolous reasons, may now be replaced by something altogether unscrupulous and barbaric. In any case, the balance of power abhors a vacuum – paramountcy there has to be . . .

Urban: You haven't answered Vaclav Havel's point that he is not worried about 80 million Germans forming a single state as long as an enlarged Germany is liberal and democratic. His words encapsulate much that we in the West have been telling the world over the last half-century.

Kedourie: The idea that war between democratic countries is unlikely is an illusion. It is, broadly speaking, the same illusion that Immanuel Kant entertained when he committed himself to the thought in his *Perpetual Peace* (1795) that wars would be ruled out if every state were a republic and these republics united in a universal 'league of nations.' In a world of scarcity there must always arise a conflict of interests between two parties, or two peoples, or two states which will covet the same possessions or advantages for (as they see it) the best possible reasons. You will recall Rousseau's explanation that tyranny came into the world when the first man put a fence around his house. If we accept that, as we should, then it is not far-fetched to say that there is a kind of 'original sin' in the very existence of states. Havel is, therefore, in error. Democratic institutions in themselves guarantee no peace. Strong armies and the determination to use them can. The Peloponnesian War was unleashed by a famous democracy . . .

Urban: But not against another democracy . . .

Kedourie: No, but the essential point is that Athens' democratic institutions did not protect the Athenians against the lure of power, loot, and profit. Nor did the democratic institutions of the U.S. prevent civil war between the North and South, nor (to demolish another favorite hypothesis while we are at it) did 'highly developed economic relations' and very similar stages of industrial development prevent Germany and Great Britain from going to war in 1914. Nor is it true that 'shared civilizations' prevent wars. Germany, France, Italy and Britain share a civilization and yet they have been at one another's throats twice this century. So I come back to my contention that only a balance of power and one's publicly proclaimed readiness to defend oneself with arms in hand can prevent war.

Urban: It is a bleak picture which few of my young friends in this country or on the Continent would willingly accept. The call for constant suspicion – for military preparedness, for cultivating an enemy image – strikes them as anachronistic and wicked. Should they go along with your pessimistic reading of history at a time when Europe is being reborn and under luckier stars than marked earlier renewals?

Kedourie: None of us can argue with the facts of history. Wars, like human illnesses, happen; often we don't know why a particular war happened; all we know is that it did happen, and we suspect that it is in the human condition that from time to time wars should engulf us. We can deplore them, but we can't ban them.

Urban: But doesn't your fatalistic analysis almost *invite* war, for might it not induce a peace-loving citizen to say: 'If wars are inevitable, I'd better get in my blow first?'

Kedourie: It does not, absolutely not, have to lead to such a conclusion.

Urban: But can we afford to ventilate opinions about the inevitability of war in the presence of nuclear weapons?

Kedourie: We have had nuclear arms on our territories since Hiroshima, but that has not prevented destructive conventional wars from being unleashed in Korea, Vietnam, the Lebanon, and between Iraq and Iran. Under the umbrella of the nuclear balance of terror, peoples and governments have found it possible and worthwhile to go to war. I cannot quite understand why a similar thing happening in Europe should be ruled out. A conventional war in the shadow of nuclear weapons could occur in Europe.

Urban: But don't you think that, even in Europe, nuclear arms would have to be used if one of the belligerents had its back against the wall and had no other means of saving itself? And wouldn't that mean suicide for us all?

Kedourie: Once a war has started, no contingency can be wholly excluded, not even the use of nuclear weapons in Europe. My point is that we should not be fooled by our own rhetoric. It is simply not the case that the internal organization of a state is, or ever has been, a guarantee against war. The Soviet Union may be more warlike or less warlike under an eventual multiparty system. So might Germany; so might any state.

Urban: The young in Europe will, in my experience, just not accept any idea that a balance of power policy is the ultimate wisdom of human affairs . . . that, unless you have a gun permanently pointed at you, there can be no decency and peace among states and nations. They feel, with Immanuel Kant, that a balance of power policy is 'the immoral sport of sovereigns.' Surely, this is a view worthy of respect . . .

Kedourie: Look: Here we are, peaceably talking in my room in All Souls College in Oxford; but our ability to do so very much depends on the rule of law in the United Kingdom and a police force which prevents somebody scaling the garden wall and shooting us down. There is, in this country, a carefully structured hierarchy of authority, starting with the monarch and parliament, which everyone accepts; hence the law prevails.

But in international relations there is no such generally recognized authority. The international system is essentially still a jungle, and the law of the jungle can only be tamed if the penalties for disturbing the peace are loudly proclaimed and imposed. That is what a balance of power policy is about.

Should one forget history?

Urban: Wouldn't you agree that the world around us appears to be going in opposite directions at one and the same time? There is, first, a move to larger, supranational formations, of which the European Community is the most convincing example, fuelled by the idea that world peace, economic prosperity, and our ecological survival all militate for supranational cooperation, coordination, and eventually a single world community. Yet we are also witnessing the rebirth of fierce nationalisms and separations both in the Soviet Union and in Central and Eastern Europe. The Yugoslav state is falling apart along the old Ottoman–Habsburg demarcation line, with Slovenia and Croatia opting for independence and a 'return' to Europe. Centrifugalism in the Soviet Union is too well-known to need comment.

Are these two developments indeed going in opposite directions, or can we assume that the separatism of Estonians, Latvians, Georgians, Albanians and all the other minority peoples is motivated, not by anti-Russian or anti-Serb feeling, but by a libertarian determination to be rid of a centralized ideological tyranny?

If the latter, then your hope that disparate nationalities can peacefully coexist in a federation or confederation would strike me as well-founded. But can we say that the independence movement of the Albanians in Kosovo is rather anti-communist than anti-Serb; or that the Ukrainians would have nothing against their Russian neighbors if the Soviet Union ceased to be communist and coercive?

Kedourie: These are difficult distinctions to make. Communist domination in the Soviet Union has been represented, for the non-Russian population, by Russians as 'elder brothers;' the tyranny of the League of Yugoslav Communists has been of predominantly Serbian coloring (even though Tito himself was half-Croatian). Resistance to one also meant, and still means, hostility to the other. But this coincidence of nationality with oppression should not mean the end of peaceful co-existence between nations of unequal size and different religions and traditions. A confederative structure based on representative government is desirable and perhaps possible once the ideological messianism of communism and fascism is removed from the mixture. Sooner or later the passions of the present nationalistic revivals may become spent, and the desire for civic peace and prosperity may become paramount. And these, in the modern world, cannot be had without wide-ranging cooperation among different national groups and a balance of power among states.

Urban: Is Margaret Thatcher, then, in error when she says that European unification runs against the temper of our time because events in Eastern Europe and the U.S.S.R. show the world moving towards national separatism rather than a faceless merger of nations?

Kedourie: Generalizations of this kind are, at best, superficial. It is undoubtedly true *at the present time* that most West European countries, with the possible exception of Britain, are prepared to surrender some of their national sovereignty to an elected and accountable European Parliament. To that extent it is legitimate to say that the militant cultivation of national identity has been eroded and the will to further a joint European 'good' prospers. Witness, under Article 3 of the July 1990 N.A.T.O. statement, the appearance of the following words: 'The move within the European Community towards political union, including the development of a European identity in the domain of security, will also contribute to Atlantic solidarity and to the establishment of a just and lasting order of peace throughout the whole of Europe.'

A 'European identity' in the domain of security is a very important addition to earlier language. It has been incorporated at French insistence, and that tells us something about the way things are moving in Paris.

But the parallel in Mrs Thatcher's argument with Eastern Europe and the nationalities question in the Soviet Union does not hold water. National resentments have come to the surface in these places not because national feeling is a constructive and innately irrepressible force, but because national rights and traditions have been savagely repressed for four and a half decades in Eastern Europe and for seven in the Soviet Union. I doubt whether any of the national groups within the Soviet state would have decided to resort to arms, as the Armenians and Georgians have done, had they enjoyed the sort of freedoms the French- and Italian-speaking population enjoys in Switzerland. The Soviet leaders now openly acknowledge that their troubles in the nationality areas are due to their own follies. For example, at the 28th C.P.S.U. Congress, G. I. Usmanov (Secretary of the Central Committee) observed:

Let's be honest! The so-called resolution of the Nationalities Question that was proclaimed in the past has turned out to be a dangerous illusion. The desire to eradicate ethnic problems based on a distorted and primitive concept of the class approach led to a situation whereby everything that failed to fall within its framework was described as nationalism. There were times when strong-arm methods crudely interfaced with the delicate fabric of interethnic relations. There was a deep gulf between the official version and what the peoples saw and knew . . .

I would, therefore, conclude that events in Eastern Europe and the Soviet Union offer no ground for inferences to be drawn either about the desirability or the undesirability, the feasibility or non-feasibility, of unification in Western Europe.

Urban: Your insistence on the good that may flow from a renewed balance of power politics sticks a pin into me. I do not dispute its stabilizing effects at various times in the past; but I wonder whether, in the utterly changed nuclear world in which we live, public opinion would stomach any recourse to a balance of power politics and sustain the attitudes that go with it.

As far as the one remaining superpower – the United States – is concerned, we saw, under Nixon and Kissinger in the 1970s, that Dr

Kissinger's Metternichian balance of power policies rendered his conception of détente ineffective because the American people either did not understand the complicated game Kissinger was playing, or, to the extent they did understand it, they found it 'un-American' and immoral. In Europe, it is true, a new balance of power politics would cause fewer eyebrows to be raised, but I think it would tend to resuscitate precisely those now well-forgotten feelings of rabid nationalism which certainly the educated young, and not so young, have spectacularly overcome.

The French and British responses to the fall of the Berlin Wall, and to the first intimations of the unification of the two Germanies, were a sobering reminder that our political masters of the older generation are stuck in the grooves of 1945, if not 1914. No sooner did the Soviet threat appear to be dissolving than conditioned reflexes came into play: language about the need for an Anglo–French nuclear entente began to be heard in the articulations of our politicians and leader-writers. President Mitterand hoped that Gorbachev would do his job for him by vetoing German unification. Mrs Thatcher conjured up atavistic images of a German menace on various memorable occasions. Anglo–Polish and Franco–Polish friendships were suddenly revived as a counter to the Polish–German border question; and in the jingoistic wing of our journalistic community dark hints began to be dropped about the impending *Anschluss* of East Germany. In July 1990, the ineffable Nicholas Ridley demonstrated clearly in the pages of the *Spectator* magazine that national and racial prejudice and a balance of power politics are two sides of the same coin.

The European public, and especially postwar generations, had little understanding for any of this. Isn't it worth asking whether it is possible, in the long term, to pursue a balance of power politics and to be constructive, burden-sharing and vision-sharing members of the European Community? In the past, balance of power politics led to war . . .

Kedourie: A balance of power policy need not go together with nationalistic intolerance. It did not do so in the late 18th century, and even in the 19th it did not become a serious factor until the Franco–Prussian war of 1870–71. A balance of power policy need not be militaristic or pugnacious. All it means is that when one state becomes too powerful for the peace and prosperity of others, the latter try to coordinate their interests so as to balance the might of the former. When Poland was under Soviet control and communist rule, it would have been laughable to suggest that General de Gaulle should sign a Franco–Polish treaty as reassurance against the German Federal Republic. Germany then had limited power and limited prospects, whereas the Soviet Union, of which Poland was a satellite, was, or so it seemed, all-powerful. But with the Soviet *glacis* in Eastern Europe gone and Germany on the verge of acquiring additional power, it does make sense for Mitterand, in the 1990s, to think of Franco–Polish friendship as a balance to German hegemony. This sort of thing is as old as history. Human nature being what it is, balance of power politics is the best mechanism men have so far invented for keeping a semblance of order in the world.

Urban: Isn't the obverse side of any balance of power politics the feeling of 'encirclement' which has cost us so dear? For balance to exist, someone is bound to feel encircled, and that leads to paranoia and worse.

Kedourie: That is far-fetched. When the French moved to create the 'Little Entente' after World War I in order to keep some form of control over Germany (and Hungary), they had a sound idea. Had the 'Little Entente' not been a cardboard contraption, we might have been spared World War II.

Urban: You said a moment ago that a confederative state on the pattern of the Habsburg Empire is one of the most desirable frameworks for the peaceful coexistence of different nations and 'nationalities' and the best guarantee against overbearing neighbors. Now you speak in support of the 'Little Entente' which resulted from the demolition of the Habsburg Monarchy. Can you have it both ways?

Kedourie: The kind of incipient multinational federalism we saw in the Habsburg Empire, had it been conducted on truly federal and liberal lines, would have been the right framework for interethnic peace and international balance. But with that gone, the 'Little Entente' was, in intention at least, the right pillar in Central Europe for the containment of a potentially irredentist Germany.

Urban: As the Europeans of the postwar generation see it, there is now a case for saying that Europe cannot be healthy as long as the central and eastern parts of it are mortally injured; and for saying that, because of it geographic position, economic strength and interests, Germany is perhaps the only, and certainly the main, European country able and willing to sanitize these cancer-ridden organs of our continent for the benefit of the whole of Europe as well as, of course, Germany's own. Does it make sense to revive the ancient suspicions, the dated vocabulary, and old power-political machinations of our grandfathers in the wholly changed circumstances of the turn of the millennium? Isn't it as important to forget some of the experiences of history when the times call for amnesia as it is to remember them?

Some of the current (1990) pronouncements of our British and French political leaders about the future of post-Soviet Europe remind me only too well of Clemenceau's backward-looking policies at the 1919 Paris peace conference. This is how John Maynard Keynes, who was present as a member of the British delegation, described them:

Clemenceau took the view that European civil war is to be regarded as a normal, or at least a recurrent, state of affairs for the future . . . European history is to be a perpetual prize-fight, of which France has won this round, but of which this round is certainly not the last . . . This is the policy of an old man, whose most vivid impressions and most lively imagination are of the past and not of the future. He sees the issue in terms of France and Germany, not of humanity and European civilisation struggling forwards to a new order.[227]

Kedourie: I can see that there is a good argument to be made for suspending the suspicions of history, erasing the past and starting again with a clean slate. I can see that this has an appeal to the young and the idealistic. I am not saying such an approach is wrong or unduly naïve. All I'm insisting on is that states do have natural interests and that these interests do increase as the power of the state increases. It is perfectly true that the West German Federal Republic is almost a model democratic state with a faultless record in its international relations. But it is precisely Central and Eastern Europe that has always been Germany's main target for expansion, and it is precisely that area which will now come under German economic hegemony.

We do not have to suppose that a united Germany would once again become an ideological, or even a conventional, expansionist power, on the pattern of Kaiser Wilhelm's Germany, to fear a certain economic imbalance developing in the affairs of Europe in the wake of the retreat of Soviet power. A prudent man will ask himself: how

[227] John Maynard Keynes, *The Economic Consequences of the Peace* (1919), 31, 33.

would Germany use its fresh economic hegemony in the long term? – because there are all sorts of ways in which a strong state can overawe weaker neighbors. What would happen if Germany did do another Rapallo? What if it said to its NATO allies: we will no longer agree to the presence of your forces on German soil unless the nuclear discrimination against Germany ends and we acquire nuclear forces similar to those which the French and the British have . . . Who could say *no* to such an approach?

Urban: Aren't we jumping a little too far ahead of history? Our current problem, which will tax our purses and our imagination for a long time to come, is how to manage the retreat of communism and rehabilitate 100 million Central and East Europeans, as well as some 280 million Soviet people, from the ravages of the communist system. Should we, in the hour of this greater challenge to our ingenuity, worry about the end effects of European recovery when the recovery itself is entirely open to question? To express in 1990 fears of 'German domination' strikes me as rather like saying: 'This surgeon will, if I'm lucky, remove my cancer – but won't that make him too powerful over my life when I've recovered?'

Kedourie: Rehabilitation is, as we know from the Third World, something for the East and Central Europeans themselves to undertake. Our assistance can be only marginal. And we have to ask whether they have the material, historical, and spiritual resources to do it. The history of the Balkan nations after their emancipation from Ottoman imperial rule is not encouraging. Nor is that of the successor states of the Austro–Hungarian Monarchy, or Hungary itself. With the exception of Czechoslovakia, they managed their affairs disastrously. What parliamentary democratic traditions existed in Poland and Hungary at various times in their history cannot be said to be alive after half a century of lawlessness under communism. They will have to write an entirely new chapter in their history – what they have in front of them at the moment are just so many blank pages. It is, therefore, by no means certain that the successor states to Soviet hegemony will manage their affairs, either among themselves or in their domestic politics, any better than they did after the retreat of Habsburg and Ottoman power.

Urban: My own analysis tells me that the Polish, Hungarian, Czech, and Slovak reserves of democracy are a bit more substantial than you have indicated. But assuming that they are as thin as they would appear to you, I am cheered by a remarkable and paradoxical phenomenon. Marxism–Leninism preached a libertarian creed and prosperity – but practised oppression and scarcity. The oppression has been overthrown but the libertarian creed has made its mark. It is now fuelling Central Europe's quest for democracy and social welfare. Communist rule has turned out to be in some ways the people's 'university.' During my recent visits to Central Europe I saw a great deal of very intelligent understanding of what democracy is about and the clear will to make it work. Constitutions are being made or amended, and institutions put on the statute books.

Kedourie: Ah, but there lies the whole problem. Democracy cannot be made to order. I don't think you can create institutions by legislation. If you look at the constitutions of the U.K., Canada, or the U.S. and ask yourself: how do they work? Are they guaranteed by the deliberations of some college of lawyers or other formal arrangements? You will find that they rest on a balanced society in which substantial interests check and control one another. It is, more particularly, economic interests, over which no one can ride roughshod, that guarantee the equilibrium and make it impossible for either a dictator or single-party rule to arise.

Most Central and East European countries have an historical deficit in these characteristics; although they might acquire them, it would be taking hope too far to say that they are likely to become democracies simply because Soviet power is on the retreat and their national independence has been restored. Your point that the spirit of democracy in Central Europe appears to be asserting itself by inspiration drawn from the 'good Marx' –

Urban: – A phrase I didn't use . . .

Kedourie: . . . and the egalitarian undercurrents of Sovietism is an interesting one. But let me say that the 'good Marx,' what is called the early Marx, was laughably utopian. He provides no basis for any practical politics. In brief, the only certainty we have at present is great uncertainty.

Urban: May I refer you to Aristotle's words about the effectiveness and ineffectiveness of constitutions: namely, that constitutions are worthless unless they are grounded in the customs and conventions of the people. It may well be true at the moment that Central Europe is without a web of countervailing economic interests, but it is certainly not the case that either the Poles, the Czechs or the Hungarians lack the traditions that make for a *Rechtsstaat* and political pluralism. Hungary's *Golden Bull* (1222), to take one example, is almost as old as the *Magna Carta* (1215) and makes comparable stipulations limiting royal privileges and prerogatives. But, coming closer to our time, we have the example of postwar Germany to consider. There was nothing in German history up to 1945 that would have induced a reasonable man to believe that from the heritage of Nazism – from the ruins of the German cities, from the human débris of the lost war, from the influx of millions of destitute expellees, the rampant hunger and homelessness – a liberal, democratic, prosperous and generous German state would arise and flourish so quickly. But it did. The most successful society in German history sprang from such inauspicious beginnings.

Central Europe today is, it seems to me, in an incomparably more fortunate situation than Germany was in 1945. The Czechs, Poles and Hungarians have housing, food, a functioning railway and a postal system. Their cities, though badly polluted, have not been laid waste, their menfolk are not in prisoner of war camps. They are all in the process of creating a free and democratic order to the applause of the rest of the world. They are ethnically entirely homogeneous (if we discount the Czech/Slovak dichotomy as a seedbed of conflict) and will soon be rid of all foreign troops. If a defeated and war-torn Germany could surmount its *Nullpunkt* in 1945–47, albeit with Anglo–American assistance, I cannot quite see why an undefeated and war-spared Central Europe should not be able to do the same – to be sure, with Western assistance, which is now forthcoming, reinforced by the prospect of eventual admission to the European Community.

Kedourie: Your comparison is unpersuasive. In 1945 the Western Powers had a keen and wholesome memory of how their victory in 1918 had been mismanaged. They were determined not to repeat the mistakes of Versailles. They were even more keenly aware that the real victor of World War II was the Soviet Union, with Stalin (and Stalinism) at the helm. A hungry and clueless Germany was waiting to fall into the hands of Stalin, from which the fall of a hungry, clueless and increasingly communist-subverted Western Europe would have followed. Western fears increased when totalitarian communist rule was extended to the whole of Central and Eastern Europe. The Marshall Plan, the creation of the Federal West German Republic and NATO followed. The German media were reorganized on American models; German trade unionism and codetermination in industry were introduced under British auspices. These were the keys to the birth and success of German democracy. Why was all this done? Because we had a vital interest in having a free, prosperous and strong Germany on our side in our contest with the Soviet Union.

Central Europe can count on no really comparable Western assistance. I am ready to concede that we do have an interest in seeing the Central European countries prosper under liberal-democratic dispensations – for we do not want them to sink into chaos. Much less do we want them to seek salvation in dictatorial rule whether of the left or the right. But the threat from the Soviet superpower is assumed to be no longer there, and our assistance is bound to be less committed than our assistance was to Germany. Central Europe will essentially have to fend for itself under difficult conditions. The West is going to help, but the analogy with postwar Germany does not strike me as convincing.

Other considerations also weigh against the analogy. Forty years and more of bureaucratic Stalinism have created layer upon layer of people with a vested interest in perpetuating the inefficiencies and corruptions of the command economy. The socialist tyranny has also utterly destroyed the legal order necessary to a free society. It will take a very long time to re-establish – and to accustom people once more to the institution of private property, and the opportunities it can open up.

You quoted Aristotle about the effectiveness and ineffectiveness of constitutions. Well, one of Aristotle's main concerns was how to forestall revolution and disorder. He was, of course, talking about very small societies and assuming that political action was organically connected with the personal virtue or lack of virtue of every citizen: 'A state is good only when those citizens who have a share in the government are themselves good' (*Politics*, Book VII, 3).

We no longer live in small societies, and we no longer link our political analysis to the virtue of the citizen –

Urban: More's the pity, . . .

Kedourie: That may well be, but we don't. Aristotle's purpose was to identify and then to remove the distemper of social extremism; and he offered certain wholesome remedies. When there is a revolution by the rich, he said, and aristocracy degenerates into oligarchy, everyone who does not belong to the victorious rich is not only dispossessed but also disenfranchised.

How, he asked, is this to be prevented? What you have to do, he answered, if you are an oligarch, is to recommend to your fellow oligarchs that your oligarchy should, first and foremost, look after the interests of the *demos*, the people, the poor. And he goes on to say that, by the same token, if the people come out on top and there is 'democracy,' it should be the first business of the people's representatives, i.e., the democrats, to take care of the interests of the rich. Now this is the kind of spirit the builders of the new democracies in Central Europe might profit from; but I doubt whether, in the wake of the passions aroused by communism, they are likely to do this in the short run.

Urban: I would say that their search for social equity is already in the making. The new democracies seem to be looking for a 'social market economy,' based more on the Swedish, Austrian, or German models than the one advanced by Thatcherism. They want to combine the productivity and abundance of the free market with a number of cushions and safety nets provided, out of general taxation, by the state. Doesn't this strike you as a modern equivalent of the Aristotelian principle?

Kedourie: In intention – perhaps. But I cannot see how it can be put into practice since these post-communist societies have as yet no private wealth from which competing political interests might issue. And if private wealth creation is to be restricted, democracy in Central Europe will have a hard row to hoe. There is and can be no shortcut to constitutional and representative government. After the war, earnest civil servants in the British Colonial Office were busy writing scrupulously fair constitutions for the British colonies in Africa. Look now at their handiwork,

Urban: But you are surely not suggesting that the inability or unreadiness of African tribesmen to create democratic societies is a clue to how the Czechs, the nation of Jan Hus, or the Hungarians, with their ancient tradition of constitutional government, will behave in the next several decades?

Kedourie: The analogy may strike you as far-fetched but it is not wholly irrelevant. It is certainly relevant to the future of the Turkmens, Kirghiz, Uzbeks, Armenians and Azeris, should they ever attain independence.

Urban: A last word about power politics: I suppose the revulsion the postwar generation feels against any balance of power politics is due (as they see it) to its transparent immorality. Fighting an ideological war – hot or cold – is morally simple to justify. When a nation is asked to put down an ideological empire – whether Nazism or Stalinism – it is asked to fight not only for the national interest, but for a conception of the world it regards as just, and against one it regards as unjust and tyrannical. But when ideological antagonists disappear and the balance of power means balancing power among states with similar institutions and a shared social order, the popular psyche is confronted with a very different problem. Democratic Frenchmen, democratic Germans, democratic Britons, and democratic Italians are then told to prepare themselves for arm-twisting and worse against one another – because this or that state is 'getting above itself,' has a better economy, or is simply overshadowing the pride, status or 'station' of others.

Those born after 1945 throughout Europe find this 19th-century manner of looking at our world intolerable; they want to see no further installments of the story 'The European Civil War, 1914–89.'

Kedourie: What is moral in public affairs is never easy to determine. Moral judgment is likewise never an open-and-shut affair. To quote Grotius, in politics and war a way has to be found between those who say that in these matters nothing is lawful and those who say that everything is lawful. In 1941 Britain and the U.S. allied themselves with Stalin's Russia, knowing full well that Stalin and his system were loathsome and alien to everything Britain and America stood for. But they felt even more strongly that the primary threat to their freedom and perhaps to their survival came from Hitler's Germany. An alliance even with Stalin was necessary in order to defeat Nazism. This was balance of power politics at its cruellest.

In the mid-1970s, former President Richard Nixon, to take another example, played the 'China card.' He made his peace with and even befriended Mao Tse Tung because he was anxious to isolate the Soviet Union. But did Nixon think that Mao and his 'Red Guards' were one whit better than the thugs the Soviet leaders let loose on the people on countless occasions? Not at all. Nixon acted on cool calculation, but in the service of a higher good which was attained.

Urban: Wouldn't you agree that in both these cases the Western powers' balance of power politics were motivated by moral and philosophical considerations? Nazism had to be defeated because it was a totalitarian despotism and a menace to the world, and the Soviet system had to be isolated and overcome for the same reason. However, in the post-Nazi and post-communist world, any balance

of power policy would involve like-minded people and identical
social systems holding one another in check by a combination of
economic pressures, military threats, and government-inspired
nationalisms. Forgive me for saying it again: The young in Europe,
the new generations, will have no truck with that. They will feel, with
St Augustine, that any peace attained by such methods is a 'peace of
the unjust' – that any further conception of 'collective security' must
not rest on insecurity. That is why, it seems to me, they support in
their great majority the unification of Europe. Can we fault their
thinking? Aren't they, in fact, advocating a higher conception of
'balance' among nations – one that would put cooperation and
integration in the place of ransom and blackmail?

Kedourie: If we are quoting St Augustine we have to remember that,
for him, justice is attainable only in the Heavenly City. You have, in
this conversation, repeatedly quoted the young and their views.
Youth in itself does not guarantee virtue or wisdom. On the contrary, to the extent that these goods are attainable, they are more
easily attained by the old. It is not for nothing that the hymn of a
demagogic movement like Fascism was *Giovinezza, giovinezza!* But
this was no rejuvenation . . .

Your mention of youth reminds me of a passage by Aldous Huxley
which it is ironical to recall in the present context. It occurs in that
marvellous anthology of his, *Texts and Pretexts*, published in 1932.
It was the first book I bought for myself as a schoolboy, and it gave
me an incomparable insight into Western poetry. Huxley has a
chapter about old age in which he quotes a couplet from the Eliza-
bethan poet Thomas Bastard:

Age is deforméd, youth unkind,
We scorn their bodies, they our mind.

Huxley goes on to say:

Things have changed since Queen Elizabeth's days. 'We,' that is to say, the
young, scorn not only their bodies, but also (and above all) their minds. In
the two politically most 'advanced' states of Europe this scorn is so effective
that age has become a definite bar to the holding of political power. Communism and fascism appeal for the support of youth, and of youth alone. At
Rome and Moscow, age has been disfranchised . . .

Later on in the same passage Huxley says: 'To a white traveller
who visited him, 'Give me hair-dye,' was the agonized cry of the
greatest of African chiefs. 'Hair-dye,' He was going grey. Not long
afterwards his warriors speared him to death.'

In its self-certainty, youth is (as the poet says) indeed unkind.

About the editors and contributors

KEITH ARMES is Associate Director of the Institute for the Study of Conflict, Ideology & Policy. Until 1990 he was managing editor of the *Atlantic Community Quarterly* in Washington, D.C., after having been on the faculty of the University of Minnesota, Minneapolis. He holds an M.A. in Modern Languages and Economics and a Ph.D. in Soviet literature from the University of Cambridge, and an M.A. in Security Policy Studies from George Washington University.

PETER BERGER is University Professor and Director of the Institute for the Study of Economic Culture at Boston University. Educated at Wagner College and the New School for Social Research, he has taught at Boston College, Rutgers University, the New School for Social Research and other universities. He served as the U.S. representative to the United Nations Working Group on the Right to Development (1981–83). He has written numerous books, including *The Capitalist Revolution, The War over the Family* (with Brigitte Berger), *The Heretical Imperative*, and *The Social Construction of Reality* (with Thomas Luckmann).

JOAN ESTRUCH holds a chair in Sociology and teaches in the areas of Sociology of Religion, Sociological Theory, and Sociology of Knowledge at the Free University of Barcelona. Born in Barcelona, Catalonia in 1943, Estruch studied at the University of Barcelona, where he graduated with a degree in History. He then obtained a scholarship from the World Council of Churches (Geneva) to study Sociology at the Catholic University of Louvain. His academic career started as an assistant at the University of Louvain. He returned to Barcelona in 1971, to establish a Department of Sociology at the recently created Free University of Barcelona. His books include: *Protestants d'Espagne* (1969); *Les juifs dans la catéchèse* (1972); *La innovación religiosa* (1972); *La secularización en España* (1974); *Sociología de una profesión* (1976); *Plegar de viure: un estudi sobre els suicidis* (1981); *Les enquestes de la joventut de Catalunya (1984); and Catalunya 77–88* (editor, 1990). In recent years he has been doing research on Weber and Freud, Psychoanalysis and Sociology, and Sociology of Monastic Life; he is now conducting a project on the Economic Ethics of some Roman Catholic Movements, under the auspices of the Institute for the Study of Economic Culture (Boston).

THEODOR HANF is director of the Arnold Bergstraesser Institute for Social Research, Professor of Sociology for the German Institute for International and Educational Research, and honorary Professor of Political Science at the University of Freiburg. His main research interests include conflict regulation in multicultural states, and the political function of education. For about 15 years he has conducted field research in Africa, the Near East and Southeast Asia. He has written and co-written several books on South Africa, Zaire, Rwanda, Lebanon, social change and development policy. His publications include *Erziehungswesen in Gesellschaft und Politik des Libanon* (1969); *Les étudiants universitaires congolais* (1971); *Education et Développement au Rwanda* (1974); *Sozialer Wandel*, 2 vols. (1975); *South Africa: The Prospects of Peaceful Change* (1981); *La société de concordance* (1986); *Entwicklungspolitik* (1986); *Urban Crisis and Social Movements: Arab and European Perspectives* (1987); and *Koexistenz im Krieg. Staatszerfall und Entstehen einer Nation im Libanon* (1990).

ROBERT HEFNER is Associate Professor of Anthropology and Associate Director of the Institute for the Study of Economic Culture at Boston University. He is a specialist on southeast Asian politics, religion and development, and the author of *Hindu Javanese: Tengger Tradition and Islam*, and *The Political Economy of Mountain Java: An Interpretive History*. He is currently writing a history of Muslim politics and conversion in southeast Asia.

ZDENEK KÁRNÍK is Professor of Modern Czechoslovak History at the Charles University of Prague, where he started as a junior lecturer on modern Czechoslovak history in 1954. After being sacked for political reasons he was unemployed as a result of *Berufsverbot* in 1970–71. His publications appeared on the Black List of forbidden authors, and he was forbidden from travelling abroad. From 1971 to 1989 he was at the Institute for Historical Landmark Protection as an expert on the 19th and early 20th centuries. He is the author of many articles and books on modern Czechoslovak history.

ELIE KEDOURIE is Professor of Politics Emeritus at the University of London, and is serving as a Visiting Olin Professor at Columbia University in 1991. Educated at the London School of Economics and St. Antony's College, Oxford, he is a Fellow of the British Academy, and has taught at Princeton, Harvard, Brandeis and other universities, recently completing a one-year appointment as Visiting Research Fellow at All Souls College, Oxford. Founder and editor of *Middle Eastern Studies* (1964–), he is the author of *Nationalism, Nationalism in Asia and Africa, The Crossman Confessions and Other Essays in History, Politics and Religion*, and *Diamonds into Glass: the Government and the Universities*, among many other books.

KATE MARTIN edited textbooks, magazines and newspapers before assuming a senior position at the Institute for the Study of Conflict, Ideology & Policy in 1989. In addition to her current publication-related duties, she is the organizational force behind the Institute's conferences, lecture series and special events. She received her degree in Journalism from Northeastern University.

MARIA MESNER is Assistant in the Department for History and Politics at the Renner Institute, which studies political and social history. She organizes conferences, such as the Vienna gathering which served as the catalyst for this book. Her other areas of interest include the relationship between state bureaucracy and economic modernization in the Habsburg monarchy as well as in the Second Republic of Austria.

DUSAN NECÁK is Professor of Modern History at the Institute of International Affairs. He studied at the department of history and art history at the University of Ljubljana. In 1972 he became foreign policy editor for the Ljubljana newspaper *Delo*. In 1980 he joined the faculty of the Institute of International Affairs. His special fields include national minorities and the nationality question, Slovene minorities abroad, and post-1945 general and Yugoslav history.

RICHARD PARRY has been a lecturer in Social Policy at the University of Edinburgh since 1983. After graduating in Politics from Edinburgh in 1974, he worked as a civil servant in the Department of the Environment in London and Edinburgh, and then as Research Officer in the Centre for the Study of Public Policy at the University of Strathclyde in Glasgow. He returned to Edinburgh University as Research Fellow in the Department of Politics, working on a project on central–local relations in Scotland, before taking up his present post. His publications on Scottish politics include *Scottish Political Facts* (T. & T. Clark 1988), 'The Centralisation of the Scottish Office' in Richard Rose, ed., *Ministers and Ministries* (Clarendon Press 1987), and most recently 'The Scottish Office in the 1980s' in *The Scottish Government Yearbook 1991* (Edinburgh University Press). He has also written on public employment (including 'Territory and Public Employment: A General Model and British Evidence,' *Journal of Public Policy* (1981), and on the history of the British welfare state (including the United Kingdom sections of Peter Flora, ed., *Growth to Limits: The Western European Welfare States since World War II* (de Gruyter 1986–87)). His main research is on privatisation.

ALFRED PFABIGAN is teaching at the Philosophy Institute of the University of Vienna. After studying law he taught political science and philosophy at the universities of Vienna and Salzburg, as well as at Franklin and Marshall College (Lancaster, Pennsylvania). His publications include: *Karl Kraus and Socialism* (Vienna 1976); *Max Adler: A Political Biography* (Frankfurt/Main 1982); *Sleepless in Pyongyang* (Vienna 1986); *The Other Bible* (Frankfurt/Main 1990); and *Presence of Mind* (Vienna 1991).

URI RA'ANAN is University Professor and Director of the Institute for the Study of Conflict, Ideology & Policy of Boston University. He is Fellow of the Russian Research Center at Harvard University. Author, co-author, editor, co-editor of 20 books, and contributor to 17 others, as well as 18 monographs and Congressional publications, his latest publications include *Inside the Apparat; Gorbachev's USSR: A System in Crisis*; and *The Soviet Empire: The Challenge of National and Democratic Movements*. His current research focuses on factional struggles and ethnic conflicts in the U.S.S.R. Prior to his current appointments, he was Professor of International Politics and Director of the International Security Studies

Program at the Fletcher School of Law and Diplomacy, where he taught for two decades. Before joining the Fletcher School, he taught (briefly) at the Massachusetts Institute of Technology, and previous to that, at Columbia University and the City University of New York. He obtained his undergraduate and graduate education and degrees at Oxford University (Wadham College, 1945–50).

BEREL RODAL is a senior official in the Government of Canada. He was born in Montreal in 1943, and was educated at McGill University and Balliol College, Oxford. His professional experience includes policy and executive responsibilities in a variety of fields in the defense, foreign affairs, international trade, economic and social policy domains, and in federal–provincial relations. He has also taught at Carleton University, and participates in the work of such research bodies as the International Institute for Strategic Studies (IISS), the Royal Institute of International Affairs (Chatham House), and the Council on Foreign Relations (New York). He is the author of a number of articles on Canadian and international affairs, and has lectured in North America, Europe, and Asia.

LAWRENCE SCHLEMMER is Director of the Centre for Policy Studies at the Graduate School of Business Administration, University of the Witwatersrand. He has served as president of the South African Institute of Race Relations and the Association for Sociology in Southern Africa. He was the organising Secretary of the Buthelezi Commission (1980–82) and served on the planning and constitutional committees of the Kwazulu-Natal Indaba (1985–86). He currently is a Trustee of the Mobil Foundation, the Urban Foundation and the Institute for Multi-party Democracy. Founding editor of *Indicator* SA, he was written over 250 research reports, books, articles and chapters, including *Transition to Democracy: Policy Perspectives 1991* (with Robin Lee; OUP, forthcoming), and *From Apartheid to Nation Building* (with Hermann Giliomee; OUP, 1989).

PETER SIPOS is senior research advisor at the Institute for Political History and assistant professor at the Faculty of Arts of the Eötvös Loránd University in Budapest. He is the author of a number of books and studies on Hungarian political and social history in the 20th century.

GERALD STOURZH is Professor of Modern History at the

University of Vienna. After earning his Ph.D. degree from the University of Vienna in 1951, he served as a Research Associate at the Univeristy of Chicago. From 1964 to 1969 he was Professor of Modern History (particularly North American History) at the Free University of Berlin. He also has been a member of the Institute of Advanced Study, Princeton (1967–68) and Overseas Fellow at Churchill College, Cambridge (1976). Major publications include *Benjamin Franklin and American Foreign Policy* (University of Chicago Press 1954, 2nd ed. 1969); *Alexander Hamilton and the Idea of Republican Government* (Stanford University Press 1970); *Geschichte des Staatsvertrags 1945–1955. Österreichs Weg zur Neutralität* (3rd ed. 1985); *Die Gleichberechtigung der Nationalitäten in der Verfassung und Verwaltung Österreichs 1848–1918* (Vienna 1985); *Wege zur Grundrechtsdemokratie* (Vienna 1989); and *Vom Reich zur Republik. Studien zum Österreichsbewußtsein im 20.* Jahrhundert. (Vienna 1990).

GEORGE R. URBAN is a writer on contemporary history, a former Senior Research Associate of the University of Southern California and Research Fellow at Indiana University. He has written *Nationalism and International Progress, Kinesis and Stasis,* and *The Nineteen Days* and is the editor and co-author of *Communist Reformation, Can We Survive our Future?, Toynbee on Toynbee, Détente, Hazards of Learning* and *Eurocommunism*.

Index